ENOUGH IS ENOUGH

Dear Mr. Camdessus . . .
Open Letter of Resignation to the Managing Director of the International Monetary Fund

Documentary Sources
for Social Change

Documentary Sources for Social Change is a series of publications presenting documents of historic significance on important economic, social, and political issues. Documents of this character frequently have limited informal circulation. Publishing such documents in this series will make them more readily accessible to all those interested.

With the assignment of International Standard Book Numbers (ISBNs), DSSC documents are treated like formal book publications and included in appropriate bibliographical databases and search mechanisms. These titles are, however, reproduced without formal editing, exactly as submitted by their respective authors who are solely responsible for their content.

Documentary Sources for Social Change is a form of publication-on-demand. Limited inventories are maintained, and additional copies reproduced in response to demand. DSSC titles are also ordinarily available in microform through the publisher.

ENOUGH IS ENOUGH

Dear Mr. Camdessus . . .

Open Letter of Resignation to the Managing Director of the International Monetary Fund

Davison L. Budhoo

Foreword by Errol K. Mc Leod
President General, Oilfields Workers' Trade Union

NEW HORIZONS PRESS
New York

This Open Letter is dedicated to the people of the Fourth World — the more than two billion voiceless, starving and diseased peoples who share our planet. They transcend national boundaries in their desperation, indicting massively their tormentors with evidence of the unneccessary horror and helplessness and suffering of their own lives.

Published in North America by New Horizons Press an imprint of the Council on International and Public Affairs, 777 United Nations Plaza, New York, New York 10017 (212/953-6920)

Distributed in the United Kingdom by New Beacon Books, 76 Stroud Green Road, London N4 3EN, England (01/272-4889)

This document is also available in microfiche. Contact New Horizons Press for details.

ISBN 0-945257-28-7

Typeset in the United States of America and printed in Great Britain by the Short Run Press, Exeter

CONTENTS

FOREWORD

The International Monetary Fund is one of the most powerful institutions in the world. Along with its 'sister' institution, the International Bank for Reconstruction and Development (the World Bank), the IMF is playing a crucial role in the reorganisation of global production. Through the rigid implementation of structural adjustment policies, the IMF and the World Bank are ensuring that the governments of countries that seek IMF and World Bank loans become faithful adherents to the philosophy of monetarism. And because the philosophy was never intended to create meaningful and sustained development, the result of the structural adjustment policies has been the deepening crisis of debt for Third World countries and rapidly growing poverty which leaves much of the peoples in these countries in a state of marginalisation at best, and abject misery at worst .

To confront an institution that has the power to implement this systematic process of recolonisation is not easy. It is also a task that requires a tremendous amount of personal courage. This publication is the result of one such act of courage. Davison Budhoo, former IMF and World Bank staffer, in a historic open letter of resignation from the IMF has not only challenged the philosophy and epistemology of the IMF and condemned its creation of mass poverty. He has gone further than anybody before by exposing massive statistical fraud carried out by the Fund in Trinidad and Tobago in the period 1985-1987.

Budhoo's resignation was an act of courage and conscience. All Third World peoples who have had to bear the economic and social weight of the Fund's "streamroller" policies are indebted to him. All those in the "developed" world of the North who are opposed to the injustice of the IMF and World Bank, are indebted to Budhoo.

The Oilfields Workers' Trade Union of Trinidad and Tobago invites others to express their indebtedness by utilising the facts and information provided in Budhoo's letter to the maximum. World public opinion must focus on the IMF's fraud. And at the same time we must collectively ensure that "Man of Conscience" Davison Budhoo is encouraged to continue his work. History is all too replete with the elites of this world using their power to break people of conscience. We must not allow this to happen to Budhoo.

For the record it must be said that Budhoo's position on fraud by the IMF in Trinidad and Tobago has been vindicated. The report by an investigating team appointed by the Cabinet of the Government of Trinidad and Tobago (which team was headed by Professor Compton Bourne of the Faculty of Economics, University of the West Indies) stated:

"(i) The Committee concludes that there have been serious statistical irregularities and technical deficiencies in the IMF's economic analysis and reporting on Trinidad and Tobago.
(ii) The likely consequences of these errors are:
  (a) Unwarranted adverse judgement of the country's economic performance and national economic management;
  (b) Inappropriate policy recommendations by the IMF and those agencies influenced by its economic analyses;
  (c) International credit problems for Trinidad and Tobago
(iii) The IMF behaved irresponsibly in not disseminating the revised statistical series and in not revising its economic assessment when the earlier ones were known to be erroneous. Professional ethics, if nothing else, should have dictated that the corrected series be given the same prominence as was afforded the erroneous data."

In addition, the predictions by Budhoo of the effects of IMF and World Bank programmes in Trinidad and Tobago have all too sadly come to pass. Sine his warnings, the people of Trinidad and Tobago have suffered through a currency devaluation, increased unemployment and layoffs, a 15 percent Value Added Tax, cuts in public sector employees' wages, cuts in social services, higher prices, loss of foreign exchange due to easing of controls on foreign exchange, impending removal of non-tariff barriers to imports, undermining of constitutionally established bodies such as the Industrial Court and the Public Utilities Commission, and willy-nilly privatisation of State Enterprises.

We however are not defeated by the burden of this weight. We have rejected these policies of structural adjustment agreed to by our own weak, spineless and uncreative political directorate. And we have redoubled our efforts and intensified our struggle to bring about economic, social and political transformation. For it is only this that will enable us to end our persistent poverty. And as we struggle, we remember and thank Davison Budhoo for the unique and historic contribution he had made to this development. Davison has pointed a way but only the unity of the people will tame the IMF/World Bank "Goliath."

San Fernando, Trinidad
February 1990

Errol K. Mc Leod
President General
Oilfields Workers' Trade Union, Trinidad

NOTE BY THE PUBLISHER

The new decade now upon us — the last of this century and millennium — has been characterized by sweeping political and economic change. Starting in Poland, this extraordinary process of change spread rapidly across East Europe and the Soviet Union.

Demonstrating the power of grassroots political mobilization, the forces behind this change quickly challenged established centers of political and economic power. The common denominator of the demands generated by these forces has been an insistence upon accountability to those whose lives are directly affected by those who wield power.

It is unlikely that this contagious mass mobilization will be easily contained in one region of the world. Nor is it likely to be confined to producing change only in national governments. Established economic and political institutions everywhere are going to be, in the years ahead, subject to demands for greater accountability for their actions.

Accountability is, in the final analysis, what Davison Budhoo's Open Letter of Resignation from the International Monetary Fund is all about. By exposing the way in which the Fund works, both generally and in specific instances such as Trinidad and Tobago, he lays the groundwork for imposing on the Fund new standards of accountability to the institutions and people affected by its actions.

Historically, the IMF has been primarily accountable to those who have provided the lion's share of its financial resources. This is no longer enough. We — the citizens of the world — are all stakeholders in the Fund. And those that have the greatest stake are the populations of countries that have had to endure the harsh economic and political adjustments imposed by the Fund as a condition of its providing assistance. By far the greatest stake of all is in the hands of the most vulnerable sections of these populations — typically, women, children, and the poor generally — because the burden of these adjustments has fallen most heavily on their shoulders.

Davison Budhoo's resignation from the Fund as an act of conscience was a courageous step into the unknown. When he took that step, he burned many bridges behind him, including a return to the safe, comfortable, well-compensated world inhabited by international civil servants. For him the risks were very large, but he took those risks because, having participated in the work of the Fund and having seen for himself the terrible burdens the Fund's actions imposed on poor and innocent people, he could no longer live with his conscience.

The Fund's initial response in threatening Davison Budhoo with legal action ill behooves a powerful public institution. Such institutions must, if they are to be truly accountable to their stakeholders, function not in a closed Byzantine environment but as though they were in a goldfish bowl. By lifting the veil of secrecy that for far too long has protected the IMF and its actions from intense public scrutiny, Davison Budhoo has done all of us who believe in the principle of accountability for public institutions a great service.

In publishing Davison Budhoo's Open Letter of Resignation, we seek to make it as widely accessible as possible as a tool for those who are striving to hold the International Monetary Fund to new standards of accountability. It will soon be followed by a new book by Davison L. Budhoo. With the working title, *Global Justice: The Struggle to Reform the International Monetary Fund,* this new book will chronicle what happened as a result of his resignation, including investigation of the charges he made against the IMF and the IMF response. It will also set forth a program for reforming the IMF and a strategy for achieving those reforms.

We hope this new book, like the Open Letter, will be useful in the struggle to make the IMF more accountable to all of its stakeholders and not just its principal patrons. We are proud to be part of that struggle for global justice.

New York
February 1990

Ward Morehouse, Publisher
New Horizons Press

AUTHOR'S PREFACE

It is almost two years since my Open Letter of Resignation arrived at the desk of Mr. Camdessus, Managing Director of the International Monetary Fund. My expectations of its impact on the Fund itself, its member governments and ordinary people around the world who might hear or read about what I had done, were greatly underestimated and, simultaneously, naively inflated.

Let me explain what I mean.

When I began writing the Letter in 1987, I though that I had one burning, all-consuming mission - i.e.; to bring to the attention of the world what appeared to me to be the criminal actions by the Fund, perpetrated perhaps sometimes unknowingly against peoples of the Third World, and particularly the poorest and most economically vulnerable among them.

I labored under the illusion then (as indeed I did for several months after the Letter appeared), that once I took the plunge and proved without question the accuracy of the serious charges that I was making, a process of internal dialogue and soul-searching, forced on the Fund by world public opinion, would inexorably be set in motion. And I felt that in the ensuing climate of flux and accommodation, the regime of reform that I had proposed would necessarily be brought into the international spectrum, along with other proposals emanating from concerned sources.

In short, I believed that there was bound to be some way through which the Fund and its powerful supporters in the developed world could be made to move away from the path of callous destructiveness and follow a humane course of fair play that makes civilization possible.

That was my thinking, but things did not turn out that way. Instead, the Fund dug in its heels, defiant and unrepentant. It turned all its anger and poison and frustrations on my person. In its own words "the Fund reserves its right to take such action against you as is necessary to protect is interests and those of its member countries." The Director of Administration who wrote these words did not, as I came to realize, have in mind legal, above-the-board action. For twenty one months I have begged them to take such action and they have refused.

Before the Executive Board in early July, 1988, top management warned that the Fund was being "entrapped" by me. And at about the same time, the Director of External Relations told the British Broadcasting Corporation's Channel 4 Television crew that the Fund was determined to take all necessary action to ensure that Budhoo never becomes an "international star." And while my person was vilified, and plans laid to destroy me, no one on the Board thought it necessary to pay heed to the charges that I had made.

Now twenty-one months later, I have eight questions for Mr. Camdessus, as follows:

(1) Does it mean nothing to the Fund that two independent commissions, appointed by the Government of Trinidad and Tobago, should have concluded that all my charges of statistical and non-statistical fraud perpetrated against that country over 1985-88 were absolutely correct?

(2) Or that UNICEF in December, 1988 should have supported, after highly technical and painstaking research, my allegations of Fund-instigated genocide of Third World peoples under the on-going, creditor-oriented, international debt strategy?

(3) Or that the governments of the entire African continent south of the Sahara, in active collaboration with the UN Economic Commission for Africa, should have vehemently rejected in 1989 the Fund's concepts and implementation of Third World "structural adjustment" on the basis of technical analysis identical to that developed in the Open Letter? And that the self-same governments, and the self-same UN Commission, should have gone on to develop alternatives that would bypass, totally in the future, the present-day policies of the Fund?

(4) Or that the World Bank, smarting from the facts of the Letter, should have begun distancing itself, in a highly visible way, from Fund "monetarism" and "Reaganomics"?

(5) Or that several world quasi-legal tribunals, including some of the world's most outstanding jurists and humanitarians, should have seen fit, over the past eighteen months, to declare the Fund guilty of fundamental violations of human rights and the perpetration of massive crimes against humanity?

(6) Or that First World and Third World voices, muted and uncertain before 1988, should now be raised in angry concert, from every corner of the globe, in condemnation of the Fund and its record of horror and ignominy?

(7) Or that so many thousands of people since 1988 should have been killed by their governments, or been maimed or arrested, fighting the Fund at street corners, and in slums and villages in countries as different and as far apart as West Germany, Venezuela, Jordan, Nigeria, Tunisia, Egypt, Algeria and Sierre Leone?

(8) Or that tens of millions of people in the Third World should have suffered needlessly and many died since 1988 because the Fund and the interests it represents still continue to dominate the pages of human history?

In the aftermath of the Letter and its initial impact - and others in due course will judge the latter more objectively and more comprehensively than I can - one important question arises: Where do we go from here? And on this matter, I will confine myself to two points, seemingly unrelated, but very much the logical outcome of the drama and the trauma of the last two years.

The first concerns the fact that the Fund remains a law unto itself, impervious to questions about its performance, its human rights record, and its accountability to its victims and others affected by its actions. In this situation, it appears that the effort from 'outside' forces for meaningful reform that will lead to civilized and responsible behavior can continue for some time to be thwarted.

Consequently, there must be an intensification of the effort to reach the hundreds of millions of Fund victims all around the world. We need to educate them about the institution that dominates their lives and to elicit a worldwide reaction sufficiently strong and broad-based and vocal to convince the High Priests in Washington and elsewhere that the day of reckoning is finally at hand. Branding the Fund's critics as "do-gooders" or "spoilers" or "madmen" or "communists," is no longer enough to get the institution off the hook or to save the over-protected skins of its staff.

Finally, I have to mention, albeit reluctantly, a systematic pattern of violation of my human rights, and the human rights of others associated with my work. On this matter, I respectfully ask to be left in peace. Let those who oppose what I am doing take formal, legal action against me, if they so wish. But covert harassment and underhanded intimidation at the personal level are, by consensus of civilized people everywhere, among the most reprehensible forms of criminal behavior, and I will never accept them as factors miniaturising my life, and conditioning my freedom. Therefore, to all concerned I say, let good sense and propriety prevail. Let us build new foundations for human understanding, not undermine further the existing fragile base inherited from centuries of broadening our tolerance, and deepen our compassion.

Washington, D.C.
February 1990

Davison L. Budhoo

Office Memorandum

May 18, 1988

To: Mr. Camdessus, Managing Director

From: Davison L. Budhoo

OPEN LETTER OF RESIGNATION IN SIX PARTS (PARTS I - VI)

I am enclosing Part I of a Six Part Open Letter of Resignation addressed to you. The remaining Parts of my Open Letter (Parts II through VI) are summarized briefly on pages 5 to 15 of Part I.

For various reasons, it is impractical to issue, simultaneously, all Six Parts of this Letter. Accordingly, Parts II, III, IV, V, and VI will be issued in that order, at fairly regular intervals over the next three months. A second "follow up" Letter to you, in one Part only, is also being prepared for release later.

All Parts of this Letter will be distributed, on the appointed dates, to the Fund's Board of Governors and Board of Executive Directors. Worldwide distribution will include political and economic organizations in the United States and throughout the world, religious leaders, human rights groups and the news media.

On the question of why I write this Letter and see fit to release it beyond the Fund, I must refer you to Part I, Section 1 for the quick answer. The more detailed answer is not hard to find either; I think that it is written into virtually every paragraph of what, unfortunately, can be seen as nothing if not a withering Indictment of Us, as an international institution, and as an over-privileged, rampaging group of men and women defying every day the world's conscience, and defacing grossly our own heritage of fair play and decency and humanity.

For God's sake, let us stop dead in our tracks and take stock of ourselves, for stocktaking is overdue. Serious, clinical stocktaking, before a knowledgeable public that, conceivably, can force us to save ourselves from what we have become is a long, long overdue act of redemption - for us, and for the mass of humankind that we have defiled and diminished for nearly two score years.

Attachment

INTERNATIONAL MONETARY FUND

WASHINGTON. D.C. 20431

May 18, 1988

CABLE ADDRESS
INTERFUND

Mr. Camdessus
Managing Director
International Monetary Fund
Washington, D.C.

Dear Mr. Camdessus,

Davison L. Budhoo: Part I of Open Letter of Resignation From the Staff of the International Monetary Fund: Reason for this Letter and a Summary of its Contents

1. THE MILIEU

(a) Why I have to Forego the Code of "Proper Fund Staff Behavior" and Write this Letter

Today I resigned from the staff of the International Monetary Fund after over twelve years, and after 1000 days of official Fund work in the field, hawking your medicine and your bag of tricks to governments and to peoples in Latin America and the Caribbean and Africa. To me resignation is a priceless liberation, for with it I have taken the first big step to that place where I may hope to wash my hands of what in my mind's eye is the blood of millions of poor and starving peoples. Mr. Camdessus, the blood is so much, you know, it runs in rivers. It dries up too; it cakes all over me; sometimes I feel that there is not enough soap in the whole world to cleanse me from the things that I did do in your name and in the names of your predecessors, and under your official seal.

But I can hope, can't I? Certainly I can hope. I can hope that there is compassion and indignation in the heart of my world, and that people can stand up and take notice of what I have to say, and listen to your reply. For you will have to reply, because the charges that I make are not light charges - they are charges that touch at the very heart of western society and western morality and post-war inter-governmental institutionalism that have degenerated into fake and sham under the pretext of establishing and maintaining international economic order and global efficiency.

You think that's all there are to my charges? No, there is more; much more. The charges that I make strike at the very soul of man and at his conscience. You know, when all the evidence is in, there are two types of questions that you and me and others like us will have to answer. The first is this : - will the world be content merely to brand our institution as among the most insidious enemies of humankind? Will our fellowmen condemn us thus and let the matter rest? Or will the heirs of those whom we have dismembered in our own peculiar Holocaust clamor for another Nuremberg?

I don't mind telling you that this matter has haunted me; it has haunted me particularly over the past five years. It has haunted me because I know that if I am tried I will be found guilty, very guilty, without extenuating circumstance.

But beyond the question of guilt, there is a far more operational matter that bothers me; it is this: what devil is there in us that will allow us to go this far into a shame and an ignominy without screaming out a protest as human beings and as men of conscience? How could we have allowed ourselves for so long to defend the indefensible?

When I ask myself that question I become disoriented. I become disoriented because I cannot cope with the consequences of the answer that I know will surface one day. Put simply, that answer will doubtlessly focus on the total preoccupation of Fund people, and Fund inspired people, with personal material gratification and with the lust for, and abuse of power placed so inadvertently, yet so completely, in their hands. It is the timeless story of human beings, faced with an exceptional opportunity to further the cause of mankind, turning around and destroying everything worth preserving because of some indefinable quirk in our Nature.

It is the timeless story of the descent of another century of history into hell.

Doubtlessly you feel outraged that I speak thus, and that I ask questions that raise the spectre of personal culpability of those who labor within our institution, and that I make what you may see as meaningless, but dramatic and eye-catching generalizations about our work and history's verdict on it. Perhaps you wish to say to me "You are mad to suggest that the Fund, or anyone associated with it, has committed such awful crimes." Well, maybe I am mad, Mr. Camdessus, to look at our operations with eyes of candor and to feel terror, rather than satisfaction, at the sight of us doing things of Dracula that we so blithely do. But I cannot help being mad thus; I cannot help feeling what I feel; I cannot help being squeamish. I guess you can say that there was always a Mr. Hyde within me, and even as I did your Dr. Jekyl work I kept looking over my shoulder at his kind face. And one day he said to me: "Take stock of yourself; the image of the Beast is blotting out all else. Your soul is becoming shrivelled up; you are becoming dispossessed of all traces of your humanity." And I replied: "It cannot be; I will never accept to be thus; I will fight tooth and nail to return to the Human Fold."

This Letter is the start of my fight back to that Fold, and in writing it, and in doing other things that I must henceforth do, I have to forego the conventional stereotype of Fund Staff "proper" behavior. Put bluntly, as from today I refuse to accept the Fund-imposed censorship on our activities in the Third World. I have also stopped obeying your directive that reports and memoranda and other printed matter that document these activities be regarded as unexceptionally confidential and "hush-hush". Equally, I reject the Fund's traditional stance that the world has no right to know details of our methodology, or be made privy to the secrets of our success in doing what we do. More comprehensively and catalytically, as from today I tear off the mask of studied ambiguity that your organization did give me twelve years ago. As from today, Conscience becomes my only guide.

(b) The Purpose of this Letter

In guilt and self-realization of my own worthlessness as a human being, what I would like to do most of all is to so propel myself that I can get the man-in-the- street of North and South and East and West and First and Second and Third and Fourth and All Other Worlds to take an interest in what is happening to his single planet, his single habitat, because our institution was allowed to evolve in a particular way in late twentieth-century international society, and allowed to become the supra- national authority that controls the day-to-day lives of hundreds of millions of people everywhere. More specifically, I would like to enlighten public opinion about our role and our operations in our member countries of the Third World. I would like...

Do I hear you bristling with disapproval? Yes, I do. "Enlightening public opinion" are nasty words in the vocabulary of the Fund; I know it; I know it. Well, not so for me. In my new dictionary, "enlightening public opinion" spells the only means to salvation. For if I can do that - if I can get people to begin to comprehend the universality and the depth of our perversion - I would have achieved something rare and precious for the starving and dispossessed two-thirds of mankind from whose ranks I come, and for whose cause I must now fight.

If only I can light a little spark of concern for the Third World from the First World, Mr. Camdessus! If only I can make others to see that the poor and the destitute are not the expendable garbage heap that our institution thinks they are! (what a garbage heap, Mr. Camdessus! What a large expendable garbage heap of three billion souls!). If only I can...

(c) What this Letter is, and isn't

Wait, Mr. Camdessus, wait! Don't breathe a sigh of relief. Don't say : "Oh, another do-gooder filled with delusion and a pitiable sense of self-importance! Another geezer striving vainly for melodramatics! Another geezer wasting my time. Now that I know who he is and what he is after, let me call in the High Priests of the Fund. They will take care of him; they will clean up the little mess that he did make. What a life! It's all in a day's work."

Mr. Camdessus, don't say these things; don't devalue my substance thus, as we devalue the currency of every Third World country that we latch on to. You know, contrary to what may be your impression after reading the first few pages of this Letter, I do not deal in wild accusations and uninformed guesses; I do not deal in diatribe. I deal in cold, stark facts - facts and specifics of time and place and Fund policies and Fund conditionalities and Fund missions and Fund meetings and Fund negotiations and Fund-related fraud, and...

And Fund-related fraud?

Yes, Sir, Fund-related fraud. You know, the term "fraud" is not mine; it was first used by your predecessor, Mr. de Larosiere; I merely pick-up from where he left off. And in so doing, I shall put under the microscope each element of the type of fraud to which he did refer; I shall dissect every element separately to show where the cancer lies.

Want an example of the technique? Want me to illustrate the method of approach that I will use to dissect our dealings in member countries?

Well, I'll respond immediately by delving into our activities in the member country of Trinidad and Tobago, a small, twin-island state in the Eastern Caribbean. I will summarize here, briefly, what we did do there from 1985 to the present time. (In Parts II and III of this Letter I describe these activities, blow by blow, in great detail.) And I'll guarantee you one thing - viz: that when I've had my say, no one in the Fund will want to laugh again today, or tomorrow, or the day after tomorrow for that matter.

2. SIX INDICTMENTS AGAINST OUR OPERATIONS IN TRINIDAD AND TOBAGO

I hereby file accusation against the Fund in its dealings with Trinidad and Tobago on six counts, viz:

(i)   We manipulated, blatantly and systematically, certain key statistical indices so as to put ourselves in a position where we could make very false pronouncements about economic and financial performance of that country. In doing so, we created a situation whereby the country was repeatedly denied access to international commercial and official sources of financing that otherwise would have been readily available. Our deliberate blocking of an economic lifeline to the country through subterfuge served to accentuate tremendously the internal and external financial imbalances within the economy springing from the dramatic downturn in the price of oil;

(ii)   The nature of our ill-will, and the depth of our determination to continue on a course of gross irregularities, irrespective of economic consequences for the country and its peoples, are clearly shown by the fact that your senior staff bluntly refused in 1987 to correct even one iota of the wrong that we had done over 1985/86;

(iii)   Congruent with action outlined in (i) and (ii), the staff has waged within the Fund an aggressive campaign of misinformation and derision about economic performance in Trinidad and Tobago. The insidiousness of that campaign is dramatically highlighted in the deliberately wild allegations made in the Briefing Paper to the last consultation mission - a paper that was cleared and approved by your good self in late June, 1987;

(iv)   As the country continues to resist our Deadliest Medicine that would put it in a position to enter into a formal stand-by arrangement with us, we continue to resort to statistical malpractices and unabashed misinformation so as to bring it to heel. Among several misdeeds, we have influenced the World Bank, apparently against the better judgement of its own mission staff, to come out in support of our trumped-up policies and stances for the country;

(v)   In our seemingly inexplicable drive to see Trinidad and Tobago destroyed economically first, and converted thereafter into a bastion of Fund orthodoxy, we have applied, and are applying, intolerable pressures on the government to take action to negate certain vital aspects of the arrangements, as enshrined in the constitution of the country, through which the government functions, and within whose framework fundamental rights of the people are recognized and protected, and norms of social justice and economic equity maintained;

(vi)   Our policy package for Trinidad and Tobago - i.e. the conditionality that we are demanding for any Fund program, and the measures that we are asking the authorities to implement as a necessary precondition for a loosening of the iron grip that we now hold on the fortunes of the country in so far as its recourse to international capital markets and official bilateral donors are concerned - can be shown, even in a half-objective analysis, to be self-defeating and unworkable. That policy package can never serve, under any set of circumstances, the cause of financial balance and economic growth. Rather, what, in effect, we are asking the Government of Trinidad and Tobago to do is to self-destruct itself and unleash unstoppable economic and social chaos. In this respect, this Letter invites you to appoint urgently an independent expert group to look into all aspects of the charges made in Parts II and III of the Letter;

Self-defeating and unethical as it may seem, what we have done and are doing in Trinidad and Tobago is being repeated in scores of countries around the world, particularly in Latin America and the Caribbean and Africa. Sometimes we operate with greater restraint, sometimes with less, but the process and the result are always the same: a standard, pompous recital of doctrinaire Fund "advice" given uncompromisingly and often contemptuously and in utter disregard to local conditions and concerns and susceptibilities. It is the norm now rather than the exception, that when our "one-for-all and all-for-one" Fund cap doesn't fit the head for which it is intended, we cut and shave and mangle the head so as to give the semblance of a fit. Maybe we bust up the head too much in Trinidad and Tobago, but have no illusions that the way we operate throughout the world - the narrow and irrelevant epistemology underlying our work, the airs and affectations and biases and illusions of superiority of our staff vis-Á-vis government officials and politicians in the developing world, our outrageous salaries and perks and diplomatic immunities and multiple "entitlements", the ill-gotten, inadvertent power that we revel in wielding over prostrate governments and peoples - can only serve to accentuate world tensions, expand even further the already bulging ranks of the poverty-striken and destitute of the South, and stunt, worldwide, the human soul, and the human capacity for caring and upholding norms of justice and fairplay.

3. A BIRD'S EYE VIEW OF SUBSEQUENT PARTS OF THIS LETTER

Each of the remaining five Parts of this Letter has been placed in appropriate safekeeping, pending release to you. In this section, a brief summary is given of each of these five Parts.

(a) Summary of Parts II and III

Parts II and III document, in considerable detail, the range of Fund wrongdoing in Trinidad and Tobago from 1985 to the present time, as summarized in Section 2 above. Part II deals with statistical malpractices and improprieties that we did perpetrate (items (i) through (iv) on page 4), whereas Part III provides evidence to support charges relating to non-statistical issues (items (v) and (vi) on pages 4 and 5). From the backdrop of our very shameful but wholly unrepentant behavior in Trinidad and Tobago over the period identified, two operational and highly relevant issues are brought into focus in later sections of Part III. The first of these reminds you that on-going Fund policy pays a lot of lip service to "evenhandedness" (or equality of treatment) in our relationships with member countries, but suggests that in actual practice this goal remains a dead letter. Firsthand evidence to support this latter position is brought to bear on a comparison that is made of our treatment of Trinidad and Tobago and Jamaica in 1987. The second matter aired is the question of what constitutes statistical fraud in the dealings of the Fund with member countries, and what are the penalties involved for entities caught redhanded in perpetrating such fraud, or otherwise indulging in statistical malpractices meant to mislead others or to misrepresent a true position. On this issue, you are urged to establish immediately an independent investigative authority to look into all charges made in Parts II and III, and in the light of the findings of such authority, to take whatever remedial action is called for in relation to established Fund procedures, notwithstanding the fact that the culprit may prove to be the Fund itself, rather than miscreant member countries for which the penalties were intended in the first instance.

(b) Summary of Part IV

Part IV is divided into three sections. The first reviews the conceptual content and the theoretical underpinning of our "program" for Trinidad and Tobago, irrespective of the statistical and other malpractices that we did commit in the process of trying to get the authorities to bite the bullet and accept that "program." The conclusion is that our "program" for Trinidad and Tobago is nothing but a hotchpotch of irreconcilable and conflicting elements and objectives. The accusation is made that the internal logic of our "program" spells comprehensive economic disorder in Trinidad and Tobago and all enfolding disintegration of the fabric of national life - economic, political, and social. Evidence is brought to show that our action in Trinidad and Tobago does not relate to any clear set of economic principles, however misguided or inappropriate such principles may be, and that we are just striking out wildly at everything and anything in our path, without reason or rationale or sensitivity to an aftermath.

The second section of Part IV asks the question: why should this be the case? How, in fact did we get into the game of giving farcical advice to member countries? In seeking an answer, another question is brought to the fore; it is this: Is the Fund staff running amok with the wholly unexpected and unexceptional authority that they wield? Are we churning out despair after despair, hunger after hunger, death after death, in the name of Bretton Woods epistemology merely to satisfy a lust for power and punish those who run against the grain of our personal or "professionalized" political ideology, while rewarding those who think as we do?

This question takes us back to the very origin of the Fund; an attempt is made to unravel the various elements of Fund history and epistemology to see how and if, to what extent and at what stage, our quest for a better functioning world became ensnarled into our personal ambitions and our burgeoning group psychosis.

On the above matters a set of inter-related conclusions are drawn. The first is that the Fund, which was established primarily to serve developed countries by overseeing the return of the industrialized world to orderly multilateral trade and payments arrangements, has never been able to come to terms with the problems of the developing world, which are fundamentally different - ie; a economic growth and diversification, and broad social change along the whole spectrum of income distribution, quality of life, social security and political instability and economic waste, and poverty and hunger and disease and desperation. Always, and under all conditions that may be encountered, the conceptual backdrop that we brought to bear on our work, and the body of economic principles that guided our action, sprang overwhelmingly from the nineteenth century vision of Pax Britanica, now writ large as Pax Atlantica - ie; "perfect competition" and "world allocation of resources" and "international division of labor" and "general equilibrium in the (western) world economy" to be achieved through the instrumentality of unbridled and "free" pricing systems domestically and Gold-Standard determined exchange rates internationally. As far as we were concerned, all the difficult dynamics and unforeseen phenomena of the developing world in the fifties and sixties and seventies and eighties of this century had no meaning whatsoever; they could be ignored or dismissed or shrugged off without the batting of an eye or the furling of a brow. Unwilling and unable to meet emerging Third World needs, we became the Neanderthaler of the twentieth century.

Why was this the case?

The third section provides the following answer, viz; sometime in the course of Fund history, our original epistemology became transformed from a system of verifiable concepts, theoretically open to change and adaptation, to a totally closed and vainglorious doctrine that has nothing to do with economic theory, but everything to do with the Nature of Man. More specifically, at some stage the Fund staff - the seeming "nondescript technocrat" who was hardly ever mentioned in our Articles of Agreement - managed to "steal" the Fund and began using it as his own personal tool to propel and shape the emergence of what I choose to call a New Nobility on Earth, wielding power and influence and control over the lives of hundreds of millions of hapless people in a New Late-Twentieth Century Dark Age, epitomized by a Continual and Never-Ending State of Tyranny and Dictatorship and Oppressiveness. Even more specifically, at some stage in Fund history, Pax Atlantica gave way to Pax Honeypot when the latter is defined to mean the easily identifiable and endless stock of almost unbelievable goodies and material Things of Life provided by the captive Fund to its triumphant and rampaging and insatiable staff. Pax Honeypot has become the be-all and end-all of everything done by the Fund in the Third World; it is the basis of all our motivation and all our objectives in countries such as Trinidad and Tobago that we would rape, and where we would commit statistical fraud, and mash up the constitution and bring poor people to further and further grief and destitution.

The following general conclusions are drawn, after close perusal of evidence.

(i) We get away with our works of Dracula hiding behind the mask of Superior Technocracy and a Greater Wisdom striving for "financial balance" and "structural adjustment" in the Third World. But the mask is becoming more and more tattered, outside observers and victims of our scorched earth policy themselves are beginning to see us as we really are. But our response to criticism is greater self- righteousness and greater indignation and sense of effrontery that anyone can dare to question our works and our methods. Can't they see that we are the only wise ones and that they are the fools?

(ii) The Fund is soulless, not because there is no scope for humanized behavior and compassion in an institution dedicated to optimum world efficiency and a more effective use of foreign financial resources in developing countries, but because its founders, in chasing their improbable dream of Pax Atlantica, overlooked all scope for exercising compassion and alleviating social injustice in certain parts of the international system that they were creating. Compassion and social justice were crying needs; they are the very roots on which we should have nurtured an evolving and pragmatic Fund philosophy for the Third World. But our Founding Fathers denied us access to them, and shrivelled our soul. So later on, when we "stole" the Fund, All Things Just and Humane became our Absolute Antithesis; we were as clinically and completely materialistic and single-minded in pursuit of Our Own Gratification (Pax Honeypot) as they were in pursuit of Pax Atlantica.

(iii) In a very meaningful way, our staff perversion is the logical consequence of our Founding Fathers' credo, just as the latter is the logical consequence of the prevailing 1944 international ethos of Superior Man and Inferior Man, and the western man and his system to be saved and nurtured, and the southern man to be overlooked and cast aside, in so far as his needs and aspirations as individuals and groups and nations are concerned.

And it is this theme - the theme of the southern man remaining in oppression under post-war multilateralism, spearheaded by the Fund, as he had been under seventeenth and eighteenth and nineteenth century colonialism - that occupies the fourth section of Part IV. More specifically, representative examples are given of the modus operandi of Fund staff as the New Nobility of Earth, out to protect and expand Pax Honeypot, and to smother all opposition to their hegemony, from whatever quarter such opposition may come. Initially, the spotlight turns to "internal" power distribution among the staff, with "core" staff from the West calling the shots and laying down, virtually on their own, Fund law at 700 19th Street, N.W., Washington D.C. Subsequently, the field of enquiry widens from "internal" matters to "external" authority wielded by sectors of our staff. In particular, the nature of power that we hold in countries of the Third World, and the methods that we use to make our power effective and self-sustaining, are brought to the fore.

On "internal" matters you are asked to take a close look at the implications of the rampant and multifaceted racism that is now an extremely operative factor in Fund staff calculations; as you are fully aware, this "internal" worm eating at our soul has created its own system of internal injustices and double standards and rank arbitrariness within the Fund, particularly in relation to staff promotion and job assignments. But, unfortunately, that is only the tip of the iceberg; the matter runs far deeper than staff issues. Indeed, racism makes itself felt in a wide range of organizational practice, some of which are eminently inexcusable, given our international nature. Among these is the classification of South Africa as a "European country" administered by our highly segregated, virtually "white staff only can work here" European Department.

But however outrageous our internal practice and organizational arrangements, they fade into insignificance when compared with the sheer temerity and dare-devil grossness of the methods and procedures that we use to keep Third World governments and peoples under our heel. And in this respect the most obvious point to be made is that we are Judge and Jury and Maker of All Relevant Laws Pertaining to the Crime Committed and Administrator of the Penal Code and Executor of the Sentence.

Yes, yes, Mr. Camdessus, in scores of developing countries that are unfortunate enough to fall within our grasp, we hold simultaneously and completely in our hand Legislative and Executive and Judicial powers over wide- ranging matters relating to national economic and financial policies. We do our own "tainted" evaluation of economic and financial performance (an evaluation that is subsequently accepted as Bible Truth by our Executive Board and by the international community); we write our own Letter of Intent under the name of the Minister of Finance and present it to him for signature; we administer the "program" specified in the Letter of Intent (this includes determining whether or not the country has met the "performance criteria" that we have established, and whether, therefore, it is eligible, on "target" dates, to draw down the financial resources that we had committed, and that other supporting institutions had promised).

The whole process of determining what is "right" for the country, to formulating that "rightness" into a legal document that specifies "conditionality" and "performance criteria", to administering and monitoring the "program", to determining whether or not the country is eligible to draw, to alerting the international community as to whether or not we did see fit to create yet another "outcast country" or "leprosy case", is performed not only solely by the Fund, or by the relevant Division of the appropriate Department of the Fund, but in most instances by a single staff member acting on your behalf and with your authority. Such a staff member would hold, for all intents and purposes, the economic fate of the country concerned, and of its peoples, in his hand; as such he becomes transformed from a human being to the Unstoppable Supra- National Authority; all his own personal prejudices and arbitrariness and hang-ups and self-interest and lust for power and mad desire to control the destiny of peoples and of nations become essential elements of that Unstoppable Authority.

It is a telling commentary on the nature of our operations in the developing world to be able to say, without any fear of contradiction - I wish you would contradict, Sir, so I can reply - that for forty years we took a particular stance and acted in a particular way that showed a total disregard and absolute contempt for the doctrine of the separation of powers - a doctrine that constitutes the true basis of everything fair and just and decent in western political and economic and social systems. Amazingly, our contemptuous disregard for, and easy dismissal of the most treasured tenets of western society, have somehow been accepted by the Third World as "normal" and "right" practice by the Fund. You know, it is Lord Acton who observed that "all power corrupts, and absolute power corrupts absolutely." That maxim could never have been truer than when applied to us. The Third World, in accepting our absolute power and our absolute corruption, is also instrumental in writing its own obituary.

(c) Summary of Part V

Part V of the Letter is devoted to a definition of the actual size and depth of our Treasured Honeypot that is the Be All and End-All of Everything for Fund staff, and to an investigation of how we use the Honeypot as a means for neutralizing and defusing "outside" elements that potentially could threaten or frustrate the exercise of our Absolute Authority in the developing world.

On size and depth of the Honeypot, details are given of salary and other emoluments, including our multifarious allowances and subsidies. On this matter, it is concluded that the salary/allowances package of a median "missionary" staff member would be in the region of from five to ten times the budgeted salary of almost every Third World head of state, and some one thousand times the per capita income of that two thirds of mankind that he is paid so handsomely to crush down into further destitution.

The salaries/allowances package, of course, tells only part of the story; beyond it, there is an amazing set of perquisites and "intangibles" that come with the job. These include diplomatic immunities and our United Nations Laissez Passer, Royalty and First Class travel everywhere we go, generous allowances for overnight stays in Europe and elsewhere on our way to perform our "missionary" work in Africa and Asia and Latin America, high class night-clubbing in Sin Cities of the world, personal secretaries on each and every of our missions, G5 Visas for maids that we bring in from Paraguay and Mexico and Jamaica and Greece and everywhere else, the very generous Group Life Insurance and Medical Benefits Plans, and the even more generous Pensions Scheme. And most satisfying of all, the realization dawning on us that we have finally made it to Ultimate Paradise.

Honeypot, of course, transcends the staff; we make others to partake of the Good Things of Life, depending on the extent to which we perceive them either as a threat to our own Unmolested Gratification, or as an aid to help us win even greater personal material benefits. Specifically, we share our Honeypot with our Executive Board and its staff, who sit at our headquarters in Washington, and whose "typical" salary/allowances package is even heftier than ours. Drawn hopelessly into our malestrom, and obviously Very Pleased with Everything Pertaining to Honeypot's Form and Style and Substance, the Board of Executive Directors-appointed by member governments as a political entity to "direct" the Fund - has become a quiescent, almost anesthetized body; it operates mostly as a rubber stamp to endorse our action and initiatives that are designed, invariably, to maintain our political and economic hegemony in Third World countries. In addition to having their teeth drawn by the faceless bureaucrat whose original purpose was to implement autonomous decisions of the Executive Board (what a reversal of function!), your attention is drawn to the consequences of a set of anomalies and conflicts of interest involving the government appointed staff of Executive Directors in their relations with "regular" Fund staff.

That we, faceless bureaucrats, protect our flanks by going far beyond the Executive Board and its staff is illustrated and documented carefully in the final section of Part V. In this respect, a representative set of action on our part involving "external" entities is highlighted viz: (a) the "carrot" (involving, of course, use of our ubiquitous Honeypot) that we offer to senior government officials, and middle-level government officials to be soft on us, and/or to actively collaborate as we construct our bogus programs based on "fixed" statistics so as to sell such "right" programs to national political directorates; (b) the cosmetic measures taken to defuse international criticism and give the illusion that the Fund is responding meaningfully to the needs of developing countries. Specifically, recent institutional innovations within the management structure of the Fund - ie; the establishment of the Group of Twenty Four and the Development and Interim Committees - are discussed from the perspective of the realistic role and function of such entities within the context of a burgeoning staff supremacy at all levels in Fund decision making processes. Equally, the true purpose of the periodic appointment of "Wise Men" (compliments of Honeypot) to do "new thinking" and undertake "independant analysis" and "objective evaluation" of our successes and failures is brought to your attention. "Wise Men" rise and fall with equally indecent haste, they say the lines that we did want them to say and then they go away. And in the aftermath, the only thing that ever becomes strengthened is the already impregnable position of the faceless Fund technocrat, and his accountability to no one but himself.

In general, the conclusion of this Part of the Letter is as follows: any outside shock wave that conceivably may serve to alter, even by one iota, the Established Order of Things, or the Equanimity of Our High Priests (senior staff) or the Irresistible Logic of the Fund in Reducing Everything to a Common Denominator of Greed and Personal Ambition, or Maintenance of the Status Quo and Further Enhancement of the Power of the New Nobility, must be expunged, necessarily and unexceptionally, from the system. However, we don't do our expunging with high visibility action or with fanfare. A willingness to ride out the criticism, or the protest, or the concern expressed by others is what is called for. Seeming reasonableness and propriety and "sweet talk" become the order of the day; we seem to feed the hog even as we stab him in the back. There is no intellectual effort, no honest search for solutions, no new thinking whatsoever. Mediocrity and an absolute slavish imitation of High Priests who have "made it" in the Fund; stultifying conformity and an amazing perfection of the art of "yesmanship" - these are the essential elements of a true Fund Person. Hypocrisy underlies everything that we do; certainly core elements of our staff have had centuries of experience in practicing it on subject peoples. And the world is no closer today to an amelioration of the ills of Imperial Empire than it was at the time of Queen Victoria. Therein lies the bequeathment of the West and the tragedy of the South. Therein, too, lies the entire history and insidiousness of the Fund.

(d) Summary of Part VI

This Part has eight sections. The first section comes back to a fundamental question raised in Part IV, viz: can the Fund reform itself so that it serves the true interests of developing countries without negating critically its role as the major plank of an international management system for economic stability and growth and for the financing of such stability and growth? In searching for an answer, a comprehensive listing is made of "reform proposals" made by your good self and by your predecessors over the past several years to change the nature and the modules of Fund operations and facilities, presumably with a view to sensitizing the institution to the needs and characteristics of developing countries. All aspects of the agenda for change and reform that you have articulated recently are classified under four headings viz: (a) resource mobilization by the Fund (eg; establishment of the Enhanced Structural Adjustment Facility financed by developed countries); (b) resource transfer by the Fund (eg; establishment of an External Contingency Mechanism to be combined with the existing Compensatory Financing Facility for assisting countries to overcome unforeseen external shocks); (c) terms and conditions for resource transfer by the Fund (eg; establishment of an interest subsidy facility and proposals for "relaxing" Fund conditionality); (d) the effect on developing countries of resource transfer under stated terms and conditions (eg; impact on the poor and economically underprivileged).

Having listed thus your Agenda for Reform, an examination is made of items on the Agenda to see just how they tie in with the wide spectrum of issues raised in earlier parts of the Letter, and how they address the rank abuses of Fund staff in the Third World - abuses that have been carefully and systematically documented throughout the Letter at a level of detail and specificity that can be checked and verified, and that can leave no scope for guesswork or equivocation. And in this respect, the conclusion is drawn that past and present "reform proposals" put forward by Fund Management are not really proposals for reform at all - certainly they do not address matters highlighted in this Letter. Instead, they are shown to be the minimum jawboning that the Fund staff feels compelled to indulge in at any particular time, to take the heat out of criticisms about our operations in the Third World made by the Board of Governors and other "important" entities. In any event, your Reform Agenda is not new; the items identified - with one exception - have been depressingly recycled, with minor modification, at almost every Fund/World Bank Board of Governors gathering over the past twenty years.

We go through motions, Sir; we have our annual charade that we call the Fund/World Bank Board of Governors Meetings; we hand out the same "reform package" to the Ministers of Finance of the Third World, and they go home satisfied, having connived in all our trickery and participated in our game. Yes, yes, we move them around the chessboard like robots. We tell them "come back for the next bodacious meeting of the Development and Interim Committees in Sin City in the Spring; Fun and Games will start anew again."

And so it goes on and on and on. And nothing changes in the developing world except more death and destitution for the people in the slums, and more power for the Fund. And with the passing of every meeting our staff becomes even more reinvigorated; they wield a sharper and more bloodied tool; an even more terrifying Executor's Axe stand poised for service everywhere in the South. And the children scream, Sir; my God, how they scream!

The only relatively new "reform proposal" on your agenda relates to the impact of Fund supported programs on poverty groups. This issue received some degree of formal recognition by the Fund in 1984 with discussion by the Executive Board of a staff paper purporting to show the impact of Fund programs on poverty levels and related matters. With slight modification the paper was published and circulated worldwide. This was unfortunate, for the paper was extremely defective technically and analytically, and its arguments highly dubious. The aim appeared to be to invent excuses from thin air, and to give the appearance of a Fund concern for this burning Third World issue - an issue that previously we had either ignored or brushed aside brusquely. In any event, the paper was seen for what it was; internationally, it was greeted with overwhelming skepticism. This forced the authors to go back to the drawing board so as to try to come up with a more credible apology. The result was another paper issued to the Board in January, 1988, and another publication circulated worldwide in May 1988.

The latter part of the second section analyses this "second attempt" paper at some depth. The conclusion is drawn that the paper can have no merit as an objective evaluation of the role of the Fund in deepening the level and extent of poverty in Third World countries and in redistributing national income in favor of highly privileged and elitist groups. In this respect, it is as equally laughable as its predecessor. More pointedly, the authors admit that they themselves had been instrumental in formulating the Fund programs being evaluated for a "poverty impact". Amazingly, those who had themselves participated in pushing our medicine down the throats of screaming victims were mandated by the Fund to judge the social damage of their work. But I should know better than to find this irregular or unfortunate in any way, given the level of ethics and morality characteristic of our institution.

Inadvertently, the paper did serve a very useful purpose. For at last Fund people have made some sort of pronouncement on the poverty issue, never mind how biased and self-serving such pronouncement may be. Now others can move on from a recognized Fund conceptual base and from a Fund related viewpoint to open up a worldwide dialogue on the true impact of Fund "adjustment programs" on poverty and income distribution in the Third World. There is no way in which we can retreat back into our shell; there is no way in which we can conveniently put the poverty dimension of our work under wraps again. Pandora's box is wide open and we had better begin to recognize that immediately.

The section ends by examining a plethora of technical possibilities through which the poverty and income redistribution variable could be made to become an integral part of Fund programming and performance guidelines in Fund supported arrangements. One by-product of this exercise is the identification of a seemingly unbridgeable chasm between Pax Honeypot and all that it stands for, and the human values that we had ignored and had lost. Starkly brought into focus is the mind-boggling extent of our violation of basic human rights throughout the developing world for over the past five years in particular. (And don't raise your hand in protest, Sir, as I say this. The evidence is there, wait to read it).

The third section of Part VI asserts that however catalytic and causative are Fund programs as tools for deepening poverty and unleasing further destitution on the South, such programs represent only the periphery of an iniquitous and surprisingly comprehensive system within whose structure the Fund operates, and whose objectives it strives to achieve. That system is responsible for massive people-oriented economic crimes, and acts of almost unbelievable horror against the poorest sectors of society in countries of the South.

A plea is made to you to start a process whereby we can be made to retrace our steps back to the Bretton Woods Conference of 1944, holding to our chest the soiled and tattered rag of multilateralism that did represent dreams and aspirations of almost two generations of southern people - dreams and aspirations that did become a graveyard and an imposed monstrosity defiling our times and our world. We have to hold that tattered rag with a contrite heart; we must be made to realize that it is an intolerable burden on our soul. Somehow we must know that we have to make amends.

The remaining five sections of this Part deal with just how we can start the process of 'making amends'.

Looking at evidence of Fund involvement in economic crimes other than through the intermediacy of our programs, the fourth section zeros in on the Fund's role in arms expenditures in Third World countries. With concurrence of the Fund, arms expenditures in developing countries rose from 7 billion in 1975 to over 14 billion in 1980 and above 21 billion in 1986. Between 1955-85, Third World military expenditures as a proportion of total world military expenditures rose from 3 percent to 20 percent. Yet in 1985 over 1 billion Third World people lived in what the United Nations has designated as absolute poverty, and over 500 million were in the throes of famine and incurable malnutrition. Throughout the entire post-war period, the Fund was content to shut its eyes entirely to the Third World military expenditure binge, in deference to the arms exporters - its major shareholders. We have no qualms in forcing governments to crush millions upon millions of their own people to death - look at the extremely serious allegations made recently by UNICEF against us in this respect - but when it comes to arms merchandising we are hypocritical enough to throw our hands up in the air and talk of "national sovereignty". That just is not good enough.

What the Fund could have done to curb military expenditures, but didn't do, is discussed at length; on this matter the issue of fungibility of Fund resources is brought to the forefront. Our cowardly refusal to undertake any sort of analysis of the arms issue, and its direct and predictable relationship to destitution and poverty in the South are also highlighted. The Letter pleads with you to try to shed for us the role of Whitewasher and Apologist on the military expenditure issue. While you cannot influence directly the arms export policies of our major shareholders, it is very much within your power to force the High Priests to undertake necessary research that could provide a base for a new and enlightened Fund position on military expenditures of Third World client states. And we should use our clout on Third World states in getting them to control the arms race, rather than forcing them to kill their own peoples for our sake.

Section five would be of particular interest to you; it deals with a theme that seems to be your own hobbyhorse; the theme of "financing versus adjustment". There is no phrase more abused and more misunderstood in the Fund than this one. We utter it loosely; to us it has really no technical connotation; it is just our blanket excuse for enslaving the South; it is Fund conditionality expressed more graphically.

So as to help provide you with a clearer perception of "financing versus adjustment" from the perspective of both the Fund and its developing member countries, a rigorous analysis is undertaken of the meaning of the term, and a conceptual base built up to show how economic efficiency can be maximised, for all the parties concerned, through use of "financing" to achieve "adjustment." This really is the heart of the aid relationship; this is the raison d'etre of multilateralism.

It is concluded that internationally acceptable and verifiable criteria can be used to determine the relevance and fairness of Fund conditionality in every instance of use of Fund resources by Third World countries, with three critical elements meshed into a matrix solution, viz.; Fund concern about the revolving nature of its resources, some criterion of international economic efficiency in resource use by the Fund, and the social welfare function of the country seeking use of Fund resources. To date, the latter criterion has been ignored by the Fund as an operative factor in its financing relationship with developing member countries. By refusing Third World countries recourse to any objective and verifiable analytical system to determine the economic worthiness of financial assistance that it is providing, the Fund has turned all post-war development economics, and all precepts underlying such economics, on their head.

In section six, the theme of the Fund turning post- war development economics on its head is tackled in a more comprehensive and systematic way. The issue hinges around the Fund's attempt to replace all development theory, from Arthur Lewis to A.Sen, with "Reaganomics" and Chicago School "monetarism". All current development theory recognizes that provision for, and administration of peoples' economic "entitlements" is an important purpose of economic management, even in the poorest countries of the South, and the ultimate rationale of government. But this is absolute anathema to Fund programs, and Fund theology. The analysis looks at the development experience of six southern countries and asks you to get your High Priests to make their choice of which of these countries have developed, and which have stagnated and regressed. I think we both know their answers in advance.

Sir, this Letter is optimistic enough, and imbued with sufficient faith to believe that there is scope for human beings, including those who run the Fund and who make decisions of life and death for the overwhelming masses of mankind, to move away from an edge - when that edge is pinpointed and its enormous dangers seen - and to seek safer ground that will allow exercise of an inherent humanity and a reaffirmation and rededication to norms of justice and fairplay. Even so, I am not so simplistic and so starry- eyed to think that the task of bringing the Fund back unto that safe ground is an easy, or an immediately attainable one. In this respect, there really are three interrelated, but conceptually different goals to be pursued in the wake of a new era of understanding on our part, and an acknowledgement by us of why and how we went astray. The first goal relates to wing clipping of our staff, or if one wants to be more blunt, to dismantlement of the modern day phenomenon of a New Nobility straddling the earth. The second involves a grappling and a coming to terms with the dynamics of the Third World; it also envisages establishment of a new and relevant epistemology that bursts, once and for all, the bubble of Pax Atlantica and ensures that Pax Honeypot will never be able to raise its head again as Fund credo. Finally, action must be taken to bring centerstage the politically-charged question of power distribution between Part I and Part II member countries within a reorganized international management system for world financial stabilization and economic and social development; or, alternatively stated, action must be taken to provide appropriate ways and means through which the Fund's changed philosophy and operational modules can become self- sustaining and its new mandate fulfilled. Sections seven and eight of Part VI deal exclusively with the first of these tasks; all else is left hanging in air for the time being.

The question of Fund staff wing clipping is discussed at various levels and from various angles, but two basic issues stand out, viz: (a) what can be done through direct means that impinge immediately on our overheavy salaries and allowances and perquisites and "privileges", to reestablish some sort of balance and sanity in our remuneration and terms and conditions of employment? (This Letter screams out that reestablishment of such balance and sanity is an absolute requirement for the restoration of professionalism and perspective and fairplay and humanity in our institution); (b) irrespective of the Honeypot that provides its stream of endless material benefits to Fund people, what checks and balances mechanisms may be created within the organizational structure of the Fund, and in the structure of relationships between the Fund and developing member countries, so as to curb the "absolute" power presently wielded by Fund bureaucracy in the Third World, and ameliorate the growing tendency for wanton abuse of that power?

On the first of these issues not much is said; the hope is that you can fill in some gaps over the next few months, as you respond, one way or the other, to my charges. I suggest, however, that there is need for some new thinking, from major shareholders, on how to halt escalating salary/allowances for Fund staff and beyond that, how to make Fund staff minimally accountable to member countries for action and stances in the developing world - action and stances that appear so totally unreasonable on any meaningful criterion of economic reasonableness. Efforts in the past to curb staff excesses have been very weak and half-hearted, and singularly unsuccessful. Proposals are made on how they may be strengthened and made more effective in the immediate future.

On the second matter, there is a distinction between (a) "internal" checks and balances mechanisms to curb staff power and restore a semblance of sanity and order among different decision-making elements of Fund management, such as senior staff, Board of Executive Directors and Board of Governors, and (b) "external" checks and balances mechanisms to halt excesses and power abuse in developing member countries - abuses that have been meticulously documented in Parts II through V of this Letter.

On "internal" mechanisms, proposals are made for the immediate establishment of those safeguards that had been built into the Fund's Articles of Agreement in 1944, but which had never been activated, mainly because of the unforeseen "hijacking" of the Fund by its burgeoning bureaucracy, and the outstanding success achieved by the latter in stifling all other potential power points within the decision making structure of the Fund. In this respect, relatively meaningless "posturing" of the past and present, including creation of the basically toothless and captive Interim Committee and Development Committee and Group of Twenty Four, as discussed extensively in Part V, must give way to a fully independent Fund Council of broad decision making powers and wide geographic representation along lines laid down in our Articles of Agreement. The Council should not be made to operate on "advice" from Fund staff; it must spawn its own small but highly proficient body of technical expertise as a counterweight to the methods and approaches of what initially may prove to be the still all-pervading power of our Retreating Nobility. In any event, it must be expected that in the short term, establishment of an effective regime of "internal" checks and balances that reflects the reality of a previously "captive" institution, will involve, inevitably, some degree of experimentation and perhaps of seeming functional duplication over a "phasing in" period of from, say, three to five years.

On "external" checks and balances the following are proposed for implementation, concurrent with the effectuation of "internal" reform: (a) establishment of an Advisory and Review Commission to be shared with the World Bank. This organ will assume the functions of the now defunct Advisory Council that was enshrined in the Articles of Agreement of the Bank. More specifically, it will act as a final court of appeal in instances where disputes of a technical nature have arisen (e.g; statistical discrepancies, relevance of performance criteria, eligibility criteria for particular facilities) between Fund (or Bank) staff and the member country concerned; (b) establishment of a series of Regional Coordinating Committees - independent of Fund staff and appointed by the Board of Governors - to review on an annual basis economic progress in each member country, and to lay down general guidelines to Fund (or Bank) staff for future operations in individual countries and regions. Regional Coordinating Committees should review all Fund staff documents (including REDs and Staff Reports to the Board) with a view to determining the accuracy and objectivity of such documents, and pronouncing on the "evenhandedness" in Fund staff stances from one country to another. Detailed comments from the Regional Coordinating Committee concerned should always accompany each and every Staff Report that goes to the Board, whether such Staff Report seeks approval for use of Fund resources or not.

In addition to action that must be endorsed formally by appropriate elements of Fund management, proposals are made for the formation, by developing countries themselves, of a Watchdog Committee to oversee their interests in negotiations with the Fund (and World Bank). It is proposed that the Committee be selected from a panel of eminently qualified persons including political figures, religious leaders, economists, sociologists, jurists and trade unionists from both developed and developing countries. The rationale for the

Committee is the existing overwhelming power of the Fund (and World Bank) in the Third World, vis-a-vis individual governments and Ministries of Finance, and therefore the extremely weak position of such governments and such Ministries in processes of multilateral economic negotiations on matters that determine their future, and the well-being or ill-being of their peoples at a particular point of time, and for several years thereafter. The Committee, which may take up the cause of any particular country only at the specific request of the government concerned, will serve to redress a long outstanding imbalance that never ever should have been made to exist. While it will have no authority to adjudicate on Fund horrors and excesses of the past, its work, conceivably, could lead to a less tortured existence for the Third World in the future.

A general recommendation of Part VI is as follows: until the above regulatory an control mechanisms, or appropriate variants of them, are established and become operative, developing countries - especially those who at the present time deem themselves to be receiving particularly raw deals from the Fund and the World Bank - may consider a strategy of freezing all relations until further notice. This will release their energies to pursue single-mindedly the very urgent, prior task of creating the type of institutional adaptations, as described above, to protect their interests in the face of current gross excesses rampant within the system. In this connection, it is pointed out that while organizational innovation within the formal structure of the institutions (e.g; establishment of an Advisory and Review Commission and of Regional Coordinating Committees) could be unduly delayed by non- Third World elements who may be opposed to the type of change contemplated, there is no reason why developing countries, perhaps through instrumentality of the G-77 or Non-Aligned Movement, or both, could not take immediate action on their own to bring into being the Watchdog Committee. Indeed, such a critical instrument for protecting the Third World could well be made to function within a six-month period, assuming that there is a reasonable degree of consensus, in the South, for its establishment.

4. A FINAL OBSERVATION BEFORE I PROCEED TO RELEASE PARTS II - VI OF THIS LETTER

Over and over again I've been told by people whose judgement I respect, that the Fund will do everything in its power to decimate me as an individual, and to destroy me as a professional economist, in the wake of this Letter. The overwhelming advice of those with my interests at heart is that I had better resist all dictates of conscience and keep my mouth shut. I refuse to do that; I will not be muzzled one iota; I will speak up; I have taken meticulous care in writing what I write; I am prepared to prove everything that I say - send me before the harshest judge and see what you will see. In any event, in the broad sweep, individuals are not important; Davison Budhoo is of no consequence. I'm a vessel and the message that I carry will get through; that's the only thing that matters; irrespective of what may happen to Davison Budhoo, the message, the whole message, will get through. And this Letter does not define anything close to the whole message; it is only the tip of an iceberg. And as to what lies beneath - well, time will tell. Soon enough, time will tell.

Follow your instincts, Sir, and let the High Priests go empty-handed for a change - at least, think very carefully before taking their advice on what to do about this Letter. For we are not speaking anymore about technical problems in international finance, amenable to technical and "convenient" solutions ("convenient" to who?) We're speaking about our role in shaping the destiny of humankind; about the horrendous part that we have played on the twentieth century world stage; about the legacy that we will leave to generation upon generation yet unborn; about man's inherent right to follow the callings of his conscience and man's efforts to try to save his soul; about the occasional sight of one individual throwing himself blindly at the feet of his fellowmen and begging for mercy and amelioration.

So think carefully Sir; think beyond the heat of an impassioned moment. Think as the man of compassion and vision that I believe you are.

Yours sincerely,

Davison L. Budhoo

May 18, 1988   CABLE ADDRESS
                    INTERFUND

Mr. Camdessus
Managing Director
International Monetary Fund
Washington, D.C. 20431

Dear Mr. Camdessus,

Davison L. Budhoo: Part II of Open Letter of Resignation from the Staff of the International Monetary Fund; Our Statistical Misdeeds and Our Statistical Fraud in Trinidad and Tobago, 1985-1988

This part of my Open Letter deals with the array of statistical irregularities that we did perpetrate in Trinidad and Tobago, in very recent times, and are still practicing today. Obviously, the provision of proof for indictments that I am making calls for extensive reference to, and quotations from documents and reports previously circulated internally, and/or to member countries and other international agencies. Even so, evidence provided here is selective, not comprehensive, and I shall be pleased to expand on the chosen themes to properly constituted investigative authority.

1. THE INDEX OF RELATIVE UNIT LABOUR COST (THE RULC INDEX) AND HOW WE ABUSED IT IN TRINIDAD AND TOBAGO

As you are fully aware, an Index of Relative Unit Labour Cost (RULC) that measures unit labour costs in manufacturing in the developing country concerned in relation to such costs in its major trading partners (industrialised countries) is a Key Economic Indicator that is used extensively in the Fund, subject to the availability of statistics. Once the series becomes available in a developing country, chances are it will feature prominently in our periodic consultation reports to the Executive Board - ie. the Report on Recent Economic Developments (RED) and the Staff Report. The prominence given to RULC reflects the perception that such an index mirrors international competitiveness of the economy concerned and indicates, therefore, the country's ability to continue to produce for export markets. In an economy such as Trinidad and Tobago, where one sector which had previously accounted for the bulk of export earnings (the oil sector) enters a phase of uncertainty and rapid price decline, the index is particularly important as a general determinant of the potential of the country to diversify successfully its export base and service its foreign debt. At a meeting in mid-June to prepare for the 1987 consultation mission, a Senior Staff member reviewed the recent, dismal performance of the country's RULC as revealed in our 1986 RED and Staff Report and commented that "this statistic is the most important one that we will ever collect in Trinidad and Tobago". In his own way he was right; no one steeped in Fund methodology would doubt those words. Certainly, we did not carry the RULC series in both the text and in the Statistical Appendix of the RED, and in highly visible graphs in both the RED and the Staff Reports of 1985 and 1986, for the mere fun of doing so. We knew fully well that the international financial community would peruse our conclusions on the RULC carefully and religiously, and that international money markets would make a decision to reschedule loans or grant new credit almost exclusively on the basis of what we were saying. In this respect, it must be remembered that the external debt profile of Trinidad and Tobago is relatively new, and that the country has not as yet had time to develop a track record of debt servicing that international banks and other financial institutions could use substantively as a guide for operations there.

Apart from providing a cue to commercial banks and other lenders, the RULC index serves a critical role in the establishment of Fund conditionality for developing countries. In fact, it is the most lethal weapon that we have in our entire bag of tricks - quite definitely, it is the one that we use most often, and most effectively, to cut short the arguments of protesting governments and peoples against the need for currency devaluation and/or other measures to cut the real wage rate, initiate mass layoff of workers in the public sector, and resort to crippling measures of "demand management". Thus, when we find a sagging index in a developing country we know, instantaneously, that the time has come to get another blighter to swallow our deadliest medicine.

And so it was for Trinidad and Tobago over the period 1985-1986. In each year we drilled home the point that the RULC was way out of line and that massive devaluation was needed; without such devaluation the country would slither progressively into mounting economic chaos. In 1985, for instance, and within the context of intense Fund pressure for devaluation, our RED (Report No. SM/85/105 of April 15, 1985) states as follows:

> "The substantial rise in wages, coupled with a fixed exchange rate and very small gains in productivity in most industries, have resulted in erosion of international competitiveness. Thus, unit labour costs in manufacturing compared with costs in major trading partners, rose by 150 per cent from 1979 to 1984."

In similar vein, the 1986 RED (Report No. SM 86/172 of July 15, 1986) comments as follows:

> "Unit labour costs in manufacturing increased by 160 per cent over the period 1981-85 due to the rapid increase in wages at a time when hours worked were declining ... unit labour costs in manufacturing compared to costs in Trinidad and Tobago's major trading partners, rose by 170 per cent during 1980- 85 ... resulting in a substantial erosion of international competitiveness."

As I said before, in 1985 and 1986 the RULC index for Trinidad and Tobago was highlighted in text tables of the RED and in the Statistical Appendix, and was plotted in graphs in both the RED and in Staff Reports to the Executive Board. These graphs demonstrated starkly an alleged position of a runaway and still rising RULC, and on the basis of such "evidence" we chastised the government severely for not taking appropriate, or sufficient corrective action to put its house in order. Even after a withering round of devaluation in late 1985 we continued to call, shrilly and insistently, for more devaluation, and more public sector unemployment and real wage cuts, and more "demand management" policies, and more price deregulation of essential goods used by the poor, and more regression in the tax system, et al.

This explicit and confrontational Fund posture is illustrated in the following excerpt from the Briefing Paper for the 1987 consultation mission, as cleared and approved by you in late June, 1987. (You may recall that that Paper became the essential reference point, and the formal basis for our discussions with the government of Trinidad and Tobago, during the course of the mission and subsequently).

The Paper reads as follows:

> "Over the ... period (1982-85), real GDP contracted sharply, and real wages continued to rise under heavy union pressure; unit labour costs in manufacturing relative to Trinidad and Tobago's main trading partners increased at an average rate of 20 per cent (per year)..."

> "A further devaluation of the Trinidad and Tobago dollar is needed ... The mission will propose a significant initial devaluation (e.g. from TT $3.6 to TT$ 5.0 per US dollar) perhaps to be followed by further small step adjustments..."

> "The degree to which exchange rate adjustment is successful will depend to a great extent on the incomes and demand management policies pursued by the authorities. The recent fall in export income makes a significant decline in real wages unavoidable ... To give full effect to the exchange rate adjustment being sought, the mission will stress the need to have exchange rate changes pass through fully to domestic prices of tradeable goods. This consideration may require a revision of the

Government's price control policy which limited the increase in domestic prices of essential imported goods following the reunification of the exchange system in January 1987".

I resort to the above quotations to establish the fact that we placed extraordinary importance on the RULC; our entire case for massive and continuing devaluation, and equally massive and continuing real wage cuts, depended on what we said was happening to that index. And this is not surprising, for there can be very few instances in Fund history where such a drastic increase in domestic labour costs over such a short period as we claimed for Trinidad and Tobago, was not followed by traumatic adjustment of exchange rates and real wages alike. As responsible international financial/economic inspectors, we were well within our right to carry a particularly poignant message to the Trinidad and Tobago authorities, and to warn them, in no uncertain terms, that we and the international community that follows us so blindly and so unexceptionally, would have no option but to turn away from the country and label it "a leprosy case" in the event that they could not see fit to drink our deadliest medicine.

But there is a catch in all this - viz: the RULC Index for Trinidad and Tobago was never close to what we were proclaiming it to be so loudly and so insistently and so definitively. What we had done over these years was to "manufacture" statistical indices - the RULC and several others - that would allow us to prove our point, and push a particular policy line, irrespective of economic realities and circumstances of the country.

Obviously, more details on just how we managed to misrepresent the RULC are needed - details of sources and statistical material and facts and figures and calculations and recalculations and Fund technical notes and Fund working sheets. And on this matter, I wish to state immediately that while I did participate in the work of all three Fund missions that visited Trinidad and Tobago between 1985-87, I did not become aware of the RULC scandal until last year, when I worked on the national income, prices and employment sectors of the economy. Not surprisingly, it has not been very easy to decipher any exact methodology underlying the 1985/86 calculations; most of the records for these years appear to have been destroyed prematurely. Even so, I have managed to put together some key elements of the jigsaw puzzle; this gives a fairly clear picture (from the technical stand point) of what we did in 1985-86. As for 1987, I have kept records of the various facets of our work on the RULC during the mission and subsequently.

On the basis of calculations made by our divisional statistician last year after the Fund mission returned from the field, the Relative Unit Labour Cost in Trinidad and Tobago increased by 69 percent only, instead of the 145.8 percent as stated in our 1985 reports, and the 142.9 percent as claimed in the 1986 Fund documents. Between 1980-85 the RULC actually rose by a mere 66.1 percent instead of our assertion of 164.7 percent made in the 1986 reports. Over 1983-85 relative unit labour costs moved up by only 14.9 percent, not by the 36.9 percent that was mooted to the world community in 1986. In 1985, instead of rising by the 9 percent that we had stated in the RED and Staff Report, the RULC Index fell by 1.7 per cent. And in 1986 relative unit labour costs slid downward spectacularly by 46.5 percent although there is no record of this in the 1987 report or anywhere else in official Fund documentation.

2. REFUSING TO "OWN-UP" TO THE TRINIDAD AND TOBAGO AUTHORITIES OR TO THE INTERNATIONAL COMMUNITY AFTER OUR "MISTAKES" WERE EXPOSED

Let me come back now to what happened in 1987 after there was "internal acknowledgement" that "mistakes" were made in 1985-1986. And let me say immediately that nothing happened - nothing at all. When, in the course of the mission last July, past misdeeds were pointed out, and a pledge won that we would "come good" once and for all, it was my understanding that we would make full amends during the consultation discussions with the Government, and that the mission's subsequent reports prepared for our Executive Board and for the international community would substitute revised figures for those of 1982-1986. But our previous "mistakes" were never mentioned to the authorities. Privately, it was conceded that in light of the corrected RULC figures, the instruction in our Briefing Paper to try to force the government to undertake more massive devaluation now and "step" increases thereafter was really beside the point. However, in statements to the authorities, and in the Aide Memoire presented to them, issues relating to the RULC in 1985, and the latter's performance in 1986 were side-stepped, and we went on glibly to ask for more devaluation, greater public sector lay-offs, further major real wage cuts and the whole gamut of demand management measures, as if the Briefing Paper's evaluation of the RULC was still absolutely valid, and eminently relevant for July 1987.

Back in Washington, the revised RULC index was prepared for publication in the RED and Staff Report. But it was not to be; all reference to RULC was deleted from all text, and from all tables, and from all charts. The reason for this action was obvious enough: public acknowledgement and publication of the corrected series, and demonstration of the dramatic downturn of the index in 1986, would have devastated the case for further devaluation now, and for the comprehensive and blistering demand management and wage/employment contraction measures that were being pushed down the throat of the Government, and for which we were seeking, ex post, formal endorsement from our Executive Board and, beyond our Board, from the entire international community. So, suddenly, what just a few weeks before had been branded "the most important statistic" that we would encounter in Trinidad and Tobago, became transformed into a nauseating irritant to be dropped as a hot potato, because it could no longer fit into the economic scenario that the Fund, with increasing insistence over several years, had tried to have enacted in the country.

3. GETTING YOUR PRIOR AUTHORIZATION FOR DRACONIAN POLICIES BY FEEDING YOU FALSE INFORMATION IN MISSION BRIEFING PAPER

Let me go on to the third indictment against Fund staff in their dealings with Trinidad and Tobago in 1987 - ie; the blatantly unfair portrayal of unmitigated confusion, and of governmental policies gone hopelessly astray, and becoming absolutely irrelevant, as painted in the Mission Briefing Paper dated June 29, 1987. Such a picture of accelerating macro-economic mismanagement and policy paralysis was deemed necessary so as to force you into giving approval to the mission for a mandate that would allow use of our iron fist.

(a) Stating the Facts

The Briefing Paper from the Western Hemisphere Department that was approved by you in late June makes the following observations:

"... Notwithstanding a downward revision of the Government's expenditure program, the overall public sector deficit rose to 20 per cent of GDP in 1986 and was financed entirely from domestic resources, including a build-up of unpaid bills by the Government equivalent to 9 percent of GDP. Because of the sharp drop in oil exports, the external current account shifted from near balance in 1985 to a deficit of US$0.7 billion (13 percent of GDP) in 1986..."

"The newly elected Government that took office in December 1986 has been attempting to design a strategy to deal with Trinidad and Tobago's economic and financial crisis... Notwithstanding (the measures they took) the approved budget for 1987 implies an overall government deficit equivalent to about 20 percent of GDP..."

"...To stem the loss of net international reserves by the end of 1987 and to begin to replenish the Central Bank's gross reserve position thereafter, it is estimated that Trinidad and Tobago would need to reduce its current balance of payments deficit to the equivalent of around 6 percent of GDP in 1987 and 2 percent in 1988. The achievement of this target would require a decline in the overall fiscal deficit to around 9 percent of GDP in 1987 and to 3 percent of GDP next year..."

"Consistent with these targets, Trinidad and Tobago is projected to need foreign official inflows (mainly from foreign banks) on the order of US$250 million a year for the next few years... It is not clear, however, that Trinidad and Tobago could secure new borrowing in the scale just mentioned, especially in view of the government's decision not to request a stand-by arrangement from the Fund."

18

"The mission will encourage the authorities to implement fully the changes in wage policy introduced in the 1987 budget ..., although these revisions have been challenged on legal grounds by the public sector unions. In addition, cutbacks in all categories of government expenditure will need to be made if the large unfinanced gap in prospect for this year is to be eliminated. In this connection, the staff will discuss the means by which the large domestic arrears incurred by the Central administration last year can be paid in an orderly fashion."

"The fiscal program also must deal with the gross inefficiencies of the public enterprise sector which received sizable transfers and subsidies from the Central Administration (which transfers amount to 14 percent of GDP in the 1987 budget). Broad- based adjustments in public utility charges and enterprise prices, as well as wide-ranging rationalization measures and lay-offs are likely to be required. The privatization or closing of certain enterprises also may be warranted".

It is on the basis of the above "facts" that the Briefing Paper went on to seek (and receive) your approval for our 1987 stance towards the country as outlined earlier. But now I must pose the question: just how true were those "facts"?

We get an inkling of where the truth lies in the Mission's Debrief to you of July 29, 1987. Grudgingly, the following confession is made:

"...the deterioration in the fiscal accounts was less pronounced than previously estimated on the basis of unconfirmed reports of a large accumulation of unpaid government bills at the end of 1986 amounting to TT$1.1 billion (around 6 1/2 percent of GDP) over and above the recorded cash deficit of the public sector of around 9 percent of GDP..."

"Contrary to expectations, the mission found evidence that real wages declined last year for the first time since the beginning of the decade signalling the beginning of an adjustment process and the adverse of the severe contraction in demand and output that has occurred since international oil prices began to decline in 1981- 82..."

"The Government reduced sharply the payment of transfers and subsidies to the state enterprises sector which had amounted to the equivalent of around 10 per cent of GDP in previous years."

"... Government expenditure has been held around 12 percent below last year and near equilibrium was achieved in central government operations in the first half of the year..."

A further insight into the truth is given in the Aide Memoire of July 21. It states as follows:

"Because of tight controls on government payments, the overall fiscal deficit has been scaled back from an estimated 8.8 percent of GDP in 1986... to a projected 5.8 percent in 1987 while the current account balance of payments deficit is projected to fall from 10 percent of GDP in 1986 to around 3.5 percent in 1987."

The foregoing excerpts from various documents tell two different stories. They tell, first, that the staff, for purposes already stated, was not being truthful to you in the Briefing Paper of June 29. But they also tell something of the staff's methodology of approach in a captive country. They illustrate the way we wheel and deal and change the justification for, and the premise of our action at every twist and turn.

That methodology of approach defines yet another layer of professional dishonesty and malpractice to be investigated. It is one thing to be untruthful so as to get your permission to use the Fund's heaviest steamroller for a joyride in a Third World country when the Moon is Full; it is quite another to knock down all signposts and shelve all pretensions at road etiquette when the ride gets underway. You know, once we get in the vehicle that you give us (let us call it Steamroller, Heaviest), the moonlight takes over and does something to us; it transforms us into werewolves. And as werewolves we become something much more dangerous than slap-happy spoilt brats of Power and Influence riding slip-shod across the country.

(b) How We Went About Fooling You so as to Get Permission to Use Steamroller (Heaviest) in Tropical Moonlight:

Falsification and cover-up before (Briefing Paper), during (Aide Memoire) and after (Debrief and Staff Report).

The following is a summary of statements illustrating Lies That We Tell and How We Cover Them Up Afterwards:

WHAT WE SAID IN THE BRIEFING PAPER OF JUNE 29, 1987	WHAT WE SAID TO THE GOVERNMENT IN THE AIDE-MEMOIRE OF JULY 21, 1987	WHAT WE SAID TO YOU IN THE DEBRIEF OF JULY 29, 1987
1)"The overall public sector fiscal deficit to 20 % of GDP in 1986":	The fiscal deficit of the public sector was only "an estimated 8.8 % of GDP in 1986"	The fiscal deficit of the public sector in 1986 was "around 9 percent of GDP
2) The fiscal deficit was financed in part by "a build-up of unpaid bills by the government equivalent to 9 % of GDP"	No mention	The statement of Briefing Paper relating to unpaid bills by the Government, was based on "unconfirmed reports." Such un-confirmed reports" in our hand at the time the Briefing paper was written indicated that the unpaid bills "amounted to TT$1.1 billion (around 6 1/2 percent of GDP). Actually, they were virtually zero.
3) "Notwithstanding (the measures that the Government took) the approved budget for 1987 implies an overall government deficit equivalent to about 20 percent of GDP."	Table 2 shows the government deficit arising from the approved budget for 1987 as equivalent to 15.3 percent of GDP	"on the basis of ... measures that the government took, government expenditure has been held around 12 percent below last year and near equilibrium was achieved in central government operations in the first half of the year"
4.) Achievement of the balance of payments target (of the Fund) would require a decline in the overall fiscal deficit to 9 percent of GDP in 1987 and to 3 % of GDP next year, which is a level that could be financed largely with external resources without worsening Trinidad and Tobago's external debt position."	"The overall fiscal deficit has been scaled back to a projected 5.8 percent (of GDP) in 1987."	"Government spending has been reduced well below last year's level ... this will result in an over-all deficit of around 6 percent of GDP this year."
5) Over the ... time period (1984-85) real wages continued to rise under		

20

heavy union pressure; unit labor costs in manufacturing relative to Trinidad and Tobago's main trading partners (i.e., the RULC Index) increased at an annual average rate of 20 percent during the period 1982-85	No mention of the RULC Index	No mention of the RULC Index
6) "A further contraction in economic activity, combined with the increase in the Government's unpaid bills, resulted in a decline in private sector claims on the financial system of 7 percent in 1986."	Table 3 shows liabilities to the private sector (deposits) declining by 3.8 percent	"Private financial savings (in 1986) actually declined by 4 percent" (Staff Report)
7) "The external current account deficit moved from near-balance in 1985 to US$0.7 billion (13 percent of GDP) in 1986."	"The current account balance of payments deficit is projected to fall from 10 percent of GDP in 1986 to around 3.5 % in 1987"	No mention is made of the balance of payments outcome in 1986
8) Government transfers to the public enterprise sector "amount to 14 percent of GDP in the 1987 budget."	No mention	"The Government reduced sharply (in 1987) the payment of transfers and subsidies to the state enterprise sector which had amounted to the equivalent of around 10 percent of GDP in previous years." The 1987 budget allocations and transfers to State enterprises was equivalent to 8 percent of GDP (Table - 1987 RED).

Except for (1) above, I have deliberately chosen to highlight figures where the true result was already known by the Fund, or could have been made easily available to us, when the Briefing Paper was written. In the case of the current account of the balance of payments, we had in our possession a detailed balance of payments statement for 1986 as well as summaries of that statement from various documents released by the Central Bank and the Central Statistical Office. And we had full access to the 1987 detailed budget documents well before the Briefing Paper was prepared. Also, we could have ascertained for most series latest updates from the authorities. I repeat and reiterate, therefore, that we chose deliberately to misrepresent the statistical series identified in (2) through (7) so as to get your permission to impose our highly clouded and subjective judgement and punishment on the country.

On Item (1) - the fiscal outcome for 1986 - I admit readily that we did not know all the facts at the time of the Briefing Paper. In this respect, the detailed figures on revenue and expenditure needed to be checked and verified by us in the field. However, we did have a fairly good idea of the size of the deficit through the budget documents, and through reports of the Central Bank and the Central Statistical Office; all these showed the deficit, on our format, to be considerably less than 20 percent. Yet the Briefing Paper chose to ignore all available evidence and make a very definitive statement about the overall deficit being equivalent to 20 percent of GDP, and the arrears of unpaid bills to 9 percent of GDP. Given these categorical and unconditional "truths", you must have found the subsequent matter-of-fact statement that information on arrears had been based on "unconfirmed reports" somewhat surprising. And why did the Briefing Paper speak triumphantly of a build-up of arrears equivalent to 9 percent of GDP when "unconfirmed reports" then, as referred to in the Debrief, had mentioned just 6.5 percent of GDP? I'm dying to know.

Although the list of items on Table 2 is far from exhaustive, it serves to bring into focus the depth of our deception in "fixing" the Briefing Paper. Translating the GDP figures of Table 2 into money terms, the following Briefing Paper misrepresentations emerge:

- we jacked up the fiscal deficit for 1986 by TT $1.9 billion over its actual level;

- we invented, literally out of the blue, TT$ 1.5 billion of "unpaid bills", by the Government (build up of domestic arrears that never were);

- we augmented the approved 1987 budget deficit by around TT$ 850 million over its actual level;

- we overstated the decline in private sector deposits in banks in 1986 by some TT$ 250 million;

- we showed the deficit on the current account of the balance of payments as being above TT$ 500 million above the actual level;

- we inflated government transfers to the public enterprise sector in 1986 by some TT$ 1 billion over the actual level.

These are not minor deviations due to technical factors, or sloppy calculations on our part. Nor can we plead ignorance of what was happening, or lack of available information.

4. HOW THE MOONLIGHT TOOK OVER AND TRANSFORMED US INTO WEREWOLVES: FUND FINANCIAL PROGRAMMING IN TRINIDAD AND TOBAGO IN 1987

So far I've been dealing with what we do to get your permission to use our spankingly exciting Steamroller (Heaviest) when the Moon is Full. But as I said before, there is another matter to be looked into viz; how the Moonlight transforms us into Werewolves, and how we go about Baying for the Blood of Innocent Victims all along the way. With your permission, I will turn now to this aspect of your staff's activities in Trinidad and Tobago by describing firstly, the joys and pathos of Werewolf's particular brand of financial programming.

You know, construction of a financial program - and it is our self-imposed duty to construct financial programs for all the countries that we visit - has been the excuse that we use to cover up almost every act of shame and ignominy that we commit on missions to the developing world. As you are aware, construction of a program necessarily involves an estimation of the gap between resource availability and resource use, and specification of ways and means to fill that gap. So at some critical stage in formulating the program we must decide on two things : (a) the financial resources presently available to the country, and how these resources may be augmented; and (b) the "outrageous" spending that the government wants to indulge in, and how we could roll back that spending so as to make (a) equal to (b). Sometimes we define the gap as a fiscal imbalance (or deficit), and sometimes we speak of a "balance of payments shortfall" (loss in international reserves). Really, for an open economy such as Trinidad and Tobago, it doesn't matter how we define the gap, because there is a fairly determinate relationship between the fiscal accounts and the balance of payments; adjustment in one implies compensatory adjustment in the other.

In recent times in Trinidad and Tobago we have defined the gap in terms of its fiscal manifestation and that's a big deal, that's a very big deal. Indeed, action on our part in making such a choice represents the totality of objective technocracy that as professional economists we bring to bear on the Trinidad and Tobago economic scene. The follow-up work that we do in specifying a gap, and in proposing adjustment measures to fill it up, can best be forgotten - mercifully so. And as I say that, don't lift your hand in protest. Don't lift it because I'm not saying that the established methodology that should be used in defining a gap - the one that we teach government officials who visit the IMF Institute at headquarters on short, technical courses - is worthless. No, no, if we practice what we preach everything could come out smelling like roses. But we never do that. Certainly, in Trinidad and Tobago, as in many other developing countries, we usually do not use the correct methodology - in fact, we usually use no methodology at all except the analytical requirements to maintain the "integrity" of our brief.

(a) Details of What We Did in Tropical Moonlight

The following quotations deal with issues of financial programming in Trinidad and Tobago in 1987, and our definition of a fiscal gap.

From the 1987 Briefing Paper:

"It is estimated that Trinidad and Tobago would need to reduce its current account balance of payments deficit to the equivalent of around 6 percent of GDP in 1987 and 2 per cent in 1988."

"... The achievement of the above defined current account balance of payments deficit target would require a decline in the overall fiscal deficit to around 9 percent of GDP in 1987 and to 3 percent of GDP next year... which is a level that could be financed largely with external resources without worsening Trinidad and Tobago's external debt position..."

"... Given the size of the current fiscal imbalance (around 20 percent of GDP) a broad range of adjustment measures will be required to achieve the proposed public sector target..."

From Aide Memoire of July 21, 1987:

"...It is projected that Trinidad and Tobago will confront large external and domestic gaps on the order of 3 percent of GDP per annum during the period 1988-1992 ... It is unlikely that refinancing or new borrowing can eliminate all of the financing gap projected over the medium term, if Trinidad and Tobago's external debt position is not to deteriorate from its present level. Therefore further adjustment measures, over and above the policy action contemplated in the government reconstruction program, should be introduced involving changes in external sector, fiscal and monetary policies."

From 1987 Staff Report:

"The mission has prepared a medium term scenario for the balance of payments and central administration operations on the basis of economic policies now in place (ie, excluding the impact of intended policies as detailed in (1) of (2) above)... The exercise incorporates targets for the replenishment of the Central Bank's gross international reserves to a level equivalent to 5 months of imports over the next 2-3 years ..."

Review of the above statements tells us in no uncertain terms that the 9 percent of GDP total public sector deficit for 1987 that the Briefing Paper was aiming to achieve through use of our Steamroller (Heaviest) was in fact scaled back to under 6 percent of GDP by the Government through non-devaluation adjustment measures that had been put into place well before the mission arrived. Of course we were shocked and dismayed to discover that the Government could have found it possible to adjust the economy thus without our intervention.

(b) Stiffening the Targets

What exactly did we do when we found that the Trinidad and Tobago authorities had already achieved the adjustment in the fiscal accounts that we were going to get them to achieve in our own peculiar way?
Well, we stiffened the targets that you had approved in the Briefing Paper, and that we were supposed to ask the authorities to achieve on the basis of the somewhat fictitious figures that we had presented to you.
In stiffening the targets we went to them and said something like this: "our detailed research tells us now

that the 3 percent of GDP deficit that we had mentioned before for 1988-92 is no longer acceptable; you must reduce it further. And have no fancy idea of reducing it further on your own. No, no, you have to let us dictate to you what to do; you have to leave room for us to use the Steamroller (Heaviest)."

Now before coming to the question of how we would make them to reduce the 3 percent deficit further, let's look at the authenticity of our initial claim that a 3 percent deficit would be unsustainable in the years immediately ahead.

We justified the latter claim with the following arguments: (i) such a deficit (of 3 percent) would entail a deterioration in the foreign debt situation; and (ii) it would not allow achievement of a reserve target of 5 months of imports (6 months in the Staff Report).

(i) Deterioration in foreign debt situation

We never did define to the authorities what we meant by this statement. What really were we after? Was it stabilisation in the debt service ratio, or stabilisation of annual amortization payments, or stabilisation of debt outstanding in relation to GDP? Was it a halt to the worsening of average terms, or a lengthening of average maturities? Why say? Nobody asked us to define anything; we had no explanation to give to anyone. What was evident, however, was that on the basis of outstanding debt and debt structure at the end of 1986, there remains considerable scope over the next three to four years, and taking into account the possibility of rescheduling, for net inflows equal to, and indeed exceeding 3 percent of GDP without deterioration in any of the debt indices identified above.

(ii) Accumulating international reserves equivalent to five months of imports (Aide Memoire of July 21, 1987) or six months of imports (Staff Report of September 25, 1987)

I want to ask a question; it is this: what developing country on earth going through the economic trauma of Trinidad and Tobago, and starting from a stock of almost zero reserves, would want to subject its people to more and more unemployment and hardship and deprivation for the sake of holding surplus and redundant funds on deposit in US and European banks and in doing its bit (in Fund parlance) to finance the US deficit? What other country on earth, placed in Trinidad and Tobago's hapless and worsening economic plight, would choose to sow dragon's teeth of social unrest and civil disturbances and political chaos so as to be able to accumulate US and European and Japanese Government bonds, not in pursuit of a policy of efficient management of a needed reserve portfolio, but merely to satisfy your staff's pique? What other impoverished country that had just seen a 20 percent cut in real wages would invite another 20 percent cut for the pleasure of helping to restore what you may choose to call "global balance" or "international financial orderliness" in a grossly inequitable and highly biased and disorderly world economic system? I will not address these broader issues now, but I want to point out that your staff's delimitation of a gross and net reserve target (gross and net reserves are virtually the same in Trinidad and Tobago since there are no significant reserve liabilities) at a time when the country is living from hand to mouth, and finding greatest difficulty to make ends meet on a day to day basis, savor of being a sick joke.

Let's make some comparisons with other CARICOM countries. In Jamaica where we have pumped over US $500 million of our own money during the last eight years, net reserves are still highly negative, and in Barbados - which, partly through our endeavors, continue to have reasonable recourse to international money markets - liquid net reserves is about US $60 million, (or 1.5 months of imports) - somewhat less than what that country borrowed from international commercial banks last year.

Or perhaps it is fairer to make a comparison with other oil exporting countries? Let's look at Nigeria (which had a stand-by program with the Fund and which is far richer in oil than Trinidad and Tobago). Net reserves there remain about two months of imports. In another oil exporting country, Ecuador, where we have a high visibility stand-by, net reserves in relation to imports are even less than in Nigeria. For all developing countries as a whole - excluding the Middle Eastern countries, Venezuela and Mexico, China, India, and Indonesia and a few other traditionally large reserve holders such as South Korea and Taiwan - net reserves in 1986 represented little more than about one month of imports. But for Trinidad and Tobago in its present economic predicament we are asking for six.

5. DISMISSING THE GOVERNMENT'S OWN PROGRAM: CONFLICTS WITH A MORE IRRESISTIBLE CAUSE

The less-than-three-percent fiscal deficit requested in the Aide Memoire (we are now squeezing more blood from them than you authorized us to squeeze in the Briefing Paper) became weighted down with a new caveat, viz; it must exclude any deficit reduction that the Government itself may achieve over 1988-90 through measures initiated on its own. In other words, "further adjustment measures over and above the policy action contemplated in the government's reconstruction program" must necessarily be put into place (ie; Steamroller Heaviest must be activated); nothing the government can conceivably do can stop that.

Let's look at the "policy action contemplated" that under no set of circumstances could save the country from the fate of Steamroller Heaviest. In this respect, the Aide Memoire stated as follows:

"The mission understands that the new government is committed to a medium-term program of adjustment and recovery in response to the economic crisis facing the country. Although many details of this program are yet to be defined, it appears that the government's medium term economic strategy involves the following key elements:

1. A reduction and rationalization of public sector operations in the economy through a reduction in levels of employment and wages, the redeployment of some existing personnel, and a reorganisation of the state enterprise sector involving recapitalisation, divestment and possibly liquidation; and

2. The promotion and reactivation of petroleum production, agriculture and tourism through an increase in private, public and foreign investment and fiscal incentives involving changes in the petroleum tax regime and reforms in the domestic tax structure and its administration."

Well, wouldn't this policy package, even if implemented somewhat sporadically over the next three years, serve to reduce the deficit, perhaps even significantly? After all, they define a set of fairly comprehensive fiscal measures (when you add to them the work being done on tax reform as part of the Government's "intended program"). Necessarily, any analysis with pretensions to objectivity would have started by quantifying with the authorities the likely fiscal impact of the Government's own program over the relevant programming period, in relation to "gap" targets on which some sort of basic consensus regarding magnitudes had been arrived at between the authorities and the Fund.

But we never even dreamt of following this procedure in Trinidad and Tobago. To do so would have been tantamount to putting the final nail in our coffin, in so far as Steamroller (Heaviest) was concerned. For if on top of the RULC's highly improved performance, we were to discover that the authorities had the beginnings of a viable program to keep the fiscal deficit in line with available financing, we would have had to return to Washington with our tails between our legs. Such a course was absolutely unthinkable; the Fund never works that way. So we steadfastly ignored the authorities' protestations that they had started on a track of major adjustment and reconstruction and that, in their view, there was a realistic alternative to our Deadly Medicine.

Of course we knew how to tell them to keep their program to themselves in a nice and polite way; in the Aide Memoire we insisted that "The Fund mission generally supports the thrust of the Government's economic strategy and policy initiatives ... but believes that those policies do not go far enough in addressing the country's economic problems and in laying the basis for sound economic recovery..."

And having thus made room for himself, Werewolf jumps on his Steamroller (Heaviest) and starts running amok. Most of the policy sections of the Aide Memoire and the Staff Report outline details of the Fund's Deadly Medicine as the only way out for Trinidad and Tobago, inclusive of massive devaluation, total freeing of the trade and payments system, escalating interest rates and domestic prices, rapidly falling real income of the poorest of the poor, massive job retrenchment in the public service.

In Part IV of this Letter the generic "whole works" scenario of the Fund, and the interlocking elements of Steamroller (Heaviest) that we were setting up for Trinidad and Tobago are reviewed at some length. Here it is enough to reiterate that we made it very clear to the authorities that nothing else but Our Deadly Medicine would do, irrespective of the rationality and relevance of any and all alternatives that would dare to take into account social factors (including the need to distribute the burden of adjustment in some equitable fashion among differing sectors of the population), and political susceptibilities. If there is anything that we can learn about ourselves from our activities in Trinidad and Tobago, it is that we will never tolerate even the slightest deviation from our Purpose.

6. STATISTICAL MONKEY-BUSINESS ONCE AGAIN: REAL EFFECTIVE EXCHANGE RATE AND THE TERMS OF TRADE

I must quote now from the 1987 Staff Report to show exactly how we managed to "sew up" the case for devaluation by asking Trinidad and Tobago once more to stand absolutely still for our convenience as we did sleight of hand on other statistical series - this time, the Indices of Real Effective Exchange Rate and the Terms of Trade.

I quote as follows:

"While recognizing that a significant real depreciation of the currency had occurred since late 1985, the staff noted that the external value of the Trinidad and Tobago dollar was still around 10 percent higher in real effective terms than in 1980, while the external terms of Trade had declined by about 50 percent since that time."

I have a question; it is this: why choose 1980 as the base year from which the chart most recent movements in the effective exchange rate and the terms of trade? What is the rationale for this procedure?

Well, we can get a fairly definitive answer by looking at the chart on page 22 A. That chart shows that from the last quarter of 1981 through November 1985 the effective exchange rate rose precipitously by 45 per cent. However, the devaluation of December 1985 sent it tumbling down by over 30 percent. And reflecting the fact of continuing depreciation of the US dollar, to which it is pegged, the TT dollar continued to depreciate further, with the real effective exchange rate falling by an additional 8.6 percent between January 1986 and July 1987.

With this little bit of history in mind let's return to the question: why choose 1980 as the base year to chart rises or falls in the effective exchange rate?

The answer is simple - we had to; we just had to. We had to because any base period after 1980 would have shown a decline in the real effective exchange rate of the TT dollar as of today, or as of mid-1987, or whatever. And of course we could never afford to show a decline in the Index; that was absolute anathema.

It was anathema because to do so would have demolished entirely whatever remaining case we thought we had for more government-induced devaluation. In the circumstances, come hell or high water, we had to "prove" that the effective exchange rate had risen - from the last century, if need be. Luckily, 1980 intervened and saved our skin.

Really, in a comparison of this nature, probably the most relevant base period would be the year when oil prices began the secular fall that was to culminate in the dramatic denouement of 1986. That beginning year, of course, was 1982. Alternatively, a case can be made out for using the year immediately preceding the start of the oil bust (ie; 1981) on the reasoning that this was the last full year or undiminished prosperity, with all systems still on "go" and with both real expenditure and real GDP still rising. Use of 1981 as the base year would show that the TT dollar's real effective exchange rate as of June 1987 had declined by 5 percent. If 1982 is used instead, the decline escalates to over 16 percent. Hardly a case for further, government-induced devaluation on the basis of a secular appreciation of the real effective exchange rate!

The same reasoning is applicable for the terms of trade, which can be defined as just a fancy way of saying what everybody knows - ie; that the price of oil, which accounts for 80 percent of the country's merchandise exports, fell progressively after 1981, while the price of imports rose somewhat, or remained relatively stable. During 1982-85 (before devaluation occurred) the terms of trade went down by less than 10 percent, but in 1986 it fell by around 40 percent, reflecting a drop in the unit price of oil of a similar magnitude. Over the last two years or so, the terms of trade have improved modestly from the trough of 1986.

Large and somewhat discordant movements in the terms of trade, as experienced by Trinidad and Tobago in recent years, cannot constitute a case for further devaluation. On the other hand, they signal a special need for international financial assistance, and we do have within the Fund - theoretically at any rate - a somewhat non-conditional facility (the Compensatory Financing Facility) to help countries in such a predicament. Will we allow Trinidad and Tobago to draw on this facility? We have continued to say no. We have continued to say "devalue first, and enter into a commitment to have a stand-by with us. Let Werewolf draw blood before anything good internationally can begin to happen to you." But I have a feeling that the Fund may want now to review its stance on this matter, in spite of the instructions in the Draft Brief for the June 1988 mission.

7. THE IMPLICATIONS FOR TRINIDAD AND TOBAGO OF OUR STATISTICAL TRICKERY DURING 1985/88

It behooves me at this stage to summarise briefly the implications for Trinidad and Tobago of our multi-dimensional statistical trickery as described so far in this Part of the Letter. And in this respect, let me say at once that what we did, had a direct and absolutely critical bearing on the country's capacity to cope effectively with the myriad economic problems that surfaced after 1982 (precipitated by secularly declining oil prices) and that turned into an avalanche of all-inclusive woes (after the dramatic oil price collapse in 1986).

Even in vastly reduced economic circumstances and with international reserves dwindling, the country opted to remain a Fund creditor under our Designation Plan until towards the end of 1986. Such a tactic was heroic or foolish, or both. At any rate, with its "graduation" from World Bank loans, and with virtually no bilateral aid programs from donor countries, the only scope for easing the burden of domestic adjustment through use of foreign savings lay in a phased program of prudent recourse to international capital markets. The scope for such recourse was considerable, given Trinidad and Tobago's relatively low debt service ratio and quite modest stock of outstanding external debt relative to GDP.

During 1984 and early 1985 - there was no Fund mission to Port of Spain in 1984 and therefore we could not, over that period, articulate credibly to others our policy stance for the country - the authorities did in fact manage to achieve their foreign borrowing targets; this served to give a much needed breathing space for effecting a range of fiscal and demand management policies consistent with norms of social justice and economic equity, including some measures to protect the poor and the underprivileged sectors of society.

Alas, our subsequent decision to start anew a virulent campaign of misinformation and statistical misrepresentation, so as to force the government into submission, resulted - as we fully well knew it would - in the sudden and dramatic freezing up of virtually all foreign funding. In turn, this has served to create a situation where the country finds it difficult to restore a semblance of financial balance, much less set its sights on the resumption of economic growth. In punishing Trinidad and Tobago for not biting our bullet, we have equally forced it to operate within a set of economic and financial parameters that not only rule out an international cooperative effort on its behalf, but subverts the logic of the market place by constraining severely the operations of international money markets in the country. In actual practice, the choice that we have given the government is either to accept our Deadliest Medicine or to go it alone as an international outcast. Either way, the consequences are accelerating economic chaos and ultimate social disintegration.

8. WHERE WILL IT ALL END?

In concluding this Part of the Letter, I want to remind you that Trinidad and Tobago is only one country from the host of Third World nations where we are perpetrating the same economic nonsense, with the same catastrophic consequences for "screaming-in-pain" governments and peoples forced to bend on their knees before us, broken and terrified and disintegrating, and begging for a sliver of reasonableness and decency on our part. But we laugh cruelly in their face, and the torture goes on unabated.

Where will it all end? Where will it? What are we doing to the world?

If only the Fund could begin to rethink, sir! If only it could disengage itself from Myth and Illusion that it is Good and Just, and ponder its verifiable role in bringing the world to new depths of shame and cynicism, and introducing in our century a new immorality where disregard of even the most elementary tenets of justice and fair play becomes accepted international practice that may never raise an eyebrow, or elicit a justifiable scream of protest from those who watch the carnage.

We need to ponder on these things, Sir, because the premise on which they are based - a merciless and uncaring and inhuman world - may prove to be one of the most monumental errors (and there are a lot of these) - that the Fund has ever made.

Yours sincerely,

Davison L. Budhoo

TABLE 1

Table   Trinidad and Tobago: Exchange Rates

	End of Period (SDR per TT$)	Period Average (1980=100)		
		Nominal Effective Exchange Rate	Real Effective Exchange Rate 1/	Relative Unit Labor Cost 2/
1979	0.316	101.4	98.2	97.3
1980	0.327	100.0	100.0	100.0
1981	0.358	105.0	108.1	129.9
1982	0.378	111.5	118.4	149.8
1983	0.398	116.1	137.5	193.4
1984	0.425	122.2	155.9	242.9
1985	0.253	124.5	162.7	264.7
1981 - I	0.339	100.8	103.0	
II	0.362	104.3	106.7	
III	0.364	108.2	111.3	
IV	0.358	107.0	111.5	
1982 - I	0.374	108.4	113.6	
II	0.381	110.5	116.7	
III	0.389	112.2	120.0	
IV	0.378	113.5	123.3	
1983 - I	0.386	114.8	132.8	
II	0.390	115.2	136.2	
III	0.394	116.7	139.7	
IV	0.398	117.6	141.4	
1984 - I	0.392	118.6	147.5	
II	0.404	120.1	152.9	
III	0.417	123.7	159.3	
IV	0.425	126.2	164.1	
1985 - I	0.420	130.4	168.4	
II	0.417	127.2	164.8	
III	0.393	123.9	162.7	
IV	0.253	116.7	155.0	
1986 - I	0.244	95.1	125.1	

Sources: IMF, International Financial Statistics; and Fund staff estimates.

1/ Trinidad and Tobago exchange rate divided by the weighted average of the exchange rates of its trading partners; the exchange rates are deflated by consumer price indices.

2/ Unit labor costs in manufacturing in Trinidad and Tobago divided by the weighted average of unit labor costs in the major trading partner countries.

TABLE 2

Table   Trinidad and Tobago: Exchange Rates

	End of Period (SDR per TT$)	Period Averages (1980=100)		
		Nominal Effective Exchange Rate	Real Effective Exchange Rate 1/	Relative Unit Labor Cost 2/
1982	0.378	112.7	122.0	140.7
1983	0.398	116.9	141.4	144.6
1984	0.425	124.4	162.3	169.0
1985	0.253	126.4	169.7	166.?
1986	0.227	83.2	117.4	88.9
1982 - I	0.374	109.6	116.5	
II	0.381	111.7	120.0	
III	0.389	114.2	124.1	
IV	0.378	115.2	127.2	
1983 - I	0.386	115.1	135.9	
II	0.390	115.9	139.8	
III	0.394	117.9	143.9	
IV	0.398	118.9	145.9	
1984 - I	0.392	120.6	153.7	
II	0.404	121.9	158.9	
III	0.417	126.0	165.7	
IV	0.425	128.9	171.0	
1985 - I	0.420	133.7	177.7	
II	0.417	129.9	173.2	
III	0.393	125.8	169.6	
IV	0.253	116.3	158.3	
1986 - I	0.244	85.6	116.5	
II	0.236	83.4	116.4	
III	0.229	81.8	116.6	
IV	0.227	82.2	120.1	
1987 - I	0.216	44.5	109.8	

Sources: IMF, International Financial Statistics; and Fund staff estimates.

1/ Trinidad and Tobago exchange rate divided by the weighted average of the exchange rates of its trading partners; the exchange rates are deflated by consumer price indices.

2/ Unit labor costs in manufacturing in Trinidad and Tobago divided by the weighted average of unit labor costs in the major trading partner countries.

TABLE 3

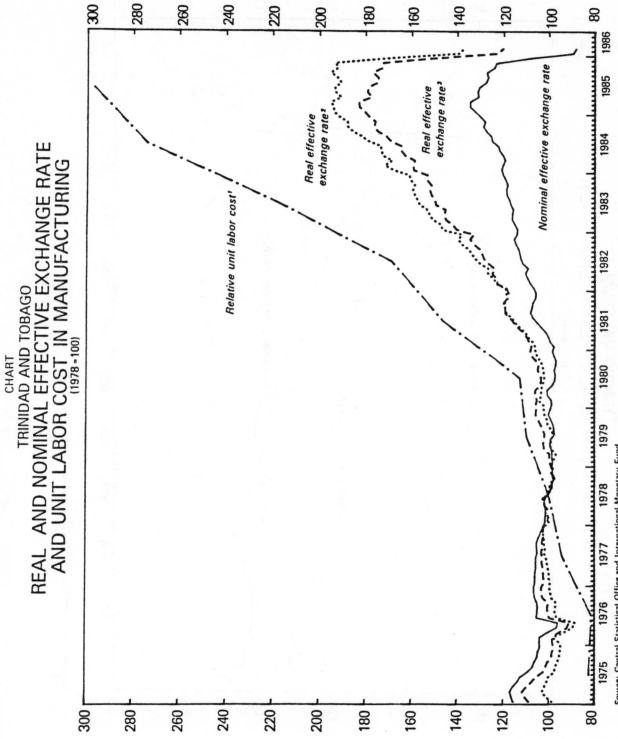

CHART
TRINIDAD AND TOBAGO
REAL AND NOMINAL EFFECTIVE EXCHANGE RATE
AND UNIT LABOR COST IN MANUFACTURING
(1978 = 100)

Relative unit labor cost[1]

Real effective
exchange rate[2]

Real effective
exchange rate[3]

Nominal effective exchange rate

Source: Central Statistical Office and International Monetary Fund.
[1] Unit labor cost in manufacturing in Trinidad and Tobago divided by the weighted average of unit labor costs in the major trading partners.
[2] Deflated by the consumer price index for Trinidad and Tobago and export unit values for its trading partners.
[3] Deflated by the consumer price indices for both Trinidad and Tobago and its trading partners.

TABLE 4

CHART
TRINIDAD AND TOBAGO
REAL AND NOMINAL EFFECTIVE EXCHANGE RATE
(1978=100)

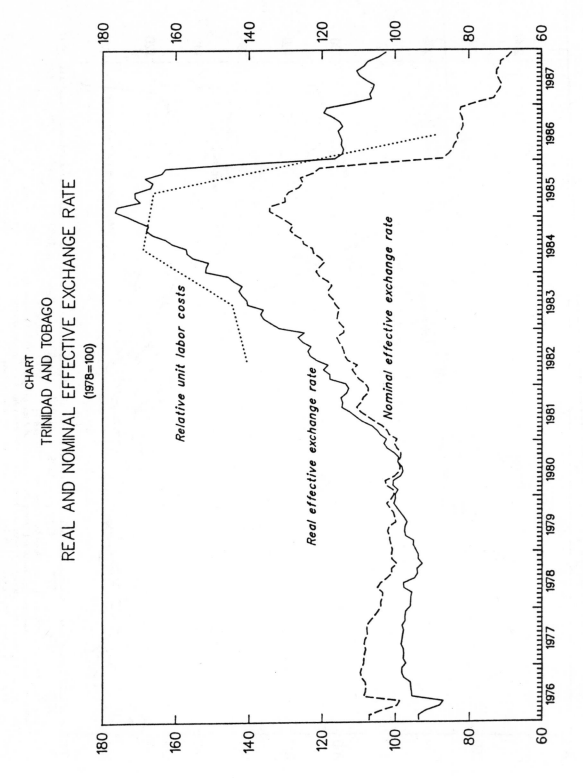

Source: Central Statistical Office and International Monetary Fund.

32

TABLE 5

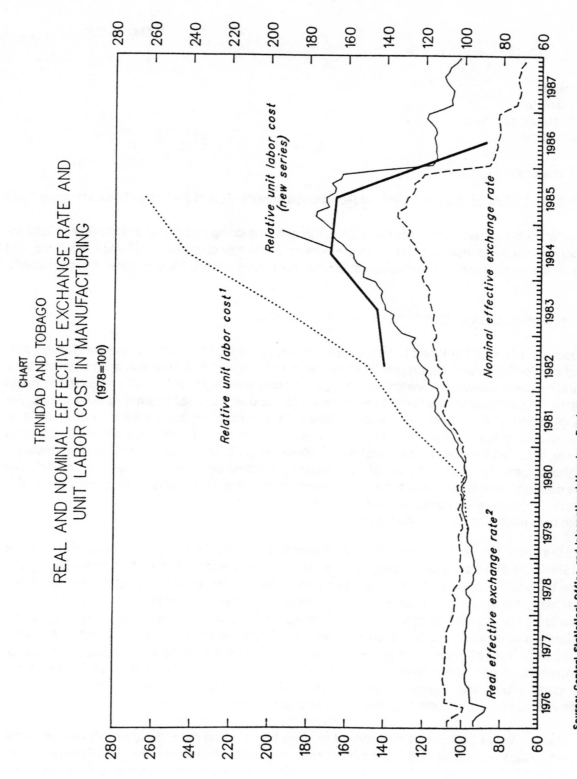

CHART
TRINIDAD AND TOBAGO
REAL AND NOMINAL EFFECTIVE EXCHANGE RATE AND
UNIT LABOR COST IN MANUFACTURING
(1978=100)

Relative unit labor cost[1]

Relative unit labor cost
(new series)

Nominal effective exchange rate

Real effective exchange rate[2]

Source: Central Statistical Office and International Monetary Fund.
[1]Unit labor cost in manufacturing in Trinidad and Tobago divided by the weighted average of unit labor costs in the major trading partners.
[2]Deflated by the consumer price indices for both Trinidad and Tobago and its trading partners.

INTERNATIONAL MONETARY FUND

WASHINGTON, D.C. 20431

May 18, 1988

CABLE ADDRESS
INTERFUND

Mr. Camdessus
Managing Director
International Monetary Fund
Washington, D.C.

Dear Mr. Camdessus,

Davison L. Budhoo: Part III of Letter of Resignation from the Staff of the International Monetary Fund

In this Part of the Letter, I turn to nonstatistical areas of wrong-doing on our part in Trinidad and Tobago. This is followed by a comparison of Fund "evenhandedness" in member countries, and Fund Executive Board definition of "statistical fraud" and remedies established for victims of such fraud or other proven malpractices.

1. GETTING WORLD BANK STAFF TO JOIN IN THE CHARADE

On December 14, 1987 the World Bank produced its first economic report on Trinidad and Tobago after an interval of over five years. That report, in white cover draft, and entitled: "Towards a Program of Policy Reform and Renewed Growth in Trinidad and Tobago" was prepared by the World Bank mission that visited Port of Spain in October, 1987 - well over three months after our own team had returned to Washington. Far more objective than us, but equally outspoken, the World Bank team did not tow our line in pushing devaluation as the solution to the country's ills. In fact, they rejected it outright on the grounds that overvaluation of the TT dollar, based on their own calculations, was relatively insignificant, and that international competitiveness, in areas where the latter had been eroded, could be restored by far less traumatic and all-inclusive measures designed to "fine-tune" specific export sectors, and protect the integrity of the government's own medium term program for economic reconstruction.

I quote from page 7 of Part 1: Main Report:

> "...the devaluation of December 1985 has restored competitiveness of the manufacturing sector to 1980 levels and manufactured exports (excluding petroleum and related products) have been growing by over 15% in each of the last two years. Nevertheless, the evidence suggests that the TT dollar may be overvalued to a small extent (less than 10%). The extent of the overvaluation has been minimized by the continued fall in the value of the US dollar to which the TT dollar is pegged. The priority now should be further reforms of industrial incentives and measures to preserve the 1985 devaluation edge through fiscal and income policies aimed at containing and reducing costs. A supplementary measure that could be considered is an export bonus for selected lines of manufactured exports, to be funded from an import surcharges on a limited range of imports. The scheme could be extended to cover certain agricultural exports and the tourism sector."

Of course the World Bank report was passed on to us before being put in final form for delivery to the Trinidad and Tobago authorities, and to the international community. And as our own High Priests and Not so High Priests read it they saw red; we contacted the World Bank; we brought "Fund/World Bank collaboration" fully to bear on this matter. And just four months after the first report was issued, a "revised" version came out that, in certain parts, was as virulently subjective, and fanatically devaluation- oriented, and statistically manipulated as any of the various Fund reports of last year that are quoted in Part II of the Letter.

But, judge for yourself, Sir, about what role we may have played in getting the World Bank to change its mind so fundamentally from one report (initial) to the next (final). And let me have the honor of setting the stage for such a judgement by quoting as follows from the revised World Bank report (Report No. 7139-TR) issued on April 18, 1988 (Main Report, page IV, of Summary and Main Issues):

"...The evidence indicates that the Trinidad and Tobago dollar (TT$) is still overvalued. In comparison with its 1976 level - 1976 is the earliest year for which data are available for this series - the real effective exchange rate, based on a basket of currencies of major trading partners, has appreciated by 16% by the third quarter of 1987, and this in spite of the continued fall in the value of the US dollar since 1985, to which the TT dollar is pegged ... A flexible exchange rate policy would further boost export competitiveness ... If foreign exchange reserves were to continue to fall, further action on the exchange rate will be required to establish equilibrium in the balance of payments. And since exchange rate adjustments play a key role in the generation of expectations, the Government will need to supplement these efforts with fiscal and monetary measures."

You know, I suspect that "Fund/World Bank collaboration" in Trinidad and Tobago over the next several months will become increasingly important. At any rate, in wake of the above report, and of Trinidad and Tobago's request that its "graduation" from use of World Bank resources (on per capita GDP criteria) be rescinded, I would not at all be surprised if the World Bank were to say something like this to the Trinidad and Tobago authorities:

"We are agreeable to the proposal that you be allowed to use World Bank resources in the future. However, use of such resources will be severely restricted, and the delivery mechanism will have to be a "policy" or "program" loan that will allow us, in collaboration with the Fund, to ensure that Steamroller (Heaviest) mow you down, rather than through loans for specific projects of reconstruction and development that will not give us any such macro-economic policy leverage. In this context, we will ask you to accept a Trade Reform Structural Adjustment Loan or some such macro-economic facility that will enable us to coordinate our structural adjustment efforts with those of the Fund. Of course, our first requirement is Massive Devaluation, and more expenditure cuts and more taxation on the poor through VAT or other such like indirect taxation measures. Drink your medicine now, Trinidad and Tobago. Drink it now, because tomorrow things may be much more difficult for you. Certainly, we will make sure that you cannot continue to defy the Fund. In this respect, please do not continue to pretend to know what are the solutions for your country's problems."

Sir, such a message may well be under preparation at this time by the World Bank - in far less graphic form, of course, but implying everything said above. Whether this Letter can prevent its delivery remains to be seen.

2. UNDERMINING FUNDAMENTAL RIGHTS PROTECTED THE CONSTITUTION

I want to go on now to the fifth indictment identified in Part I - ie; the glib way in which we go about undermining people's fundamental rights as protected by the constitution of the country. Of course, once we set ourselves up as part of the State Machinery that would deny benefaction to certain groups while promoting the welfare of others - and we necessarily do this when we force the government to bite our bullet - we become, by definition, a domestic political force in the job of redistributing national wealth among social groups in a particular way that can enhance the effectiveness of our "program". We may say that we are merely out to ensure that adequate adjustment occurs in the economy - ie, that "economic and financial balance" is restored - but that's only a fancy way of saying that we are taking a direct hand in reallocating the national cake to suit our own purpose and that we are punishing certain groups and rewarding others so as to further our own cause. Now in Part IV of this Letter I will go into a lot of details to show exactly how "our own cause" conflicts with what we may call "the cause of the country." Here I will just restate what I have been saying all along - ie; that when we enter the national arena to punish or to reward, we leave nothing up to chance; we push our weight around; we never stop until we get what we want. And in our mad rush for self-fulfillment, everything in our path that potentially can threaten achievement of our welfare redistribution aims are thrown aside. And, invariably, we find that the constitution and the constitutional conventions of the country, whether written or unwritten, are impediments in our path. And we always brush them aside irritably, as if swathing a fly.

You know, not so long ago, the colonial power, in circumstances where the colony concerned was perceived to be errant, would just go ahead and suspend the constitution and take over power directly and brazenly and unceremoniously. We don't operate that way today; internationally that is unacceptable, and logistically it is impossible, but we get the same results through other means. And unlike the colonial power of yesteryear, we can fine-tune our intervention so that we take away today only those rights and constitutional guarantees that it is necessary to take away in order to achieve our immediate ends (which of course may change from time to time). In other words, we undermine constitutional rights gradually, and in a non-visible sort of way. And before we know it (if our relationship with the country concerned is intensive and sustained enough, and if we perceive that Great Things are at stake for us) we render the government naked and defenseless and on its knees before us, and we go about our business of doing absolutely as we please. And nobody, in retrospect, would seem to know how on earth we could have managed to subjugate both government and peoples thus, and how such a state of affairs could ever have been made to exist in the first instance.

Well, as I said before, how far we are prepared to go in this neo-colonialist game depends on our vested interest in the country concerned. Because that differs tremendously from one place to another, our tampering with constitutional guarantees run the whole gamut, from Jamaica to Zambia to India to China. Given this fact, one would have thought that Trinidad and Tobago would have been relatively safe and tamper-free, for it has never used our resources, or been involved in any Fund "arrangement". But surprise, surprise! Trinidad and Tobago was not allowed to remain virginal; over the years 1985-88 we tried to dig our tendrils into the constitution of the country and relieve certain sectors of the population from some of their most cherished rights.

Congruent with my method of approach in this Part of the Letter - ie; not to seek comprehensiveness, but merely to give examples of Fund wrong-doing in specifically identified areas - I will confine my remarks on the subject of our miniaturisation of constitutional rights to two matters.

The first relates to our concerted attempt over three years, to make the Public Utilities Commission a rubber stamp of a particular brand of government policy that we wanted to see implemented - a brand of policy that serves exclusively the interests of the shareholders of the companies, and which, demonstrably, is anathema to the interests of the people of Trinidad and Tobago - themselves the raison d'etre, as consumers, for public utility services.

The controversy between the Government and the Fund on public utilities pricing stemmed basically from our policy stance that cost increases should be passed on automatically and unexceptionally to the consumer, irrespective of the cause of such increases, or the technical and managerial efficiency of the company concerned. In 1986 the matter was discussed extensively during the course of our mission, and the Public Utilities Commission saw fit to make the following policy statement (as written by the Fund mission) in the course of a meeting with the Fund:

> "The Commission makes it a policy to avoid any rate increase necessitated by operational inefficiency. In granting rate increases, the Commission attempts to balance the needs of the utility companies and consumers, as well as political considerations. In particular, the Commission's policy concerning utility rates takes into account the government's social policy objectives."

The position that we developed after listening to the views of the Commission was that cost inefficiencies were not immediately verifiable, and their removal, or partial removal, could not be guaranteed in the short term, and should not be a consideration in deciding whether or not to grant a price increase. We felt, moreover, that "social policy objectives" which implied elements of subsidy for the poor were inappropriate in the aftermath of the 1986 oil price collapse and the growing fiscal crunch of the Government. During the course of the 1987 mission, we debated extensively whether we should make a formal request to the government to force the Commission to award immediate and substantial rate increases across the whole gamut of public utility services within its purview. In this debate, the plea of some mission members that the Commission was an independent body established by constitutional convention and could not, or should not be "forced" by the government to implement a Fund policy based simplistically on marginal cost pricing and blissfully unaware of broader social considerations, was vehemently rejected. Instead, the mission took the view that irrespective of constitutional propriety, the Commission must be made to tow our policy line, and that responsibility for making it to become as a captive Fund instrument was the government's. While the final version of our statement of "advice" to the government on the role of the Commission was toned down somewhat (presumably in deference to internal mission dissent), the message that it conveyed, and the implications that it carried for formal constitutional guarantees, were straightforward enough. Certainly, there can be little room for equivocation when you tell a government that public utilities' finances must be improved "by means of a more flexible and automatic processing of tariff adjustment by the Public Utilities Commission" while ignoring entirely the other very wide range of cost increase inducement factors, apart from our pet theme of "over-staffing", and the imperatives of "retrenchment".

Yes, Sir. Just establish that costs have increased and the Commission, foregoing its constitutional responsibility and bending to the will of the Fund, will do an "automatic processing" - ie; will come up with an identical, or near identical percentage increase in user prices. Matter closed. Next utility take the stand. The Fund is in control here ...

The second area of "constitution busting" that I want to highlight touches on the role of the Industrial Court - another creature of constitutional convention - in awarding wage and "pay package" settlements after established procedures for arbitrating industrial disputes had become exhausted.

Already in mid-1986 the Fund's stand on what it expected of the Industrial Court was crystallized, having been determined by the staff with due rubber-stamping by our Executive Board. I quote as follows from the Staff Report of July 3, 1986:

> "The authorities noted that the decision of the Special Tribunal of the Industrial Court will be binding, and that a wage award higher than that proposed by the Government would pose a major problem."

> "In this connection, it was noted that some of the criteria used by the Industrial Court in arriving at its decisions, including the principle of comparability with settlements previously agreed outside the court, might hamper the adjustment process, and the mission wondered whether it would be feasible to give more weight to ... (other) ... considerations ..."

Just how strong were our objections to criteria used by the Industrial Court, and how determined we were to undermine its authority, can be gleaned from remarks made in the Briefing Paper of June 26, 1987. In that document, the mission sought your permission - and obtained it - to "encourage" the government to "implement fully" all changes in wage policy announced in the 1987 budget - ie; the freezing of salaries and the removal of COLAs for all public sector employees - irrespective of whether such changes, based on unilateral action, were subsequently approved by the Industrial Court, or whether they were otherwise deemed to have legal foundation, or to confirm to established bargaining processes and procedures. Again, as in the case of the Public Utilities Commission, there was heated discussion among mission members on the propriety of action by the Fund to "request" the government to refuse to abide by the judgement of the Industrial Court in the event that the court ruled against the government. Sadly, in this case too, those who pleaded for respect of the constitution and for the laws and legal conventions of the country were overruled. Although the wording of the instruction in the Briefing Paper was softened somewhat, Fund staff was given explicit authorization to "encourage" the government to ignore constitutional propriety and legal authority in its dealings with the public sector unions. Specifically, the mission's mandate was to "encourage the authorities to implement fully the changes in wage policy introduced in the 1987 budget, although these revisions have been challenged on legal grounds by the public sector unions."

Need more be said? I think not; the implications are clear enough.

3. EVENHANDEDNESS OF THE FUND IN DEALINGS WITH MEMBER COUNTRIES: A COMPARISON BETWEEN TRINIDAD AND TOBAGO AND JAMAICA

You know, Mr. Camdessus, your predecessor, Mr. de Larosiere, had a pet phrase that he used to utter quite a lot; it was "evenhandedness in the Fund's relations with different member countries." I don't know if you yourself have been vocal on this matter, but certainly "evenhandedness" is a principle that you would not have difficulty in accepting. So let's deal with it. Let's deal with it, however, by referring, for the moment, to two Caribbean countries only - ie; Jamaica and Trinidad and Tobago. And also, let's limit our examination of Fund "evenhandedness" in these two countries to cover one subject, viz: our treatment and transformation of "raw" data into key statistical indices and other indicators of economic performance that can draw international praise or condemnation, and that can elicit "thumbs up" or "thumbs down" in so far as international financial assistance is concerned.

Since a new government was installed in Jamaica some eight years ago, the Fund has been continuously - virtually on a day-to-day basis - in consultation with the authorities of that country on their economic and financial policies, and except for brief aberrations on a few occasions, Fund programs have been current there from 1980 to the present time. Indeed, Jamaica is one of the most heavily indebted countries to the Fund (in percent of quota) and our per capita disbursements there are among the highest in the world. The sight of Jamaican officials in the corridors of the Fund is so commonplace that sometimes they are mistaken for regular staff members. Nor does the Prime Minister himself shy away from visiting Washington and holding forth with you and with our High Priests; some two years ago he attended an Executive Board Meeting and made an interesting presentation on economic performance and prospects of his country.

After several years of economic backsliding and open talk in the Fund that Jamaica was nothing if not a basket case and a blatant liability that we should drop like a hot potato, the Fund and the World Bank and the Jamaican authorities seem finally to have put their act together in what some people are saying is a remarkable example of effective international cooperation for the good of the country. In any event, the economy, seemingly, is rebounding strongly (if our figures are anything to go by) and we keep saying that economic performance under the just concluded stand-by, has been good and sustained, even exceptional.

Alas, however, I must be a spoilt sport and burst the bubble. Or should I? Perhaps I should not, for if I do you will brand me a destroyer of good and wholesome things, and a harbinger of wicked news. So I will take a back seat and put our staff on stage; let them tell their own story the way they want to tell it. And to do that I will call to the witness stand staff members who are either High Priests or near-High Priests. High Priests 1 and 2, Sir, sit on one side of the room, High Priest 3 sits on the other side.

Now let us sit back, too, and ...

How stupid of me! I forgot to say what the charge is all about! Well, it seems to be this: High Priests 1 and 2 appear to be upbraiding High Priest 3 for seemingly collaborating with the Jamaican authorities in fudging the statistics, and deceiving our Executive Board and, beyond the Board, the international community that equates a Fund pronouncement on Jamaica with Unconditional Words of Wisdom Straight from the Horse's Mouth.

Excerpts from Memorandum of High Priest 1 (dated some time in February 1987):

" ... the Bank of Jamaica is not providing data in a sufficiently up-to-date or detailed way. In the past, the authorities have provided such data and the resident representative has had open access to the ledger account on a daily basis. The authorities must keep the ledger up to date for the efficient conduct of the Bank and, therefore, the information must be available. By not supplying the resident representative and headquarters with these data, they are in direct contravention of Article VIII, Section 5a, "the Fund may require members to furnish it with such information as it deems necessary for its activities ..., and Section 5b, "Members undertake, however, to furnish the desired information in as detailed and accurate a manner as is practicable and, so far as possible, to avoid mere estimates." We know the authorities must maintain a current ledger account and we should require that they conform to the Articles of Agreement they have signed."

"In at least (two other cases) ... the Fund has delayed program implementation until acceptable data were provided. It seems something similar (suspension of drawings) should be considered in the case of Jamaica."

High Priest 1 felt very strongly about the non-cooperation of the Jamaican authorities and the resulting misrepresentation of the actual figures used for the performance criteria. Indeed, in a follow-up memorandum a few days later, High Priest 1 wrote as follows:

"The Staff Report (EBS/87/22) does delineate the various components of the overall fiscal deficit. However, no mention is made of the difficulties of obtaining data, the lack of cooperation of the authorities, and the reason for adopting the particular quarterly quantitative performance criteria ... on the overall public sector net financing requirement. The only hint that all is not well with the data might be conveyed to Board members by the "others and discrepancy" line in Table 4; a residual discrepancy fluctuating between 0.6 and 4.1 percent of GDP in the last six years does suggest that the other figures might not be too reliable for monitoring."

"It does seem reasonable to ask the Jamaican authorities to carry out paragraph 6 in the notes. They should also be offered technical assistance to improve their data (paragraph 5). If they demur, they should be reminded of their obligations under the Articles of Agreement (paragraph 4), and their attention drawn to the examples of other countries and their cooperation in providing data (paragraph 5). The authorities should be told that the monitoring device is only a stop gap and we expect that, with STA assistance, if necessary, they will be able to use their ledger accounts to produce monitoring data in the normal framework within three months."

"Finally, even if we are not mentioning any of this to the Board, I suppose management's attention should be drawn to these issues?"

Well, apparently the Department concerned did not find it possible to change its ways, or that of its client; certainly a policy that would ensure the use of "ledger accounts to produce monitoring data in the normal framework within three months" was never implemented. Indeed the alarm bells were still ringing, and far more stridently, eight months after High Priest 1 had written. I take up the story with comments by High Priest 2 sometime in October 1987:

"Our major concern with this staff report (of October 1987) is that it is based on a total consolidation of the nonfinancial public sector and the Bank of Jamaica not only for monitoring, but also for analytical purposes. Furthermore, we also expressed concern that the staff report does not make a sufficiently convincing argument for the modification of the domestic asset ceiling for the Bank of Jamaica."

"With regards to the fiscal analysis of above-the-line developments and targets, it was disconcerting that it is essentially limited to a partial analysis of the Central Government..."

"Although (High Priest 3) was strongly urged to change the fiscal format in the present draft he indicated that he was unable to do so at present, partly because of time constraints..."

Well, the new Staff Report on Jamaica to which High Priest 2 refers was recently issued, but I do not find in it, or in the previous one, any "footnote" or other entry that draws attention "to the unusual features of the data" and that indicates "that data difficulties were the reason for ...deviations from standard concepts and definitions."

What I do find is an unmitigated praise for the way the authorities are managing the economy and cooperating with the Fund in meeting the aims of our program. Really, that is not too surprising, for we seem in Jamaica to be prepared incessantly to modify the performance criteria; last year, the number of modifications in the program targets that were effected was probably a record for the Fund over such a short time; doubtlessly this reflects an unusual flexibility on our part in keeping the program alive. Obviously, one feels pleased about this development. The only regret is that the same thing cannot be said in relation to our dealings with some other countries in the Caribbean and Latin America and Africa.

Sir, will you consider setting into motion procedures to investigate Jamaica's treatment by the Fund vis a vis that meted out to Trinidad and Tobago in 1986/87? Probably such action is necessary, you know, because evenhandedness can never be just another assertion to be made when it suits our purpose to make it. Like justice, it is a highly visible quality that must not only be done by all parties concerned, but that must be seen to be done at all times, and at every stage of the process in hand.

4. OUR EXECUTIVE BOARD'S DEFINITION OF STATISTICAL FRAUD AND ITS RULING ON PUNISHMENT FOR CULPRITS

I want to turn now to the question of what constitutes fraud in our penchant for misreporting in developing countries. And in this respect let me refer you to a Fund Executive Board meeting on May 24, 1984. Your predecessor, Mr. de Larosiere, summed up that meeting with the following words:

"Directors considered that misreporting ... is a matter of legitimate concern, for various reasons.

(1) On a technical plane the effectiveness of Fund policies and of adjustment programs depends on the provision of accurate data.

(2) The credibility of the Fund and of its "seal of approval" is at stake; numerous financing arrangements depend on it, and if there were doubts in the minds of outside observers about its reliability, the institution itself could be endangered.

(3) The revolving character of Fund resources is also directly related to the quality of reporting; and if the Fund lets misreporting problems become more frequent, it might well have great difficulty in increasing its own resources.

(4) A relationship of mutual trust and good faith between members and the Fund is the essence of an institution based on cooperation.

(5) Equality of treatment demands that misreporting must not give one member any advantage over another member that complies with its reporting obligations."

He went on to state as follows :

"I was interested and heartened to note that the Executive Board, in its majority, had wisely warned the staff not to try to assign to the Board the judicial role of having to pass judgement on the reasons for the misreporting and to identify fraud as opposed to error. The magnitude of the misreporting ... is a relevant basis for action; however, if fraud is flagrant and established beyond any doubt, it should be an element in the judgement of the Board, which has said that in such cases the Fund would probably be justified in imposing the maximum sanctions."

"All cases of misreporting, whether motivated by an intention to conceal information and to draw on an illegitimate basis, or whether only the result of inaccurate reporting, should be brought by Management to the attention of the Executive Board, which should decide what to do on a case by case basis."

The above board discussion, and Mr. de Larosiere remarks, related exclusively to situations in which a reporting country was deemed to have provided, or to be providing, inaccurate data to the Fund. The reverse, and much more common scenario is when Fund staff itself misrepresents country data to the Executive Board and to the international community so as to achieve some ulterior, and invariably politically motivated end that conflicts fundamentally with the spirit and letter of the Fund's Articles of Agreement and the interests of the member country concerned. This latter situation has never been discussed by the Board - indeed, as far as I am aware, misrepresentation of member countries data by Fund staff in the field and at headquarters has never previously been brought to the attention of Fund management. However, I presume that the same guidelines for determining fraud and punishment that apply to miscreant countries would also be made to apply to miscreant Fund staff. At any rate - and irrespective of whatever action a victimized country may see fit to take against the Fund in cases where serious wrong- doing by our staff is established - a very large number of people everywhere will be watching the action that the Fund itself may take in such instances.

5. HUMANKIND'S CONSCIENCE TO THE RESCUE

Sir, let me end this third Part of my Letter by telling you something that you may find somewhat chilling, it is this: more and more evidence is coming in to show that the world is no longer prepared to shut its eyes to the shocking misdeeds of your staff in the Third World. Part of that evidence lies in the growing incidence of spontaneous mass protests, demonstrations, strikes and even civil disobediences launched by aggrieved folk in individual countries against the operations of the Fund - countries such as Egypt, Peru, Ghana, Tanzania, The Dominican Republic, Brazil, Mexico, Argentina, Jamaica and even Trinidad and Tobago. But however virulent may be the expressions of grass roots rebelliousness by those whom we torment, they are far outpaced by the growing wave of admonitions and disaffection and expressions of concern and pleas for mercy and humanity from civil liberties and human rights organizations around the world; from national and world religious leaders; from Heads of States and Ministers of Finance; from regional and world groupings of countries, such as the Organization of African Unity, the Group of Seventy Seven and the Non-Aligned Movement; from Universities and Research Institutes everywhere; from the trade union movement in virtually every country of the South, from perceptive and influential sections of the world press and mass media; from private groups, and from individual men and women of conscience.

Yet all that we do - all that we continue to do in scores of countries around the world - suggest that we have chosen to ignore entirely this growing focus on us; all that we do suggest that we deem ourselves to be above the law, and extraneous to the mainstream of human behavior, where conscience and decency and justice vie for pride of place with other, and less noble motivations propelling the human machine.

But no longer, Mr. Camdessus. Somehow, you know, I have a gut feeling that the game is up and that, in the future, we will no longer be able to get away with the excesses of the past. No longer will the grossly overpaid and nondescript bureaucrat choke us all to death through statistical trickery, et al. No longer will he or she be able to hide behind a mythical cloak of evenhandedness, and pose as an impartial dispenser of good housekeeping seals; no longer will there be sauce for the gander and death for the goose.

You know, Sir, I want to ask a question; it is this: Is it wrong to have the world to step in and take a cold, hard look at us? Is it wrong to cry out for a rescue? You know, we have got ourselves into a terrible rut. Perhaps a scrutiny by the peoples of the world, who ultimately are our employers and our raison d'etre, provides the last hope for us to try to pick ourselves up, and move forward again as professional people and as human beings.

Or perhaps it is too late for that?

I have my own views on this matter, but in these dying seconds of this Part I will keep them to myself. All I want to say now is that I am absolutely convinced that it is only the force of world public opinion, brought strongly to bear on our psychology and our operations and our methods in the Third World, that can serve to set the stage for a new world policy to rescue two-thirds of humankind from the horrific fate of more and more debilitation and disease and stunted growth, physically and mentally, that is imposed through our iron fist and other reinforcing arms of what others insist in calling the Present Day World Economic Order, but which in Part IV I shall dub simply as the Bretton Woods System.

For the moment, back to the question of the rescue of that poor and starving Two Thirds of Mankind. It must come, Mr. Camdessus. It must come and I will be there, with all other men and women of conscience and goodwill, hopefully including yourself, fighting for it. And one day the chains will be broken, and we will all be free.

Yours sincerely

Davison L. Budhoo

May 18, 1988

Mr. Camdessus
Managing Director
International Monetary Fund
Washington, D.C.

Dear Mr. Camdessus,

Davison L. Budhoo: Part IV of Open Letter of Resignation from the Staff of the International Monetary Fund. A History of the Fund, or How We Moved From Pax Atlantica to Pax Honeypot

In this Part of the Letter I will turn to the role that we play in developing countries outside of our lust for dabbling in seeming fraud and misrepresentation of facts and figures. For, really, we should not get caught in the trap of thinking that once we mend our ways on the figure work and begin to focus more on the technical norms (vis a vis our alarming penchant for politicisation and victimization and bias), our problems with the developing world would be ameliorated, and our relations stabilized. Far from it. Indeed, I would go as far as to say that the epidemic of irregularities in our work, as undertaken from the backdrop of the particular epistemology that we bring to bear on our outlook and operations in the Third World economies, is in a sense a red herring. I don't want to put a floodlight on the herring merely to have the whale slink away unobserved. No, no, we cannot afford to do that; we must latch on to the fins of that whale; we must tackle the problem at source. And to do that, we must go back to our preconceptions, and our doctrine, and our theoretical underpinning that strike fear and trembling in the hearts of hundreds of millions of people in the South everyday of every year.

1. THE TRINIDAD AND TOBAGO PROGRAM RESTATED : EVERYTHING IS AD ABSURDUM

You know, let me tell you something, Sir. As I read through our July 1987 Aide Memoire to the Trinidad and Tobago authorities, and indeed our latest Staff Report on that country I get goose bumps; there is an acute despair within me because of the growing irrelevance of what we say to Third World countries and what we try to force them to do in the name of financial adjustment. Yet that irrelevance and that forcing is not neutral or benign; our policies in the Third World are becoming more and more synonymous with economic and social bedlam. In Trinidad and Tobago, for instance, if we had our way - and in certain Departments of the Fund there is a feeling of great optimism that we are finally about to get our way - we would have the authorities taking the following measures:
   - significant devaluation immediately with more to come, a la Jamaica;
   - removal of domestic price controls even on the most basic essentials used by the poorest of the poor (and creation of a brand of desperation and destitution unknown to the country before);
   - further accelerated reduction in the real wage in each and every sector of the economy (a further precipitous drop in the living standards of the unskilled and semi- skilled and a drastic redistribution of income in favour of those most able to cope);
   - total removal of import duty exemptions to all producers and investors, save exporters (virtual dismantling of import substituting and processing industries and those catering for the domestic market);
   - subversion of the Industrial Court and the Public Utilities Commission, leading immediately and automatically to a serious erosion of constitutional and democratic rights of the Trinidad and Tobago people;
   - removal of exchange controls on external capital and current transactions, so that a privileged few could legitimately drain the country of the remaining dregs of foreign reserves that it still possesses;

- spectacularly large cuts in the (annual) public sector wage bill through massive firing of people and drastic reduction in the nominal wages of those fortunate enough to remain employed;

- deep and incisive reductions in transfers to persons, inclusive of benefits and subsidies to the aged and the sick and the handicapped;

- deep and incisive reductions in social services, including health and education;

- removal of import controls so that the domestic market become flooded with a plethora of consumption-related imports from non-regional sources (thus putting another nail in the coffin of the local manufacturing and agricultural sectors and creating a new wave of unemployment and social unrest);

- systematic increases in interest rates, without rhythm or reason that relates to domestic economic conditions, so that domestic producers who constitute one of the major catalysts for enhancing income and employment throughout the economy become squeezed out of the market, and find it impossible to borrow domestic funds generated from domestic savings (leading to even more generalized business failures and bankruptcy in all sectors of the economy);

- structural change in the taxation system to increase significantly its regressiveness, with indirect taxation as a proportion of total revenue escalating significantly through the imposition of a withering VAT and introduction of other elements of indirect taxation that fall disproportionately on those least able to bear it;

- massive and indiscriminate divestment of public enterprises, a la Jamaica, that reduces significantly the stake of nationals in the capital stock of the country, liquidifies, at outrageously discounted prices, public capital assets for current consumption, eliminates overnight the social rationale for government action - all for the pleasure of momentarily satisfying the Fund, and "window dressing", unsustainably and fleetingly, the fiscal accounts and balance of payments;

Need I go on? No, I won't; it is too painfully embarrassing. Even for your High Priests who cooked up the above defined "adjustment program" it must be too embarrassing. For the bits and pieces of our "program" just don't jive together in relation to any type of objective, whether it be domestic retrenchment for correcting financial and economic imbalances, or resource reallocation to create greater overall economic efficiency, or balance of payments viability, or "structural adjustment", whatever that may mean, or economic diversification to broaden the economic base and generate new growth points, or restructuring of the Trinidad and Tobago economy to further the cause of general equilibrium in the world economy, or any such like aesthetic Fund dogma. Quite frankly, our "program" is nothing but a hotchpotch of irreconcilable and conflicting elements and objectives; it reduces economics to a farce. It is the recipe for comprehensive disorder and all enfolding disintegration of the fabric of national life - economic, political, social - without reason or rationale or sensitivity to the aftermath. More pointedly, our action in Trinidad and Tobago does not relate to any clear set of economic principles - however misguided and inappropriate such principles may be. We're just striking out wildly in every direction and at everything in our path; we strike out thus and we create maximum grief and confusion. It's like a terrorist attack, you know, splashing around rifle fire and bazookas and even nerve gas indiscriminately so as to get the highest death toll in the shortest possible time.

2. A QUESTION TO BE ANSWERED: HOW DID WE GET INTO THE GAME OF GIVING FARCICAL ADVICE TO MEMBER COUNTRIES?

In the aftermath of our recent dealing with Trinidad and Tobago - and I must emphasize again that such dealings is but one example of scores of senseless and disastrous Fund/country relationships that define nothing but frontal attacks on peoples minding their business in their own homes and in their own countries all around the world - it behooves us to take a deep breath and sit down calmly, reflectively and ask ourselves a simple question; viz:

How on earth could we ever have got ourselves in a position where, with a straight face and without the batting of an eye, we could ever offer this brand of professional "advice" to the myriad of developing member countries in our midst? My God, my God, what have we wrought unto ourselves and unto the world?

Frankly, Mr. Camdessus, I don't have a clean and clearcut answer; I don't know exactly how our dogma did crystallize into such monstrosity. But I do have some ideas of why we are what we are, and how we did become that way, and I want to pass on these ideas to you. Probably you will find them worthwhile, probably not; I don't know. What I do know is that we cannot continue to dodge the issue anymore; we cannot keep sweeping it underneath the carpet, pretending that it doesn't exist. We cannot continue to ignore the howls of pain of those in the developing world who drink our senseless medicine of death and destruction every hour of everyday. We cannot continue to mete out our own brand of punishment and justice to leaders who have the guts to stand up to us and say "no". We cannot continue to hold the whole world and its peoples to ransom to satisfy some undefined, and catalytically destructive quirk in our nature.

You know, Sir, since you came to us just over a year ago, I have been following with great interest the initiatives that you have taken relating to the role of the Fund in Third World countries. I know that you are worried, and I hope that you are big enough, and open enough to listen to what other people (High Priests aside) have to say. Who knows, maybe there can even be a meeting of minds, at some (low) level, between you yourself and those who see the Fund and the world in perspectives different from those of your High Priests, and who are therefore branded by the latter as natural Fund "enemies"? You think that's too ambitious? I'm not so sure.

(a) A Link between Fund Staff Material Aspirations and Fund Epistemology

The first question I want to ask is perhaps a shocking question; at least you will think so, so let me ask it quickly, and get it over with. It is this:

Is the Fund staff running amok with the wholly unexpected and unexceptional authority that they wield? Are they churning out despair after despair, hunger after hunger, death after death in the name of Bretton Woods epistemology merely to satisfy their lust for power and punish those who run against their personal political ideology, and reward those who think as they do? Or maybe the creation of that despair and that hunger and that death is the way to promotion and personal aggrandizement within the Fund? Maybe it is the passport to an office as big as a church, and stuffed sofas to sit on there, and high heeled secretaries constantly in attendance; and Young Economists listening gratefully to advice on how "to make it" in the Fund? Or maybe it's a combination of all these things?

Be that as it may, I am firmly convinced that there is a close, and indeed watertight, link between our perverse role in developing countries and the epistemology that guides our action and the personal aspirations of our staff. More specifically, there is a widespread perception among Fund staff that personal progress and career advancement can best be served - indeed, can only be served - by an attitude that would deny, as being legitimate or valid, the aspiration of "the teeming masses" of the South for a better life. Thus in our day-to-day work we must trump up a missionary zeal to put the skids, carte blanche, on any effort of any government to alleviate destitution or to redistribute the gains of economic advances or to lighten, for the poor, the burden of economic adjustment. Put differently, the staff through time has twisted and changed whatever may have been the original epistemology of the Fund into a dogma that says that irrespective of reason, or conscience, or necessity, or professional etiquette, Fund staff has an inherent right, springing from the Bretton Woods philosophy of 1944, to emasculate the Third World, and particularly the economically underprivileged of the Third World, and to wield unholy power there, and to line their pockets with the good things of life for doing so, and to solidify the myth that they are above the law and that they are The New Nobility of Earth, and to say that they are...

Halt! No more! I don't expect you to agree with what I've already said, much less to what I was about to say. But really it doesn't matter. The important thing is that, whatever your own thinking on who we are, and why we are what we are, you are prepared to concede that we must try to get to the bottom of the whole question of staff motivation in doing the things that we do. So let us proceed, hopefully in a systematic way, to unravel the various elements of Fund history and epistemology to see how and if, and to what extent and at what stage, our quest for a better functioning world became ensnarled into staff personal ambitions and lust for power and more material comforts. And to do this we must go back to the very origins of the Fund in 1944; nothing less would suffice.

(b) The Origins and Theoretical Underpinning of the Fund

The Fund was created in 1944 to oversee the return of the developed world to orderly multilateral trade and payments arrangements, mainly through currency convertibility and exchange rate realignment in the United States and Western Europe after the debilitating disruptions of the inter-war period and World War II. We never did do as much pioneering work in the developed world as our founders intended; from about the mid-fifties our attention turned increasingly to the developing world.

Of course the problem there was not the creation of workable arrangements for more world trade and freer capital movements, but one of economic growth and diversification, and the need for urgent change along the whole spectrum of income distribution and quality of life and social security and political instability and economic waste and poverty and hunger and disease and desperation. Yet this whole gamut of problems was never conceived when the Fund was founded in 1944; people then never realized that the institution would come to play the catalytic role in the developing world that it plays today. This being the case, no mechanisms were built into the Fund's organisational/management system or policy structure so as to allow it to deal specifically with Third World concerns and priorities; recognition was not even given to their existence.

Okay, Mr. Camdessus, you may say: "such recognition was not necessary then; an institution can change with time to meet new needs as they arise." True, true, Sir, but the point remains that the Fund never did change. In a sense that is an aberration from all normal expectation; perhaps we can say that the Fund is the Neanderthaler of the twentieth century?

Why was this the case?

Well, it is probably due to the fact that concomitant to a quite separate role in developing countries, we continued to play our part in the process of coordinating economic policies and ensuring "sustainable" balance of payments in and among developed ones. As we proceeded thus to serve the developed world, management of the Fund - predictably drawn from that world itself - began to develop the airy-fairy idea that our role in the South was nothing if not a symmetrical extension of our First World role. In the circumstances, it was not perceived that any fundamental change in our outlook or in our way of doing things was required as we jetted from the affluence of one world to the desperation and disease of the other. Always, and under all conditions that may be encountered, the conceptual backdrop that we brought to bear on our work, and the body of economic principles that guided our action, sprang overwhelmingly from the nineteenth century vision of Pax Britannica, now writ large as Pax Atlantica - ie; "perfect competition" and "world allocation of resources" and "international division of labour" and "general equilibrium in the (western) world economy" to be achieved through the instrumentality of unbridled pricing systems domestically and Gold Standard - determined exchange rates internationally.

The logic of Pax Atlantica as described above, in so far as staff priorities were concerned, was that the self-same staff should operate to ensure that economic policies of Third World countries be made to satisfy a "means" test, viz: that irrespective of what such policies did or didn't do for general economic welfare in the developing country concerned, they must meet the key criterion of improving economic conditions in western market economies. Always our staff felt duty bound to judge their work in the Third World as "good" or "bad" in relation to that criterion. In other words, Pax Atlantica demanded that everything done by the Fund in the Third World be reduced to a common denominator of maintaining and increasing welfare in the First World; all else was incidental.

No wonder then, that all the difficult dynamics and unforeseen phenomena of the developing world in the fifties and sixties and seventies and eighties of this century had no meaning whatsoever for the staff or for the Fund; such phenomena could be ignored or dismissed or shrugged off without the batting of an eye or the furling of a brow. Adam Smith and the utopian, absolute laissez faire political economy that goes with him seemed to be the guiding light of everything. But if truth is to be told, the dream of a self-regulating world system for the 1950s tending always towards perfect competition was the dream of a few hard- lined and misguided neo-classical economists desperate for a return of western prosperity within the framework of Pax Atlantica reigning supreme in the post-war world. Yes, yes, these nostalgia hunters would have us all return to the nineteenth century reality of master and slave, of colonial powers and colonized peoples saying prayers in mosques, and lining the streets to beg and die, and dancing naked in the jungle in blissful submission to those who were divinely ordained to rape the heritage of others and drain their substance.

And for forty years, we chased that western dream of more and more prosperity and economic hegemony for North America and Western Europe. We chased it in the most unlikely places and at incalculable cost to hundreds of millions of hapless people in the South. And we knew no justice or fair play, and we had no conscience or soul. And today, still in pursuit of that dream, we point our loaded gun at the Trinidad and Tobago economy and at the economies of scores of other hapless Third World countries, and commit statistical malpractices, and cheat and lie and wheel and deal on the rationale that this is the only way that can safely allow us to plug in "right" figures in our "financial program" - "right" figures that in turn will place us in a position to sing our theme song and fool ourselves that the nostalgic dream of our forebears may yet become a reality.

Devalue! Tax the poor! Remove all transfers and subsidies to the underprivileged! Fire the people! Cut out social services! Let the children starve! Let malnutrition of all in the shanty town be our Performance Criteria! Increase prices of bread and yams and soap and water! Negate the constitution! Kill all hope and aspiration from the heart of the downtrodden! Go back again to saying your prayers in the mosque, and begging in the street, and dancing in the jungle! Turn back the clock two hundred years and let us again be the masters and you the slaves! Lay yourself out in a garbage heap as grist for our Steamroller, our Heaviest Steamroller! Play, Developing World by the rules of the Dream to be Recaptured! Lie prostrate - lie obediently prostrate as our Heaviest Steamroller plough through you for glorification of our Founding Fathers and for the pique and career development of our present-day staff!

You don't believe me? Then I ask you to do one thing. Analyse critically our "program" for Trinidad and Tobago - even if you can ignore all the lies and the cheating we had to do there to put "substance" in that program. Analyse it on its merit, as a means of "restoring financial balance", and "structurally adjusting" the Trinidad and Tobago economy. Analyse the existing programs that we have for Peru and Brazil and Guyana and Grenada and the Dominican Republic and Venezuela and Nigeria and Tanzania and Zambia and the Sudan and Vietnam and Bangladesh. Analyse them carefully, Mr. Camdessus, and come back and tell me with a straight face that what we are doing in the Third World is not a total farce that turns all economic logic on its head. Come back and tell me that the mess that we are making of the Third World is not motivated by considerations that are alien to the needs and realities and aspirations of the countries concerned. Come back, Mr. Camdessus, and tell me that - if you can.

3. SECOND QUESTION TO BE ANSWERED: CAN WE RETRACE OUR STEPS AND START FROM SCRATCH AGAIN?

When the analysis mentioned above is undertaken - when the answer is in - one important question will arise; it is this: Can we retrace our steps back to 1944, recognize our tremendous errors, and start from scratch again? Can we ask the world to give us a second chance? Can we say we will learn from our mistakes, horrendous and catalytic as they may have been? "World, be assured that we are on the right path now; it took us forty years to get there; a few hundreds of millions of souls were lost in the process, but what the heck, that's the way life is. Forgive us; let's start anew again; we'll do a better job the second time around." Can we do that, or must the world dump us in the garbage heap of history as one of civilization's greatest shame?

For what it is worth I will give you my answer to the above question; it is this:

It will be a very brave and optimistic man who would say that we can change from within; I am neither that brave nor that optimistic.

More specifically, I do not think that our problem is a matter of adaptation of epistemologies and organisational/administrative structures and financing mechanisms and operational criteria to enhance a predetermined end of helping those we serve to help themselves within a self-reinforcing system with mutual rights and responsibilities. If it was that, we would have changed a long time ago. You know, I have gone through almost everything written over the past decade within the Fund in self-examination, and on the need to alter our ways in response to mounting international criticism, particularly on "conditionality" that we impose on

Third World countries that become forced to use our resources. What struck me most in this review was the tone of self righteousness and the seething resentment, and the sense of effrontery that others could ever perceive us to do wrong in any respect, or in any aspect of our work. Yes, Sir. Our files and our history are littered, not with soul searching, or suggestions for fundamental change, or recognition of our growing irrelevance, or admission of our cheating, but with self congratulation for what we are, and insistence - we always insist - that there can be no concessions whatsoever to those who do not regard us as The Epitome of All That May Be Perfect. And as "outside" criticisms pile up on us, we say more and more emphatically: "the whole world is stupid, and it becomes more stupid every time it dares to criticize us. When will others begin to realize that we are the only wise ones and they are the fools?".

You know, we are so wedded to the Grand Illusion that we can turn, by sleight of hand, our lies and our deception into the Absolute Truth that everyone else must accept and obey, that the mere thought that there could be scope for self-criticism becomes a heresy, and anyone who suggests it becomes immediately an institutional outcast and a threat to the balance and sanity of the Fund. As far as we are concerned, there is a halo of Superior Wisdom all around us; we can do no wrong.

(a)   The Making of a New Nobility on Earth

You know, Sir, at some critical stage in the course of our history a terrible event did happen within the Fund.

Let me try as best as I can to describe that event; it is as follows: somehow, sometime, our original epistemology, as described above, became transformed from a verifiable system of concepts open to change and adaptation to a totally closed and vainglorious doctrine that had nothing to do with economic theory, but everything to do with the Nature of Man.

That totally closed and vainglorious doctrine is as follows: Fund staff is above the law and can do no wrong. And the seeds of what we are today were sown when we hijacked thus the Fund's already simplistic and inappropriate dream of Pax Atlantica, and made it to become our testament of personal infallibility and our justification for resurrecting the ancient myth of the Divine Right of Kings and Princes and foisting it on an unsuspecting, late twentieth century world, itself already weighed down by the same troubling problems of Gross Materialism transcending everything else, and diminishing drastically man's own conscience and man's own humanity.

(b) "Core" Staff as Successors of Colonial Civil Servants

The concept of Pax Atlantica as a body of ideas had its counterpart in the "core" people who populate the Fund, or were meant to populate the Fund (and, of course, its sister institution, the World Bank); the subsequent hijacking of the Fund was undertaken by the self-same "core" staff. You know, Mr. Camdessus, the "core" of our staff, and the overwhelming majority of our High Priests, are still "technocrats" from the developed world, "trained" at "prestigious" North American and European Universities, or their mimics from the developing world who aspire to be just like them. It is these people who, two centuries ago, would have gone into the Colonial Service of their respective countries as colonial administrators, or would have migrated to "their" colonies as entrepreneurs or plantation managers or slave owners. Times and employment opportunities have changed, but ingrained attitudes after hundreds of years of ruling the developing world as vassal states, and as contemptible appendages of the metropole, have not. In more explicit terms, a lot of the seething contempt, and the "higher than thou" and "better than thou" and "natural right to rule thou" attitude of our staff vis a vis our developing member countries, have their origin in the history and national mores, and pre-conceived expectations of our "core" staff. I hesitate to say it, but the "white man's burden" mentality that is the root cause of so much of the troubles of our age, is as evident in the Fund today as it must have been in the United Kingdom, or France, or Holland or any other western colonial powers three hundred years ago.

Of course it goes without saying that service in the colonies meant privilege and social status and high emoluments and perks - extremely high emoluments and perks - for material gratification was the motivation for everything. So it was then and so it is today. The multi-faceted implications of the ridiculously high Fund staff salaries and allowances and privileges are discussed in Part V; I will not pursue that matter here except to say one thing; it is this. Within the Fund itself, as you must be aware, there is a very underhand and un-written, yet highly operative and effective system for promotion and career advancement that contrasts stark-ly with the formalized and written one; unfortunately racial considerations have played a very dominant role in superimposing the former system on the latter. Nor must it remain unsaid that certain Departments of the Fund are virtually segregated along racial lines, and "internal" race relations are deteriorating further, even as our relations with "black" and "brown" countries seem to worsen. And if you want to go further into an in-ternal worm that's eating at our soul, I will ask one simple question: Why is South Africa classified as a European entity in Fund organisational structure and operational modalities? Is it not in Africa? Shouldn't it be within the African Department? Why is it administered by the European Department - a Department, as you well know, that remains highly segregated along racial lines, in total contradiction to the international na-ture of the Fund. What if Trinidad and Tobago, given the deal that it has been getting from the Western Hemi-sphere Department, was to ask for reclassification as an Asian country supervised and monitored by the Asian Department? Would you agree?

What I ask are not frivolous questions intended to embarrass our institution. They are fundamental is-sues that demonstrate the way in which the present is still governed by the ethos and prejudices of the past. They bring into focus an important aspect of that bigger theme that I have posed - i.e, our capacity or in-capacity to shed the errors of forty years of shame, and to start anew again.

(c) The Fund as Judge and Jury and Prosecutor and Legislator and Administrator in Developing Countries

I turn now, to the rules of the game that we play so successfully in developing member countries to en-sure our omnipotence there. And in this respect, I want to highlight certain matters relating to the nature of power and authority that we wield in these countries, and the ways and mechanisms through which an All-Enfolding Fund Power is manifested over indigenous populations and their governments.

The most obvious point to be made is that we are Judge and Jury and Maker of All Relevant Laws relat-ing to the Crime committed and Administrator of the Penal Code and Executor of the Sentence. Yes, Sir, in scores of developing countries around the world that are unfortunate enough to fall within our clutches through use of our resources, we hold simultaneously and completely in our hand Legislative and Executive and Judi-cial powers over wide ranging matters relating to economic and financial policies. We do our own "tainted" evaluation of economic and financial performance (an evaluation that is subsequently accepted as Bible truth by our Executive Board and by the international community); we write our own Letter of Intent under the name of the Minister of Finance and get his signature after minor modifications that we may concede. (If he refuses to sign, our wrath can take very practical forms; the sky may begin to fall down all around him; his country may be made to join that group of leper countries that no other international agency or financial in-stitution will want to touch). And having thus "negotiated" a program, we go about "administering" it; this in-cludes determining whether or not the country has met the performance criteria that we have established, and whether, therefore, it is eligible, on "target" dates, to draw down the financial resources that we had com-mitted, and that other "supporting" institutions had promised.

The whole process of determining what is "right" for the country (consultation or "negotiating" mission), through formulating that "rightness" into a legal document that specifies "conditionality" and "performance criteria" (Letter of Intent), to "administering" and "monitoring" the program (appointment of Resident Representative or provision of other staff inputs breathing down the necks of the Minister of Finance and President or Governor of the Central Bank and keeping them trembling in their boots), to determining whether or not the country is eligible to draw ("satisfying" performance criteria or providing "waivers" if there is "non-performance"), to alerting the international community that a new outcast exists (assuming that, in our Su-perior Wisdom, we adjudicate that the country should not be allowed to draw), is not only performed solely by the Fund, or by the relevant Division of the appropriate Department of the Fund, but in most instances by a single staff member (Mission Leader or Division Chief) acting on behalf of the Fund. Such a staff member would hold, for all intents and purposes, the economic fate of the country concerned, and of its peoples, in his hand; as such he becomes transformed from a human being to the Unstoppable Supra-National Authority with Heaviest Steamroller Crushing Down All in Its Path.

It is no wonder that individual staff members - and sometimes relatively junior ones at that - have achieved extreme notoriety in certain member countries - Peru and Egypt and Jamaica in the mid to late 70s, Tanzania and Zambia in the early eighties, are good examples. At the time of Peru's torment, one analyst reportedly insisted that at the mere mention of the name of the Fund staff member concerned, little children from the slums would run to their mothers, crying and disoriented, "as if they had just seen the Devil Incarnate or heard his voice."

Well, we don't need to cite such an extreme example to realize that the one-sided and wholly unbalanced system of rights and responsibilities in Fund/developing member country relationships has become intolerable. In this respect, Lord Actons's maxim that "all power corrupts and absolute power corrupts absolutely" is particularly relevant. You know, for forty years we took a particular stance and acted in a particular way as if the doctrine of the separation of powers - a doctrine that constitutes the true basis of everything fair and just in western political and economic and social systems - could never ever be made to apply to us in our dealings with the Third World. Amazingly, our assumption of the role of Monster Leviathan, wielding multidimensional economic power in the developing world seems to have become crystallized as acceptable late twentieth century practice. Just how we managed to get away with such an assertion of irresistible power at the national level for over several decades is probably one of the most puzzling and unresolved mysteries of twentieth century international politics.

4. THE BIGGER PICTURE

Sir, I have been trying, in this Part of the Letter, to give some examples of factors that impinge on staff motivation and action and responses to particular situations, real or trumped up, in developing countries. Doubtlessly, the things that I outline are important in themselves, but they are also part of a much bigger picture of staff privilege and exemption and almost unbelievable financial reward. Now I am at the stage where I have to stop giving examples and go on instead to discuss that Much Bigger Picture of Privilege and Emoluments and Exemptions, for that Much Bigger Picture is the Be All and End All of Everything pertaining to Fund staff action; it is the root from which all else spring, and I call it the Honeypot.

Honeypot?

Yes, Honeypot. Honeypot of All the Good Things of Life that our organisation does proffer to its employees. Honeypot is like Eternity; it has no end, and when everything is said and done, it transforms us into tinsel gods and goddesses; it is the source from which comes the already-mentioned New Nobility on Earth.

5. THE FOUNDING FATHERS, THE HONEYPOT AND THE NEW NOBILITY

You know, Sir, I don't know if our Founding Fathers in 1944 did ever envisage emergence of us as a New Nobility drinking endlessly from a Honeypot; I suspect that they didn't. I think that they saw us merely as a necessary input in the overall vision of international institutionalism being harnessed to help restore the economic greatness of the western world, and to help satisfy the aspirations of its peoples for greater employment and a better quality of life. And they were so taken up with laying down Articles of Agreement that would serve these Bigger Ends that they failed entirely to grapple with problems of internal organisational balance; certainly they never conceived that the nondescript and "neutralized" army of neo-colonial civil servants that they were creating could ever dare to "steal" the institution and wear its spoils on their chests, as Knights of an Equally Dark Age would wear Orders of Merit and Baubles of Exclusivity.

How simplistic were those Founding Fathers, Mr. Camdessus! Didn't they know anything about human nature? Didn't they have before them the lessons of our ten thousand years of failure and ignominy because we could never suppress the Devil's Lust within us? Didn't they have any inkling of the impact of their mean little vision on the psychology and motivation of ordinary men and women who would be asked to serve that vision and seek to realize its most essential features?

I tell you, Sir, despite all the technical expertise of key figures like Keynes and White, the Bretton Woods Conference remains a prime example of human shame and failure of perspicacity. Not only were our Founding Fathers preoccupied with the foolish and wholly unworthy vision of Pax Atlantica - of western aggrandizement to maintain and increase western prosperity at the expense of all else - but in the process of trying to weave that vision into the warp and woof of post-war world institutional structures, they left the door wide open for the faceless bureaucrat, ignored by everyone at the beginning, to slink in unobserved and take charge and transform everything into a credo of Massive Personal Power and Massive Personal Material Advancement. With the Fund mask on our face, and your approved Briefing Paper in our hand, we roam through the world in our hundreds. We roam like Caesars and Gengis Khans and Hitlers. We roam, from one fiefdom of our creation to the next, dispensing harsh and summary justice on the poor and the defenseless and the underprivileged.

For us, it's harvest-time. For transformation of the Bretton Woods creed from a Vision of Atlantic economic supremacy to an irresistible quest for staff gratification is nothing if not a logical and wholly-to-be-expected progression. Materialism breeds materialism, whether it be at the international or at the personal level, and what started out as a vision of western materialism unencumbered by considerations of humanity, or calls for greater social justice for the poor and destitute of the developing world, has merely slipped into a different gear to become a vision of personal material bliss for the staff, unrestrained by norms of professional propriety, or by pangs of conscience.

Let me tell you, Sir, that the Fund is soulless not because there is no scope for humanized behavior and compassion in an institution dedicated to optimum world economic efficiency and a more effective use of foreign financial resources in developing countries, but because its founders, in chasing their improbable dream, overlooked all scope for exercising compassion and alleviating social injustice in certain parts of the international system that they were creating. Compassion and social justice were crying needs; they were the very roots on which we should have nurtured an evolving and pragmatic Fund philosophy for the Third World. But our Founding Fathers denied us access to them, and shrivelled our soul. So later on, when we "stole" the Fund, All Things Just and Humane became our Absolute Antithesis; we were as clinically and as completely materialistic and single-minded in pursuit of our Own Gratification as they were in pursuit of Pax Atlantica. So in a very meaningful way our staff is the logical consequence of our Founding Fathers, just as the latter are the logical consequence of the prevailing 1944 international ethos of Superior Man and Inferior Man, and the White Man and his system to be saved and nurtured, and the black/brown colonized man to be overlooked and cast aside, in so far as his needs and aspirations as individuals and as groups and as nations are concerned.

If truth is to be told, late-twentieth century international economic institutionalism is just another reenactment of the theme of the Possessor and the Dispossessed, and just another rerun of the mechanics of ensuring Greater Possession for the Possessor and of letting the fortunes of the Dispossessed to hang on the irresistible and unconditional and vainglorious and exclusive aim of Those Who Possess. What we are seeing is nothing if not the recurring motif of man's history with the Downtrodden and Dispossessed playing the part of Sisiphus, going up falteringly only to be swept down again, ad nauseam. The only difference today in relation to the past is that the management system for sweeping down (as represented by our institution) is worldwide, whereas before it was at the "Empire" or the national, or the group level. It is chilling to realize that virtually the whole world is involved; hardly anyone can escape responsibility; we are either culprits or victims.

6. A PERSONAL PLEA

Forgive me, Sir, but I smile wryly as I write these words, and I shut my eyes, and I shake my head over and over again and I swallow and nonchalantly I thrust my pen into the cotton sheet of my bed and the ink spreads there slowly, and as the blue blob grows and grows I think of how idealistic and hopeful I was twenty-two years ago when I first joined the staff of the World Bank, and how disillusioned I am today as I leave the Fund. And I remove the pen from the sheet, and I throw it away from me. And I say to myself: "let it be; let it be. Close this Part of the Letter now; don't write another word. Go outside instead; take a brisk walk in the cold; try to calm yourself tonight.

But I cannot do that. I cannot bring myself to conclude this Part without at least begging you to affirm that we share something in common as members of the human race. For only if we can admit existence of that minimal commonalty that I have tried to define in the opening paragraphs of Part I, can there be any hope, however fragile it may seem to be, of seeing eye to eye on issues raised in this Letter, and of being able to use the period immediately ahead to reevaluate the state of our institution from the backdrop of some acceptable code of civilized behavior, and from an agreed benchmark of human conduct that can serve, at some future date, to validate our relationship with others.

You know, Sir, we are not the cold and dispassionate technical inter-governmental agency doing cold and dispassionate and technical things unrelated to the warp and woof of the broad stream of human life that flows through our planet. Your High Priests, in blissful illusion and with the Honey of our Pot dripping from their lips, would claim that we are the Innocuous Eunuch of twentieth century international society, keeping Due Order in the Harem on behalf of Master Sheik, untouched by the pathos and tragedies and triumphs of Haremdom that swirl around us. Sir, they are wrong in that evaluation, for we are part and parcel of the tide; we make or break human life every day of every year as probably no other force on earth has ever done in the past or will ever do again in the future. And we've botched it all up; there's dust and ashes everywhere. The only things that grow in Size and Stature are our Honeypot, and those who suck at it. That's unsustainable; that's eminently unsustainable; there will come a day when we will have to go down unto our knees to pick up the pieces of our Horror and our Infamy. Pick them up carefully merely to thrust them away from us again to show the world that we are contrite. And on that day, and at that stage the world will tell us where we must go from there, or - more realistically - whether there is any place at all for us to go from there.

As we stand waiting for the world to speak thus - and it will speak, Sir; it will speak sooner than you may think; much sooner - I want to ask some questions about our common humanity. If I'm insistent, its only because I'm worried; very worried. Sometimes I have nightmares, and I wake up in a cold sweat, and I say to myself: "Maybe Mr. Camdessus will not understand; maybe we are on entirely different wavelengths. I fear that he will never see my point of view." So let me find out now, Sir; let me find out once and for all, and let your answer pitch me into a further dismay, or provide a new hope.

I don't know, Sir, if you ever did wonder why the history of the Fund should have been written by our High Priests with such effervescent satisfaction and self-congratulation. I don't know if you ever noticed that it is only those who worship unreservedly at our altar of Inhumanity and Savage Thirst for Blood when the Moon is Full who can be made to belong to and find his or her ultimate Potential within our Fold. I don't know if you ever became nonplused as you wish your staff Godspeed, and send them to roam the Third World everyday, and create new chaos there. I don't know if your heart did ever bleed to see all around you in the Fund such a complete lack of human worthiness, and such an easy divestment by human beings of their birthright of humanity, and such nonchalant denial of their capacity for compassion and fair play toward others. I don't know if you ever felt uneasy in an environment where there is such evident joy and self-satisfaction of the Over-Privileged in tormenting further the innocent and the hapless and the diseased and the malnutritioned and the little children of the South. I don't know if you ever sensed the dark and dank cloud of shame that hangs around us all the time, stifling us, blotting out all vision beyond our physical and material gratification, mirroring faithfully what we are and what we do to others. I don't know if you ever saw terror in the eyes of at least one of your staff members and thought to yourself: "My God, my God, maybe there's some devil that he sees that I cannot see as yet; I wonder if it is more than a hallucination that I see in his eyes?" I don't know ...

I don't know; I don't know. I wish I did; I wish I could be reassured. For I want to stop addressing you as an economist, or as a central banker, or as an appointee with a mandate for Pax Atlantica, or even as a Man with Even Hands. I want to stop addressing you thus, and to subsume all your variegated roles as Fund

Boss into the much bigger context of one human being seeking to establish dialogue with another on matters of overwhelming mutual concern that test our soul, and prove or disprove our common humanity.

Yours sincerely,

Davison L. Budhoo

INTERNATIONAL MONETARY FUND
WASHINGTON. D. C. 20431

May 18, 1988

CABLE ADDRESS
INTERFUND

Mr. Camdessus
Managing Director
International Monetary Fund
Washington, D.C.

Dear Mr. Camdessus,

   Davison L. Budhoo: Part V of Letter of Resignation from the Staff of the International Monetary Fund;
Details of the Honeypot

   The Honeypot - I want to get on with the juicy details of the Honeypot. And in doing that I will refer to my own situation. Admittedly that is not a very good example, for my Fund career has been punctuated with rebelliousness and non-conformity. Certainly, I have incurred the wrath of your High Priests; I have been put on short rations and my access to Honeypot's Voluptuousness has been calculatingly restrictive. But given the fact that I do not want to reveal the Salaries and Allowances and privileges of others, I will have to speak about myself. So for what it is worth, here's my salary and Benefits Package as I leave the Fund :

1.   MY SALARY AND BENEFITS PACKAGE (GROSS) AS A FUND STAFF MEMBER AS OF MAY 18, 1988
(excluding all benefits and emoluments on official travel and on mission and Fund representation work)

	(In US Dollars)
Total salary/benefits package	143,000
Of which:	
Basic annual salary	114,000
Other Emoluments and subsides gross, calculated on base of $114,000 annual rate), inclusive of education, family and home-leave travel and allowances, interest subsidy on loans for allowable purposes and other subsidies	29,000

   Sir, I want you to note that I am being specific, so that the figures I give can be checked. If I am wrong in any detail, please issue a statement of denial; I shall be pleased to correct certain technicalities if I have to. But I suspect not. I suspect that I will not have to revise anything downward. In fact, I may have to augment, perhaps significantly, my estimated figures of our Honeypot's largesse to our "missionary staff".
   A word of caution is necessary as one tries to interpret the above package in relation to norms for other Fund staff members. That word of caution is as follows: my allowances are relatively modest because my family group is small. So let's increase the size of my family group and see what happens. Assume, for instance, that I had my grandmother residing with me in Washington, and I had chosen to have five children attend school/college in say, Geneva. In such circumstances my gross package would shoot up towards the US$200,000 mark per annum. If, in addition, I was on field assignment in say, Guyana, as Fund Resident Representative (I was, you know, some years back) I would have earned close to US$300,000 per year.
   My annual package, much less that of Big Family Man in Washington, or on assignment overseas, is more than the annual budgeted salary of almost every Head of State in the world; it is anything from five to ten times more than what virtually every President or Prime Minister of the Third World would get on his basic pay check. The Big Family Man with my identical basic pay but on assignment in the Third World even as his five kids learn Social Graces in Geneva, compliments of Our Honeypot, would receive more than the basic pay of every head of state in the world, including the President of the United States and the President or Chancellor or Prime Minister of every West European country. In relation to the developing world, his gross

earnings would probably be about ten to fifteen times more than the budgeted salary of a typical African, or Latin American or Caribbean or Asian Head of State, and about one thousand times more than the per capita income enjoyed by two thirds of mankind.

Well, that's a handy little package of gold, you know. It is, indeed, a very handy little package of gold for a very handy job well done. You see how lightning did strike one day, several years ago, and brought me a-rushing unto Honeypot's ample bosom for a milk?

Oops! I forgot to mention the intangibles that come with the job. Like diplomatic immunities and our United Nations Laissez Passer that we flash before the eyes of cowering custom officers of Third World nations, even as officials from Foreign Affairs Ministries whisk us from VIP airport lounges to our Twenty Star Hotel in the capital city of the particular fiefdom that we are visiting. Like Royalty Class and First Class travel everywhere we go, and generous subsistence allowances for overnight stays in London and Paris and Copenhagen and Frankfurt and Rome and Rio de Janeiro and Caracas on our way to bust up the natives in Africa and Asia and elsewhere. Like high class nightclubbing and such-like follies in Sin Cities, Compliments of Honeypot - always compliments of our Lustful Honeypot. Like personal secretaries on each and everyone of our "missions". Like maids that we bring into the United States on G-5 Visas, and at our pleasure, from Paraguay and Mexico and Jamaica and Greece and India and the Philippines and everywhere else. Like the very generous medical benefits plan and the Group Life Insurance Plan and the even more generous Pensions Scheme. Like the realization dawning upon us that we have finally made it to Ultimate Paradise.

2.   SHARING THE STAFF BLISS WITH SELECTED NON-STAFF ENTITIES: ENDLESS HONEYPOT SPREADS HER WINGS

I've spoken so far of Our Honeypot for Fund staff, and indeed the staff has always been the core recipient of All That There Is To Offer. But Our Pot transcends the staff; she radiates like a Glowing Flame from our headquarters in Washington; she is seen throughout the world as the Emblem of Easy Money, and High Living, and Exclusive Jet-Setting for Faceless People with Pretensions to Economic Technocracy. As such, she draws into her orbit pent-up hopes and aspirations and way-out fantasies of bureaucrats, and has-been politicians, and self-seekers from all around the world. They hope and aspire, and fantasize about getting a piece of the action, and a select few achieve their goal of consummation - at least at that minimal level that serves to tickle the pallet and make them ask for more.

You lift your eyebrow, Sir, and you ask: "Just how generous is Our Honeypot to her myriad suitors of every creed and nationality?"

My answer, simple and straightforward, is as follows: "Exceedingly Generous, Sir, exceedingly generous indeed."

(a) The Executive Board and Its Staff as Recipients of Honeypot's Largesse

Our Executive Board and their staff - and both Board and staff sit permanently at our headquarters in Washington - are as equally subject to the Charms of Our Pot as we are, and she, in return, is generous to them to a fault. All the goodies that she bestows on us she gives to them, and more. Many years ago, as staff salaries became unrealistically inflated, salaries of Executive Directors and their staff became even more so, given the Fund's policy of maintaining percentage differentials between the emoluments of the faceless bureaucrats and those of our political directorate. Thus was the Board drawn into the fragrant bosom of beloved Honeypot, seemingly Very Pleased with Everything Pertaining to Her Form and Style and Substance. The Board remains in general a happy but quiescent, almost anesthetized body. At any rate, it seems to operate today as a rubber stamp for action and initiatives of the staff, especially in relation to our Third World role.

You know, Sir, let me tell you something. One of the most depressing experiences you can have as a Fund staff member is attending Executive Board meetings to hear Executive Directors singing staff praises and going through motions and repeating uncritically the data and conclusions that we serve up to them in

RED and Staff Reports. In this respect, it is interesting to note that at the relevant Board meeting last year on Trinidad and Tobago, no Executive Director or his representative seemed willing to ask the staff to explain why they should have discontinued the RULC index so abruptly, and so unceremoniously, or to query changed statistics in several of the series previously presented. Such questions, had they been asked, could have brought to light some of the staff's statistical malpractices over 1985/87, but they seemingly went a- begging. Is the Board not interested enough in objectivity and accuracy and consistency in Fund staff "data" and "estimates" and "analysis" to take a stand at some stage? Obviously, the High and Not-so-High Priests responsible for the Trinidad and Tobago trickery thought that it was not. They surmised that no capacity could be made to exist on the Board for asking the right questions; they relegated the Board to an inconsequential blob of complacency and head nodding.

Sir, while I'm at it I should make another observation, it is this: even as the Board is becoming more and more immobilized as an effective decision making body, and as the monitor of Fund staff activities, Board staff members (who normally would serve for fixed and relatively short periods in Washington on nomination of their governments), seem to be aspiring more and more to remain in their present Glorious State, drinking ever more from the Honeypot. Indeed, a casual enquiry will show that the incidence of formal and informal applications from Executive Board staff for regular or fixed term Fund staff employment is increasing alarmingly; several members of the politically appointed staff of the Board have in fact been placed in the bureaucracy of the Fund. Of course, if you are supposed to be serving your government but are at the same time looking over your shoulder for a job in the Fund, invariably you will begin to play up to those High Priests who hold the power to give or to deny you the job; you will tend to butter them up and bend down to them even while you sit on the Board, or prepare policy positions for those who sit on the Board. Well, perhaps you'll tend to do even more than play up to them - perhaps you'll find it right to grovel at their feet and clap your hands in delight even as they rape the country that you represent, or otherwise distort the policies and the credibility of the government that had elected you to the Board Staff in the first instance. What I'm saying is that a clear and easily identifiable conflict of interest is inherent in the current practice of recruiting Fund "technical" staff from the ranks of aspiring Board staff members, and it is surprising that nothing has been done to halt this trend.

(b) Honeypot Goes to the Third World

(i) Top Brass Government Officials in Make-or-Break Try to Seduce Her

In scores of Ministries of Finance and Central Banks around the world, the hearts of aspiring "technocrats" flutter when a Fund mission is announced, for hope springs eternal in the human breast - hope to gain access to the Honeypot's Lusciousness by picking-up a "big work" in Washington. The means to achieve this dream, of course, is by being "nice" to and by "cooperating" with Fund missions, or to call a spade a spade - by doing all the things our Visiting Priests would have them do. Put another way, it can be said that active and "I-scratch-your-back-and-you- scratch-mine" collusion between national government officials and Fund mission staff is becoming more and more prevalent. The purpose of such collusion is to set the stage and pave the way for All the Nasty Games we Love to Play. The modus operandi for this relatively new dimension of our operations in the Third World is to identify beforehand those key officials who are most vulnerable and influential (in the sense of aspiring to Honeypot's goodies and of having "clout" with the political directorate). Thus preselected, we make it clear to them that that their cooperation and ability to "deliver the goods" could conceivably make them to win friends and influence people in High and Mighty Places.

(ii) Not-So-Top-Brass Officials Find a Place in the Sun

Have no illusions that in any particular country of the developing world, Our Honeypot is not made available to a much wider range of "cooperative" and deserving officialdom than the one or two top level technocrats or self-serving politicians that we preselect for special treatment and lightning-striking magic. "To each his own", says the poet, and we follow that principle rigorously in our dealings with the younger, middle-level government bureaucrats who we encounter and interface with at the technical level at the Ministry of Finance or the Central Bank or similar key policy economic making government departments of the Third World country concerned. Our line vis a vis this brand of raw up-and-coming bureaucrat is not a top job in the Promised Land, but a "top training course" at our own Training Institute at our own Washington head-quarters. We offer several different courses in several different languages for "deserving" middle order offi-cials. This, of course, is laudable, except that the selection process seems to favor overwhelmingly officials who had been particularly helpful to us on missions in the past, and who we deem to hold out a promise of even greater "cooperation" in the future.

3. OTHER EXAMPLES OF HONEYPOT'S LURE

They come like moths to the candle; they can never fight her irresistibility.

You remember, Sir, how, some years ago, we instituted new organs in the management and decision making structures of the Fund and World Bank so as to give developing countries a greater say in the decision making process on Matters of Great Moment? You remember how the Development Committee and the Group of Twenty Four came into being? You remember the lofty aims that we touted for them? Whatever did become of those aims? Whatever happened to the concept of the Third World taking the bull by the horns and carving out from all the Bretton Woods stickiness and illogicalities an institution sensitized and respon-sive to the needs and realities and multi-faceted dynamics of the South?

Nothing happened, nothing at all.

Sure we established a Development Committee. Sure we created an Executive Secretariat for that Com-mittee at - of all places - the World Bank, to operate virtually as just another facet of the staff of the World Bank and the Fund. Sure we brought the Ministers of Finance of the Third World and their hordes of Advisors to Washington far more frequently than they were wont to come. Sure we built a spanking new Conference hall and facilities in the Fund for them to sit and talk through fancy new microphones with simultaneous trans-lation in several languages. Sure we got them to issue press communiques. Sure we appointed Chairmen and Vice Chairmen and sub-committees and sub-sub-committees and Working Groups and Consultants. Sure we released Members of our Executive Board (our citadel of Fund and World Bank staff "Wisdom") to be Prompters and "Think Tanks" to the Committee. Sure we implemented, honestly and faithfully, all the mechanics of setting up another White Elephant in our shop, programmed to gesticulate wildly, harmlessly, when we turn on the batteries. Sure we did all the cosmetic things that we needed to do to take the mount-ing political pressures from off our backs.

But nothing happened. Nothing except what I have described in Part I of this Letter - ie; accelerated abuses by our staff of the powers that they wield in developing countries, and more and more Fund programs and program proposals that turn economic logic on its head, and greater politicisation of the Fund, and an even more uneven distribution of power and influence in the Fund in favor of Part I members (First World). And more Death and Destitution in the Third World because our institution operates the way it does.

I could go on and on with other examples of how we respond to political pressures to mend our ways. I could go on and on about new institutionalization and "new thinking" and "independent analysis" and objec-tive evaluation of our successes and failures, and of "Wise Men" rising suddenly to say their lines that we had taught them to say and falling back into oblivion again with equally indecent haste. I could go on about us writing our own history and undertaking bogus-like exercises to judge our own relevance, and pronounc-ing from within on our own exalted place in history. Or if you prefer, I could turn the coin over and proceed to show how our Honeypot has the peculiar knack of turning up in the most unlikely places, mesmerizing everybody and corrupting everything, and making nonsense of the angry resolutions of Third World leaders at Annual Bank/Fund Meetings, or at G-77 Ministerial Meetings, or at Non Aligned Movement Heads of Government Meetings, or at UNCTAD and several other international fora.

But I will not, because I must not upstage Part VI.

4. REDUCING EVERYTHING TO A COMMON DENOMINATOR OF GREED AND PERSONAL AMBITION

What I have said so far serves to define fairly clearly the usual pattern of response by Fund Staff to any perceived threat that arguably could endanger the Joys and Privileges of Honeypot Wallowing. In this respect, any "outside" shock wave that, conceivably, may serve to alter, even by one iota, the Established Order of Things or the Equanimity of Our High Priests, or the Irresistible Logic of the Fund in reducing everything to a common denominator of Greed and Personal Ambition and Maintenance of the Status Quo, and Further Enhancement of the Power of the New Nobility, must necessarily be expunged from the system. But we don't expunge with high visibility protest and formal resistance - how can we do that when those who cause us grief and heart palpitations are themselves our nominal masters and members of our Board of Governors - ie; Third World Ministers of Finance? Such a situation demands patience and finesse on our part. A willingness to ride it out with Honeypot at our side, able and willing to make her contribution in any way whatsoever, is what is called for.

So in all that we do publicly, seeming reasonableness and propriety and "sweet talk" become the order of the day; we seem to feed the hog even as we stab him in the back. There is no intellectual effort, no honest search for solutions, no new thinking whatsoever. Mediocrity and an absolute slavish imitation of High Priests who have "made it" in the Fund; stultifying conformity and an amazing perfection of the art of "yesmanship" - these are the essential elements of a true Fund Person. Hypocrisy underlies everything that we do; certainly, core elements of our staff have had centuries of experience in practicing it on subject peoples. And the world is no closer today to an amelioration of the ills of Imperial Empire than it was at the time of Queen Victoria. Therein lies the bequeathment of the West and the tragedy of the South. Therein, too, lies the entire history and insidiousness of the Fund.

When all is said and done, Sir, we are nothing if not a vainglorious spider weaving an enormous web. The flies around irritate us; we cannot stand their buzzing; we fear that they have a power to bust up our web and, besides, they are succulent; they titillate our taste buds. So we stalk them. We sing songs of love and adoration. We lure them into our web and then we kill and eat them; they become part of everything that we are; they are assimilated into our system; they nourish us. And at the end of the day we are fatter and more secure than ever before and there is peace and quiet in our house, and no flies will dare approach us tomorrow. Maybe the day after tomorrow they will venture by again; but not tomorrow; already we have bought tomorrow's peace with today's labor.

Yours sincerely,

Davison L. Budhoo

MULTILATERAL ECONOMIC NEGOTIATIONS ASSISTANCE GROUP (MENAG)

SUITE 188 □ 4807 BETHESDA AVENUE □ BETHESDA, MARYLAND 20814 □ UNITED STATES OF AMERICA □ TELEPHONE (301) 229-8817

September 20, 1988

Mr. Camdessus
Managing Director
International Monetary Fund
Washington, D.C. 20431

Dear Mr. Camdessus,

I am enclosing Part VI of my Open Letter of Resignation, dated May 18, 1988. Please note that Section 3, (ii) entitled "The Fund as Agent of Powerful Shareholders to Change Third World Political and Economic Systems" is being renamed, revised and extended. This sub-section will be resubmitted to you at the earliest possible time.

Yours sincerely,

Davison L. Budhoo
President

May 18, 1988

Mr. Camdessus
Managing Director
International Monetary Fund
Washington, D.C. 20431

Dear Mr. Camdessus,

> Davison L. Budhoo: Part VI of Open Letter of Resignation from the Staff of the International Monetary Fund. Reform of the Fund - Psychology, Epistemology, Organization, Operations

In this final Part of the Letter I would like to come back to a question I asked in Part IV - ie; can the Fund reform itself so that it serves the true interests of developing countries without compromising its role as the major plank of an international management system for economic stability and growth and for the financing of such stability and growth? I suspect that you will raise your hand immediately and say yes; over the past year you have affirmed repeatedly that the institution is on the right track; the garden is in seed or blooming; where there are bare patches something is being done to turn the latter green; in every instance there is, full awareness of what potential still exists for further cultivation; everything will turn up trumps. There is a toasty feeling of comfort - of quiet confidence - because the staff is Wise and Dedicated, its Vision Piercing and Untramelled and Unspoilt. "Aren't I a lucky guy?" you seem to tell the world: "Look at the Expertise and Unwavering Commitment of my International Band of Hard-Working and Over-Extended Economists and Movers and Shakers and Jet-Setters. What an International Treasure resides at 700 19th Street! The Board of Governors and of Executive Directors and the Group of Twenty Four and the Development Committee propose, but my Good and Trust-worthy staff dispose! Hurray, my Staff! World, let's sing a song to them! Let's sing "For They Are Jolly Good Fellows!"

Now, now, Sir, don't wag your finger at me with that little fierce frown to which I've grown so accustomed. Don't try to admonish me now. We're in the salt mines. There is no time for venting a fury here; there's too much work yet to be done. We'll quarrel later if you like, during Happy Hour, after we have returned to our respective bases, and are able to meet on common ground.

There, I'm straying again. I'm being extravagant and smiling to myself. Steady on, Davison Budhoo! Steady on as you tackle the Weighty Issue of Reform in the Fund. And since you must be punished for straying from your subject, you'd better go the whole hog and tackle the Weighty Issue of Reform in the World Bank as well. Tell Mr. Camdessus everything you know about that.

World Bank reform? Please don't ask me to elucidate on that subject; it'll only serve to confuse my readers. Why bring it in here? Why not just write a separate letter to Mr. Conable - another story, another time, another place; you know what I mean. Write him a Letter in several Parts, just as I'm writing you. Make it a post-resignation Letter, several years afterwards. I worked for many years in the World Bank too, you know. I worked there a long time ago, and I resigned, as I'm resigning from your institution now, in protest and indignation and in sorrow. The World Bank and its High Priests remain as a part of me that I cannot brush off. I follow events there avidly, and I know ... what I know. So why don't I write a post-resignation ...

Give up, Budhoo, give up. You strayed from your theme to Mr. Camdessus, and you deserve to be punished; in this Part you MUST write about reform in the World Bank; that will be your punishment; there can be no escape. Of course you remain free to bring in the matter of World Bank reform as you see fit; blend it into your remarks about Fund reform. After all, the World Bank and the Fund are different sides of the same coin, aren't they? Use your discretion, Budhoo. Use your sense of occasion...

See Attachment 1. It says all I want to say at this time about World Bank reform.

1. YOUR PERCEPTION OF FUND REFORM

Sir, if there is one thing about you of which I am certain it is this - viz; when we speak of reform you'd equate that with proposals being made, or on-going policies being implemented, in relation to the raising of financial resources by the Fund and the transfer of such resources to Third World countries, inclusive of the modules and mechanisms for such transfer and terms and conditions that we impose on those who use these resources. That's how reform is defined nowadays in the Fund itself and in member countries too. In the circumstances, it certainly would do your heart good to read the following rough and ready classification that I have made of virtually all aspects of your on-going and contemplated "reform agenda" for the Fund in the Third World. All quotations in the classification, except otherwise stated, are from statements that you yourself have made in recent months.

Table 1: Your Agenda for Change and Reform in relation to developing countries

(i) Resource Mobilization by the Fund

a) Establishment of the Enhanced Structural Adjustment Facility (ESAF) financed from contributions by developed member countries.

(ii) Resource Transfer by the Fund

a) Establishment of an External Contingency Mechanism to be combined with the existing Compensatory Financing Facility for assisting countries to overcome unforeseen external shocks.

b) Proposals for another SDR allocation

c) Proposals for enhanced quotas (Ninth Review)

d) Proposals for enlarged access and the limits on access to the Fund's resources

e) Proposals for the Fund and World Bank to collaborate more closely and strengthen their joint effort in providing financial assistance to developing countries

f) Proposals for revitalizing the Extended Fund Facility designed to provide financial assistance over a longer period to members engaged in "structural adjustment".

(iii) Terms and Conditions for and Effect of Resource Transfer by the Fund

a) Establishment of interest subsidy on certain Fund facilities used by developing member countries (Subsidy Account)

b) Establishment of lower interest rates and longer maturities for loans under the Enhanced structural Adjustment Facility

c) Proposals for reexamining Fund conditionality in light of changes in the conditions facing member countries and in light of the increased emphasis being placed on growth-oriented adjustment

d) Proposals for identifying "aspects of structural adjustment that the Fund should be involved in and how the Fund can best support effective implementation of (structural adjustment) policies by members."

e) Completion of staff study "examining the impact of Fund supported adjustment programs on the poor in selected sample countries. This study "will attempt to identify issues which are of relevance to the design of Fund supported adjustment programs."

Well, having listed your agenda for reform, let us examine carefully the nature of the items on the agenda and see how they tie in with the wide spectrum of issues raised in this Letter, and the sequence of causation identified here. And let me start off by telling you that in the broader order of things, your proposals are really not proposals for reform at all. They are the minimum jawboning that the staff feels compelled to do to take the heat out of criticisms made by the Governors (Ministers of Finance) about the Fund's operations in developing countries. On closer examination, they exhibit the following two characteristics:

(a) They are not new. They all relate to statements made by Fund Governors from developing countries over the last twenty years or so, demanding the following: (i) greater access to the Fund's own resources, or resources borrowed by the Fund from Part I countries; (ii) easier terms (lower interest rates) and longer repayment periods for Fund facilities; (iii) more flexible "conditionality" by the Fund (ie; "adjustment policies" should be more sensitized to social and political conditions in the developing countries concerned, more relevant economically, and more supportive of domestic aspirations); (iv) more attention to long term developmental needs in Fund-supported programs, vis a vis an on-going, almost total concentration on short term "financial balance" as the focus and objective of Fund programming.

(b) You will find most of these proposals, sometimes formulated more vaguely, sometimes more explicitly, in almost any random sample of reform proposals that had been put forward by any of your predecessors over the past twenty years. Indeed, all of your proposals, except the one relating to the impact of Fund programs on poverty levels, are perennial staples - eg; the Fund as financing intermediary, SDR allocation, enhanced quotas, enlarged access, closer Fund-World Bank collaboration, the need for more focus on structural adjustment lending and growth-oriented conditionality, interest subsidy, longer repayment periods. Your highly touted initiative in getting the ESAF established was precedented in 1979-80, with equal fanfare, by the Extended Fund Facility which was to be the Fund's final answer to the critics' carp of our total concentration on short term adjustment and demand management, at the obvious expense of development and structural change.

Whatever happened to growth oriented adjustment, Sir? Whatever happened to "supply side" economics? Never mind, never mind; the ESAF would put everything in perspective again; it is the start of a Brave New Third World; let's just formalize cross-conditionality between the World Bank and ourselves and all will be well... As for debt ridden middle income countries, well the Extended Fund Facility is still theoretically there, although hardly any country these days would think of using it...

For at least twenty years, Sir, the developing world has been reciting a litany of demands centered on your proposals; for at least twenty years the Fund has been doing "new thinking" and putting forward "new proposals" and establishing "new facilities" and implementing "new guidelines" and suggesting "new mechanisms" and ordering "new studies". Now and then we repackage the past; we put on new ribbons; we mend the edges that had become too jagged and too threadbare from over-exposure and misuse. We do these cosmetic things, and then we send out the "package" again; we send it out to the developing world, and we sit back and wait for the known, predicable sequence of annual events to unfold itself.

Of course the highlight of that sequence is the Annual Meeting of our Board of Governors - viz: the arrival in style and in pomp of the world's Ministers of Finance and their hoard of Advisors in Washington, or Seoul, or Manila, or Berlin, or other such city where they can be properly protected and accommodated and entertained. We set up (need I say?) our Administrative Unit from the Treasurer's Department to reimburse them for their First class and Royal Class travel and to provide all necessary, Magnified Subsistences from Honeypot's Largess for their stay in our selected city of Virtue and of Sin. We send them out on intensified rounds of social engagements and cocktail parties, we set up a big and impressive Conference Hall where, in between the socializing malestrom they can go and make their speeches, sometimes patting us on the back for being able to present such an updated "reform package"; sometimes expressing the same concerns that they had expressed ten years ago about the Perennial Package being Perennially Put Forward but never being Implemented; sometimes optimistically making proposals for slight modification of this year's Perennial Package to be incorporated in Next Year's Perennial Package; sometimes becoming so bold as to ask us to incorporate in Next Year's Package, corrective measures that can serve to alleviate streams of new troubles and new instabilities in the world's economic and financial system (the debt problem is a good example of this).

We listen politely to them; even as we wine and dine them we listen politely to them. For us it is Open House; we will them on to feel for one week the same toasty feeling of comfort and well-being that we ourselves experience during the whole year. But then we send them back empty-handed to their countries, and to their poor and to their desperation. We will them on to believe that they have a friend in us, and that we are an honest and supportive and highly professional group of men and women working tirelessly on their behalf, and doing our best in difficult and almost unbearable circumstances, with adverse exogenous influences running amok everywhere, and threatening our efforts to keep their houses in order and their economies afloat.

"Let's meet again next year", we tell them, "same time, same package, perhaps same place. Let's do it all over again, as we have done it over the past forty years. Let's go through our motions, and play our tune, and dance, and pack our bags and go home. Let's go home until the next bodacious meeting of the Interim and Development Committees in Sin City in the spring, when Fun and Games will start all over again."

And having dismissed them thus with smiles and back-slapping - having accomplished thus our public relations marathon - we sit back and breathe a sigh of relief. And in the months following the Annual Meeting we get to work on the package again, fine-tuning it here and there, doing "new" studies, establishing "new" mechanisms - going through the same farce that we have gone through decade after decade, so that nothing can be made to rock our boat. We go through the farce of twiddling our thumbs, waiting for them to come back next year; waiting for them to partake again in the same social roller-coaster that they have partook in, ad nauseam, in the past; waiting for them to revise last year's speeches and go through the motions of delivering them on the podium with pomp and ceremony and conviction.

They are set pieces, you know, and they must play their part, as we must play ours; they must connive in our game.

It is all a matter of juggling with words; it is double-speak. If there is a concession on Enlarged Access to our facilities, it is accompanied by hardening conditionality to ensure that Enlarged Access is never used. If there are new modules on which to pin conditionality, they must be designed to enforce the same conditionality as before. If we say "no more credit ceilings as performance criteria under the Expanded Structural Adjustment Facility, no more Letter of Intent that we would force the Ministers of Finance to sign", it is only to give an appearance of major change in the most dehumanizing parts of our work. If we say that in collaboration with the World Bank we will use a Policy Framework Paper as the basis for negotiation and the focus of performance criteria, because this module can allow us to pay more specific regard to structural adjustment objectives, and bring to bear on our work a broader economic and social perspective, we are equally saying that this mechanism will enable us to implement an inflexible regime of wide-ranging cross-conditionality between the Fund and the World Bank that developing countries protested so vehemently five years ago, and that both the Bank and Fund disclaimed at that time. If we say that the Fund, over the past two years, has recognized anew the urgent need for growth-oriented adjustment and is trying to restructure its programs around a growth objective, we only have to refer to our policy package for Trinidad and Tobago, as outlined in Part IV, and check it against our "growth orientation" prescription as publicly stated by senior Fund staff in recent months, and published extensively by the Fund, to realize that the two set of prescriptions are nothing if not identical. Put starkly, if we say that what we did in Trinidad and Tobago is an accident or an aberration, we are equally saying that what happens in all Third World countries are accidents and aberrations.

From what, Mr. Camdessus? From what are they accidents and aberrations? In the Fund, we know of no other philosophy, no other method, no other valve system, no other conduct or standard of professionalism. We know of no other world but the false one in which we are so hopelessly, yet so blissfully, encapsulated. Sorry, Sir, to raise the temperature again, but your "reform proposals" are of that world, they were born and bred there; they fit beautifully into our history and into our unique brand of personal foibles and institutional ethos. Whatever new material that we put in, the mill transforms it into the homogenized product that bears the trademark of Pax Atlantica and Pax Honeypot and staff stealing the institution and Unbridled Power and New Nobility et al.

As I said before, pleas for change in conditionality or modules of operation come mainly from protests and indignations and perceptions of unfairness and injustice by the developing world, as represented by developing countries authorities themselves, at the Group of Twenty Four or the Development Committee or the Board of Governors. Representatives of developing countries fight to get their cause mentioned in the final communique of the particular meeting concerned. It is the staff who will follow up proposals made at the meeting, and in fighting thus, developing countries delegates are equally begging the staff to take up their concerns and formulate them into detailed proposals for change. In other words, they are asking the staff to put itself in their own shoes and represent their own point of view. But in every probability, the latter is anathema to that of the staff; that is why "concern" about staff action arose in the first instance.

On the question of our staff presenting and implementing the views of developing countries - the head nodding Board of Executive Directors will invariably endorse whatever the staff says - two questions arise, viz: what capacity resides in the staff to think through and to implement something different from what had been thought through, and implemented in the past? What philosophical underpinning and method of approach different from those of the past, can the staff bring to bear on whatever reform proposal it may choose to write up so as to express a "concern" by the Board, or by an organ of the Board?

As the staff sees it, its purpose is to write up a reform proposal that sounds credible enough to the developing world, but which can be reduced to the same common denominator of all Fund policy, as described in Part IV. Your staff, Sir, is incapable of doing anything else.

Why is this so?

The major motivation of course, is Pax Honeypot; the uncertainties and insecurities of branching out in something new; the overwhelming intellectual lethargy; the need to maintain the status quo, as described in depth in Parts IV and V. But there is another compelling reason that has not been mentioned before.

That reason, quite frankly, is sheer technical incompetence and lack of technocracy outside of a very narrowly defined set of fiscal and monetary variables within whose framework we operate as financial analysts and policy makers. Take us out of the narrow technical environment and jargon of the so-called "monetarist" and we are as fish out of water. Although the Fund has been paying a lot of lip service to the design of Fund programs for "growth oriented" and "structural" adjustment - as already stated, two of our major facilities, the Extended Fund Facility and the Structural Adjustment Facility are three year programs whose purpose is to elicit "growth" and "structural adjustment" in recipient member countries - our staff has only the vaguest and most imprecise notion of the existence of concepts such as economic planning, sectorial resource allocation, for optimal development, input output ratios, criteria for financial and economic feasibility, optimum developmental infrastructure, and measurement of the efficiency of investments - all necessary inputs and analytical tools in any strategy to look at alternative paths for, and progress towards longer term development. Well after a decade since we started our high publicity program design for, and financing of longer term development and structural change, our staff remains virginal and totally unexposed to all and every aspect of the techniques of development programming. It is not only that we refuse to learn; we really have never been told to learn. And even in 1988 as we shout loudly to the world that 62 developing countries are eligible to use our Enhanced Structural Adjustment Facility, we do not at all seem prepared to take even the first tentative step towards learning the most basic lessons about the mechanics of economic development and the role of the latter in helping to transform Third World economies.

Of course in our "structural adjustment" lending we cover our technical shortcomings by proclaiming that we "lean" on the World Bank - that's what Bank/Fund collaboration is all about. But as we saw in Trinidad and Tobago, we do not really "lean"; more often than not, we bully the World Bank to comply to our "program" wishes as based on the most diehard Fund dogma of Heaviest Steamroller crushing down all. Really our experience with the three- year Extended Fund Facility is that is is nothing but a series of three "bunched up" one year stand-by arrangements, uncomfortably put together with an almost total concentration on short term "stabilization" and punishing demand management in lieu of longer term measures to generate supply responses in the economy. And the Structural Adjustment Facility, Sir, in which you have taken such a keen personal interest, is no different from the Extended Fund Facility, in spite of its changed module (Policy Framework Paper in collusion with the World Bank, as against the customary monetary ceilings and Letter of Intent).

Indeed, within the Fund itself there is a growing concern that a module that lays down a specific timetable for major concerted adjustment measures that directly hit hardest the poorest of the poor, and that provides little scope for forgiveness, or exemption through waivers, will lead to an even harsher and more inflexible regime of conditionality and desperation in the South. Nothing that has happened since the SAF became operational in 1986 suggests that the experience will be otherwise; an African country, currently under the discipline of the facility, is about to be cast aside as an international leper and made ineligible for further use of our resources, and several other countries, particularly in Sub-Sahara Africa and in the Eastern Caribbean, may never be able to use the Facility because they see it as an instrument that will propel political chaos and social disintegration nationwide and regionally and internationally.

You know, with both Bretton Woods institutions now having to agree on "common conditionality" and having virtually identical financing facilities for poor countries - ESAF in the Fund and Structural Adjustment Loan (SAL) in the World Bank - it seems to me that the Bretton Woods Conference of 1944 has come full circle. Certainly the very clear distinction made then between establishing conditions for freer international trade and payments and providing finance for long term development do not fit into the respective, intended present day roles of the institutions anymore. Perhaps with the type of history we have behind us, and our present day enslavement in sham and irrelevancy, it would have been better to let the EFF die a natural death, and miniaturise, mercifully, the work of the Fund in developing countries while letting the World Bank, through IDA, assume an expanded role in the development process there. You chose instead to go for the heroics and bring the Fund center stage again with the Enhanced Structural Adjustment Facility, accompanying this highly expanded role for our institution with glowing praise for the capacity of our technical staff to perform, seemingly with perfection, all additional tasks that may be thrust on their backs in a discipline where they do not know their ears from their nose. Tactically and intrinsically, Sir, I think you were wrong, just as your predecessor was wrong in accepting an expanding role for the Fund as analyst and catalysis for the Baker Initiative on Debt. Before we take on these tasks we have to put our internal house in order, otherwise everything we try to do in the Third World lead to grief and confusion and death. And how can we put our house in order if we don't even want to recognize that disorder exists?

2. FUND-SUPPORTED PROGRAMS AND THIRD WORLD POVERTY

I want to turn now to an area where we have been forced - literally forced - by "outside" pressures to do some internal thinking and some reevaluation of our policies - ie; the question of the impact of Fund supported programs on income distribution and poverty levels in countries of the Third World. Until 1984 we had resisted growing international criticism that our programs in the Third World led, directly and predictably, to a redistribution of income in favor of the "better off" and economically advantaged sectors of society to the detriment of the poor and economically underprivileged. Our stock response to this mounting criticism was that the world misunderstood our purpose and the nature of our operations in the Third World. Ad nauseam, our External Relations Department made it known to all and sundry that we did no more than provide balance of payments support to those of our member countries with balance of payments disequilibria, and that so benign a task could have no income distributional or poverty effects within the society concerned. Amazingly, in 1988 your External Relations Department was still using this as an argument to counter criticism of the Fund on the poverty issue.

Well, that key Department must have got its propaganda wires crossed, because about five years ago Fund management decided that the balance of payments excuse had lost all credibility, and could not be used anymore. Indeed a Fund publication in 1984 - the first ever of its kind - stated that "while (Fund) policies are focused primarily on external financial flows, they also inevitably affect the domestic income distribution. Thus, although the Fund officially maintains that distributional issues are primarily an internal political concern, it, indirectly, has always been concerned with distribution and resource allocation issues and has recognized the relationship between external and domestic policies in its adjustment programs."

Of course the staff protested vehemently - as perusal of your files will show - its alleged "concern" with "distribution" issues and about its presumed "recognition" of a link between "external" and "domestic" policies, including redistribution and poverty effects of such policies. The staff consensus on this matter will read something as follows: "If for political reasons our management feels compelled to admit that we are in the business of redistributing income and influencing poverty levels, well, let them do so. But whatever our management says, let it remain words spoken, and nothing else. As far as we are concerned this poverty thing is just a red herring in the path of Steamroller (Heaviest). We will continue to ignore it entirely, as we have always done, and get on with the business of joy-riding on moonlit nights, and crushing all in our path."

What I'm saying, Sir, is that the Fund's officially-expressed concern with the income redistribution and poverty issue has not changed one iota the attitude of our staff and its intention to bypass this matter entirely. And when, about one year ago, you requested the staff - in pursuit of what you may sincerely believe to be an important Fund goal - to carry in the Basic Data Sheet of each Staff Report a few "country" social indices (level of education, nutrition, health) you were seen as something of a little green man from Mars who had landed on earth for the very first time. In any event, we continue to do the chore - whatever you are, you're the boss anyhow. So as we write our reports we check the World Bank's hopelessly dated social indices and mechanically put in our little table in the Basic Data Sheet with the pathetically meaningless information that can be anything from five to fifteen years old. Of course no mention is made of this information in the text or anywhere else. Our attitude is : "You want it; you get it. We have done our job. There."

I mention this to highlight the difference between what we do, and what we lead others to think that we are doing. For the impression one can get after reading our publications on the poverty issue - the 1984 paper was followed by a more analytical one in 1988 - is that the staff is trying to come to grips with this issue in country financial programming and in laying down performance criteria for Fund programs.

Nothing could be further from the truth. Of course on the fly sheet we quote your "convictions" about adjustment and poverty - ie; "that adjustment does not have to lower basic human standards", and "that the more adjustment efforts give proper weight to social realities - especially the implications for the poorest - the more successful they are likely to be." We quote you thus, Sir, as a public relations gimmick. Or perhaps you are simply telling your staff and the world that Fund programs of the recent past have been so eminently unsuccessful because we have failed entirely to take account of income redistribution and poverty considerations? Perhaps you are even more perspicacious than any of us could have believed? How I hope so, Sir!

In spite of the staff's continuing resolve to ignore the poverty issue, formal and unequivocal recognition by the Fund that our Third World programs are inherently imbued with major income redistribution and poverty effects is a breakthrough for the South and an event - woefully belated as it may be - that will please people of goodwill everywhere. What one has to do now is to take up the Fund on its statement, and force Fund management to put the staff in line and to set up procedures and guidelines that will ensure that your statements on the poverty issue, as quoted above, become operative criteria in Fund dealings with developing countries.

Because the two publications mentioned above will be a first focus of attention as a renewed "outside" effort is made to have Fund policy harnessed to the poverty issue, I will make some brief remarks about them. And the first thing to say is that there can be nothing but considerable disappointment that the authors of the first study perceived themselves as unabashed Fund Apologist, rather than as objective researchers; their conclusions, really, in the light of subsequent studies, including the Fund's 1988 paper, can best be forgotten. However, it did try to be comprehensive, analytically speaking, and to examine all major Fund induced "demand management" measures from the perspective of income redistribution. But its conclusion that "the issue is: ... not whether various income classes, socio-economic groups, or factors of production are affected by a Fund-supported program ... (but) whether income size and distribution in the medium term without a Fund supported program ..." does not only beg the question, but dismisses entirely the burning issue of the immediate, or "first flush" impact of a Fund program on wealth redistribution and poverty levels. In the medium or long-term, you know, we are all dead, as Maynard Keynes once said. In this sense, the paper dodges everything.

The 1988 paper is of the same genre, although it is more prepared to admit that specific adjustment measures in particular Fund programs analysed did have highly negative impact on poverty levels and disadvantaged groups. Yet everything is fudged by the recurring motif of a wholly speculative, alleged longer term salutary impact, and by the following counterfactual and equally speculative argument, viz: what are the alternatives, and what may be their likely impact as compared with that of a Fund program?

You have taken up this theme, Sir, and you have addressed the poverty issue by posing the question of if there are alternatives, let the country concerned come out and say so. You know, ultimately, this is a highly charged political question that cannot really be answered, given the international political environment that constrains, sometimes very severely, the spectrum of political and economic choices open to a weak and economically fragile developing country. I think that it is a lead question that the country may want to answer, but cannot. And it smacks of the cat that ate the cheshire cheese; it smacks of gloating. I think you should stop asking countries to identify their alternatives to the Fund, and follow a different path, if they dare. It is really not in the spirit of good faith and supposedly mutual understanding to pose so stark and unanswerable a question.

There is another point I want to make. Putting the poverty issue in these terms, as you have done, has a far more serious implication for the future of our institution and for the well-being of our developing member countries. For what really we seem to be saying is as follows: "We know Fund programs have withering adverse effects on income redistribution and poverty levels. We can do nothing about that; you have to accept it. If you don't want to accept it, go find yourself an alternative and see what you will see."

Well let me tell you, Sir, that the Fund cannot continue to say this as an excuse for doing nothing about the horrific impact of its programs on world poverty. For, really, I do not think that the conscience of the world would let the Fund get away with it. Sooner rather than later, pressures will become so unbearable that the Fund will have to sit down and think through ways and means that it must use to reduce, and ultimately eliminate, the highly adverse income distribution and poverty level impact of its programs. At the present time pressures from sister United Nations agencies such as UNICEF and the Economic and Social Council are already building up; they will become irresistible, and rightly so.

Before that time comes you must take the bull by the horns. It is important that the world perceives you to be acting in a particular way not because you are forced into a corner from where you must make minimal and superficial concessions to those who have "won out" on you, but because you know that it is right to do so - because you know that multilateral economic institutionalism can only begin to take root and meet the burgeoning aspirations of twentieth century mankind only when it begins to assume a face of compassion and humanity, and when it demonstrates a willingness to learn from past mistakes and serve with alacrity and in good faith its confused but still hopeful global constituency.

Sir, an organization like the Fund could never belong to its employees and its technical bureaucracy; they should never, never have been made, even for one second, to capture it all in the first instance. Our Fund must either belong to the world, or to nobody. That is the lesson your staff has to learn. It is the hardest lesson of all, after forty years of grossly misguided perceptions and Fund staff self-centered, and wholly selfish material personal expectations. And it is your responsibility to begin to teach it to them; you can never have a more urgent, or a more important task in hand.

Stand-up, Sir, and take command of our institution. Instruct the High Priests to do what they have to do, and tell them, in no uncertain terms, that if they cannot, they will have to find employment elsewhere. Tell them that; and you will see how fast they will rally to your cause.

And that cause, as I see it, is straightforward enough in so far as the world poverty issue is concerned.

For there can be no choice now but to incorporate as formal performance criteria in Fund supported programs, desirable and mutually determined, income redistribution and poverty alleviation variables adequately quantified and capable of being monitored.

Lest you say that this is too ambitious, let me insist that it is far more modest than some proposals coming from your sister institutions such as UNICEF. Certainly, in most recent times, the argument has been made within the UN system that macro-economic adjustment programs, whether Fund supported or not, should be used as a tool to modulate the adverse distributional impact of exogenous external shocks and as a paramount vehicle to improve the welfare of poverty group. According to this argument, all macro-economic variables that are "country" desiderata, such as GDP growth and internal price stability, must be made subject to a prior condition of quantified change in income redistribution and poverty levels; everything must start from this irresistible aspiration. To me this may be somewhat unrealistic as un immediate mandate for all countries, given differing national perceptions, given the way the world economic system is constructed and works, given existing international economic and political ethos and level of awareness of the horror and insidiousness of destitution and deprivation. While it may be true that poverty alleviation as an overwhelming world economic and social objective must remain for some time on the back burner, this does not mean that the Fund cannot take a giant step forward now in coming to grips with the poverty issue in its Third World operations. And it can do this, and try to redress somewhat its past crimes against humanity, without compromising its capital base, or its creditworthiness, or "the revolving nature of its resources" - a term that your High Priest always resort to when other excuses fail them.

In very specific terms, I think that the Fund, as a matter of great urgency, must now begin to look at three things viz: (a) the technical possibilities that exist for smoothly integrating into fund programs as a significant variable, the income redistribution and poverty alleviation factor; (b) the hitherto philosophical and policy constraints that had precluded any consideration being given to the poverty issue in past fund-supported programs for the third world, and how these constraints could be immediately ameliorated; ((c) the scope for taking a bold international initiative to devise a meaningful and internationally recognized index of social welfare relevant for developing countries - an index that can become the basic starting point for quantifying poverty and destitution, and for marshalling concerted international action including action on Fund-supported programs, to deal with this vital economic and social issue.

It is necessary that I repeat to you, Sir, that whatever is done about the poverty issue must be done now; the world must know that corrective action, specifically identified by the Fund, is underway.

You know, Sir, expectations need to be generated in the Third World that significant change within the Fund is being effected, and that there is realistic scope for substantive improvement in modules, and for sensitizing Fund programs, and Fund day-to-day operational norms, to quantified, and non-controversial basic human needs in Third World countries. Without that assurance, Third World frustrations will begin to run amok; a whirlpool will develop; multilateralism will be swept aside sooner or later. And we will be just another blot in the history book, another concept of human self-help that failed not because it was wrong, but because it could never take root in the human condition of greed and selfishness in which it was spawned. Is this how you want it all to end?

3. THE FUND AS MANAGEMENT SYSTEM FOR INTERNATIONAL FINANCE AND WORLD POVERTY

Tactically, Sir, the Fund would devoutly wish to fight the question of its role in deepening poverty in the Third World on the basis of the design and implementation of its programs; in this respect, what I have said above will certainly lead you to breathe a sigh of relief. "Budhoo rightly recognizes", you may say "that we have made a start. All his protestations about the staff not towing the line can be dismissed - he himself says that we can get them to implement concerted poverty alleviation policies if and when we so wish. All we have to do now is to mark time and tell the world that lack of adequate statistical data and other technical country-related problems in the design of Fund programs would prohibit considering the type of optimistic changes that the Third World may want. Phew! For a time here I thought that he was coming with some sort of indictment of us that would justify his high-flown and out- of-place emotional outburst in Part I about 'blood running in rivers.' He spoke of a mountain, you know, but when the time came for delivery he could only produce a mouse."

Not so fast, Sir; hold back the joy. Don't think for one second that I'll let you get away with the tactic of covering up the Fund's role in spreading Third World poverty and destitution on the sole criterion of what the Fund is or is not doing, in the design and implementation of Fund- related programs - although even in this sphere, what you may choose to call my "emotional outburst" can be fully justified. But let's not dwell on that now; I have chosen another medium (other than this Letter) to provide the reams of shameful evidence from our files and elsewhere.

Really, Sir, what I want to say here is this : however catalytic and causative are Fund programs as a tool for deepening poverty and unleashing further destitution in the South, such programs represent only the periphery of an iniquitous and surprisingly comprehensive system within whose structure the Fund undertakes, directly and with premeditation, massive people-related economic crimes, including the performance of acts of unimagined horror in countries of the South.

And don't be happy that I speak thus. Don't say "Budhoo can now be branded as a voice to be embraced only by what the Fund and the International Establishment perceive as a way-out fringe group of spoilers and anarchists who want to see organized society destroyed as an objective in itself, irrespective of rhythm or reason, merit or demerit, cause or effect."

Perhaps you can say that; you know, and get away with it in certain quarters, but before you do so there is the little irritating matter of having to navigate some very muddy waters ahead; really there are seven rivers to cross, and each is in flood. Best of luck, let the High Priests try to navigate out of this mire as best they can. Let's see if their tactic of continuing to say "No Comment" to all and sundry will not unravel in their face.

4. THE FUND AND ARMS EXPENDITURE IN DEVELOPING COUNTRIES

Expenditure on arms and other military equipment, and establishment of an indigenous operational infrastructure for use of such supplies, constitute by far the most important single factor underlying real budgetary expansion in the Third World since 1945.

Consider the following in relation to relatively recent periods: In 1980 Third World countries utilized about $60 billion as military expenditure; by 1983 this had risen by 50 per cent; by 1986 it had doubled. In 1975 developing countries imported armaments amounting to $7 billion; in 1980 this had increased more than twofold; in 1986 it had quadrupled. And at the latter date over one billion people - considerably more than in 1945 - lived in what the United Nations has designated as absolute poverty, and over 500 million were in the throes famine and incurable malnutrition. At the present time over 75 per cent of the population of the Third World have no access to potable drinking water; a much higher proportion have no access to sanitary facilities. As for the consequences of arms imports in the Third World, Professor Saadet Deger Birkbeck College, University of London concluded in his recent enlightening book on Third World arms expenditure that 16 million lives have been lost in Third World wars undertaken on Third World soil since the Second World War.

Let me put the figures on Third World military expenditures and their stream of tragic consequences on the one hand and Third World economic and social development on the other, in a different perspective by showing relative growth rates. It is estimated that in real terms Third World military expenditures galloped ten fold between 1955- 85. Over this period Third World military expenditures as a proportion of total world military expenditures increased from under 3 per cent to over 20 per cent. Over the last two decades the annual rate of growth in military expenditures in the developing world was over 10 per cent, as compared with an annual growth rate of such expenditures in developed western economies of less than 3 per cent. The University of London study referred to above shows that Middle Eastern countries multiplied their real military spending by 56 times between 1952-83; the comparable figures for Africa (excluding Egypt) and for the Far East (excluding China) was 30 times and ten times respectively.

As against these mind-boggling multiples in the growth of real military expenditure, real per capita GDP in Africa, and most countries of South East Asia remained stagnant or may even have fallen, and indices of social welfare for two thirds of the population of the Third World - indices such as health, education and basic facilities such as the quality of shelter, continue to decline alarmingly.

"Hey!" you may say. "What you say may or may not be true - your figures need to be checked - but what does all this have to do with the Fund? We can't tell developing countries what to do with their resources; if they want to spend the latter on importing arms from the west and elsewhere, who are we to say no? That's a matter of sovereignty of the nation state. The latter must decide its own security needs. If, in taking such a decision, it pays little or no heed to economic considerations, that's its own business. Eternal vigilance, you know - we must always bow to that security consideration. What I mean is that we must never question it; we must not even appear to be interested in it. We must just shut out eyes and look the other way."

The authorities having decided how much of available resources they want to spend on defense - be it 5 per cent or 99 per cent of total budget allocations - we must automatically subtract that from the national cake and begin to work our black magic - ie; establish our financial program for allocating the remaining 99 per cent or the 1 per cent as the case may be. We must work our black magic so as to achieve our own brand of "financial stabilization" and "structural adjustment" for the economy. Of course our financial programming for the 99 per cent or 1 per cent would revolve around lambasting the poor and the economically disadvantaged sectors of society - literally squeezing blood from store in the shanty town; literally cutting off all government subsidies and transfers to them while at the same time increasing prices and indirect taxation to take whatever little crumbs of bread they may dare to hope to put in their mouths. Yes, yes, our trade off between "financing" and "adjustment" have practical significance mainly for the poor; we must punish them until they die. They must be punished thus for being poor in the first instance."

"Yes, Mr. Budhoo," you may continue. "We must persevere with our noble work. We must persevere like Rumpelstilskin doing the thing we have to do in a single- minded way. Remember Rumpelstilskin's own words? Remember him dancing and singing in the forest, joyful and contented in his usual environment, bursting over with happiness as he performed his tasks? So he was then; so we are today."

Yes, I remember, Sir. I remember very well Rumpelstiskin's own words:

Today I brew; tonight I bake.
Tomorrow I shall the queen's child take,
For guess as she may she never will know,
That my name is Rumpelstilskin!
Ho! Ho! Ho!

That's us, Mr. Camdessus; That's us. We are the Rempelstilskins of the late twentieth century. And to think that I chose to call us the New Nobility of Earth! No,no; we are just the Instantaneous Marauding Fraternity of ... Oh! Oh! Let me not call our name, lest the magic of our operations be destroyed. You see, Sir, although I'm now away from the Fund, there are still some Fund secrets that are inviolable.

Back to the salt mines, eh, and let me tell you, in very specific terms, that I have very strong objections to the standard Fund response on the defense issue.

The source of all my objections are as follows:

Why does the Fund say that the defense expenditures in developing countries are entirely beyond the realm of economics and economic adjustment for stabilisation and growth? Why should it conclude that such expenditures are not amenable to economic evaluation? Why should it conclude that the burning issue of the opportunity cost of defense spending is taboo, and is a matter that may never ever be raised by us at any level whatsoever in the Third World?

You know, Sir, about twenty years ago the UN Committee on Development Planning took the position that the single most important constraint on economic and social development in the South was the worldwide expenditure on defense spending, and this position has been eminently borne out in the plethora of research on this issue within the UN system itself, at universities around the world, and by private, pioneering scholars. In most recent times, research has focussed on technical questions to be posed and answered, relating to the economics of military expenditure in general, and more specifically to the economic causation that such expenditures generate in the spending country concerned. And econometric modelling, the backbone of our own "monetarist" research, has been used extensively as an analytical tool to throw light on a wide range of matters relating to the defense spending.

With our immense research budget and our highly-trumpeted research capabilities, have we done anything whatsoever to join this military expenditure analytical stream, and to give it momentum? No, we haven't - not in the least. Well, you may wish to applaud this position and say that there was no need to do this type of research, for it can have no relevance for the Fund. But that position is unsustainable, you know; any right-thinking and fair-minded person will have to disagree with you vehemently, once he or she know the fact.entirely.

Well, there are two reasons for the vehement disagreement.

To begin with, defense expenditure is invariably the cause of Fund programs - many countries are put in the position where they must drink our medicine only because they have spent, and are spending, far too much on arms imports from the industrialized North, given tenuous resource bases, and extremely fragile budgets. And secondly, in many instances Fund programs have collapsed because it proved impossible to get the government concerned to reduce the public sector deficit by another 1/2 or 1 per cent of GDP through "demand management" type of adjustment measures - ie, more taxation on the poor, more unemployment of unskilled workers, more cut-back on social services, more price increases on basic foodstuffs, more death in the slums. In the developing world as a whole, military expenditures in recent years averaged over 10 per cent of GDP. If 1/5 of this could have been diverted to "adjustment" instead of non-productive expenditure maybe the role of the Fund in developing countries would have been miniaturised dramatically! Certainly a lot of Fund programs that went astray would have been saved.

Sir, in the past we should have taken time off to do some rigorous, military expenditure-related analysis. Specifically, we should have devoted our energies to researching the all-enfolding economic consequences of military expenditures and the spectrum of trade offs at the margin between increasing such expenditures and reducing further the incidence of starvation and destitution and death in the South. If we had done this, in an honest and objective way, and if our conclusions had been articulated nationally and internationally, developing countries as a whole would have been in a much better position to make rational choices between sheer economic survival and further militarisation. Even if we couldn't interfere ourselves - a position that I reject entirely (see following sub-section) - we certainly could have provided others with something of an economic base for decision-making on this literal matter of life or death.

Well, let me be rigorously correct and give the devil his due. In fact in 1982 we did do some preliminary work on the question of the cost of the trade off between military expenditure and economic and social development. We brought to attention matters concerning the relationship between capital investment and military expenditure; the extent of urbanisation and defense spending; the size of the public sector and the defense budget. However, that study was very heavily weighted with expenditures in developed countries, and besides, there was no follow-through. It seemed that an interesting experiment in research that could have led the Fund on a path of sympathy and support for the poor of the South, was cut off suddenly, before it could develop steam.

There can be no doubt that today, logic and good sense and necessity professionalism will tell us that we must retrace our steps back to our tentative and highly inconclusive study of military expenditures in 1983; we must pick up our analysis from where we left off; we must zero in on the Third World. Let me hasten to add that in saying "we must pick up our analysis" I'm not giving any vote of confidence to our research staff. I know that any such study - like the ones on the impact of Fund programs on poverty - will end up by being nothing but another whitewash of our existing policies and perspectives. But the content of such a study will not in itself be the issue; what will be important is that any such "official" pronouncement will help clear the air and establish a Fund position that the world may latch on to and establish criteria to make us more accountable in this most vital aspect of our Third World operations. If, Sir, we would just open up on this issue, the stage would be set for an entirely new debate on our operations in the Third World, and the impact of such operations on poverty.

But you say no. If such a study may conceivably serve to expose the soft under-belly of the Fund you'll say : "No study whatsoever, whether now or in the foreseeable future. Mr. Budhoo, you're trying to bait me; you're trying to get me to instruct the High Priests to commission research that may be used as a base to develop a position favorable to developing countries, as against our usual policy stance of choosing research topics that would score heavily in favour of our major shareholders of the developed world. No, no, I wouldn't fall in any such trap. You see, the purpose of the Fund is ...".

That's precisely the point, Sir. That puts my position on this issue in true perspective. That position is as follows: why should you feel scared to tackle an issue of greatest operational and intrinsic relevance for the Fund (from any possible definition of "relevance") Why should you want to sweep an issue under the carpet simply because it could start a chain of events that may eventually lead to a change in existing policies - a change that may serve to further enhance the Fund's oft stated objective of encouraging stabilisation and helping economic growth in the developing world? Are you scared that research, on the variegated aspects of our Third World operations, however initially biased in the Fund will ultimately serve to open up a Pandora's box? Are you scared that such analysis, once started, will ultimately end up by putting the Fund in a position where its whole Third World policies over 40 years will be shown to be a fake and an imposition?

For it will be shown to be just that, you know. Any position that your staff may initially take as Whitewasher and Apologist on the military expenditure issue will immediately provide the analytical base from which others will go on to show the following:

a) The Fund's insistence on crushing the poor deliberately - of physically and mentally maiming the economically weakest sectors of society, or if you prefer to be more formal, the spectrum of social effects of its typical adjustment program that I have described at great length in Parts II and III and IV - and the extension of its tendrils in every nook and crevice of national economy and polity (including constitution busting) defines a total subjugation of the nation state to a rampaging supra-nation authority (remember how our staff members hold Executive and Legislative and Judiciary Powers simultaneously in their hands in countries of the South?).

b) When you control nations thus, governments are nothing if not puppets and rubber stamps in your hands. If it is an accepted norm that the Fund may withdraw, at its beck and call, fundamental constitutional rights of a people, forcing thus the government concerned to sentence masses of its own poor to even greater economic hardship and deprivation, how can the argument be sustained that on the peripheral issue of surplus arms purchases from developed countries "national sovereignty" must be meticulously respected and maintained? A country will sell control over the fate and well- being of its population for the right to determine the number of antiquated tanks it may buy from the US, or the UK or France? Objective research will laugh in your face, Mr. Camdessus, when you speak of "national sovereignty" on subsidiary issues, once you can be left in control of the nerve center.

c) Your argument that military expenditure is untouchable contradicts the elementary but internationally recognized principle of fungibility of financial resources. All Fund conditionality and Fund involvement are based on this principle. How come, all of a sudden, military expenditures become exempt from the general rule? If the country didn't have our resources, and the resources of others that we, as catalyst, bring into a program, wouldn't it have been forced to reduce its military spending that our developed member countries were imploring it to increase, in a situation where the choice was either more jet planes (that couldn't become operational for many years yet because there were no crews to maintain/fly them), or immediate catalytic economic collapse? Sir, the fact that we did provide resources opened up the capacity of the country to get those jet planes, you know, at the cost of massive human misery, generated by the conditionality for use of our resources, and those of supportive donors. Put another way, in a variety of cases where use of our resources serve to provide the wherewithal for arms imports, provision of such resources could not lead, in theory or in practice, to stabilisation or "structural adjustment", but merely to more human suffering and to a new burden of debt for military hardware that was already nothing but sunk capital the day that it arrived.

Go on Sir, raise the military expenditure issue, even if only to give your High Priests a chance to cover it up. Do that, Sir, and see if in the end it would not lead, after a lot of trauma within the Fund and outside, to exactly the above conclusions. As I said before, open up the Pandora Box. The Fund owes it to the world, you know. And I suspect that the latter may insist ...

5. "FINANCING VERSUS ADJUSTMENT"

Let's look behind the easy jargon.

Over the past five years, and coinciding with our new thrust to enlarge the Third World human garbage heap, the phrase "financing versus adjustment" has surely been used more than any other within the Fund. It is in almost every Briefing Paper and Back to Office Report, it is referred to in virtually every seminar on working group meeting, it slides glibly from the pen of the Fund apologists who would want to extol our virtues in FINANCE AND DEVELOPMENT and other such Fund self-congratulation publications. Your Board of Executive Directors seemingly love the way it trips off the tongue, your High Priests and public relations staff use it in every public appearance that they make; it is your own stock-in-trade at press conferences, and when you are on the lecture trail you never fail to pay your respects. Throughout the world it is synonymous to the Fund's blanket excuse for enslaving the South's poor.

What really does it mean? Well I guess nobody knows except that, in a commonsense sort of way, "financing" is seen as an alternative to "adjustment", and the Fund and other major donors must be extremely careful to ensure in every instance of a Fund program "adjustment" that the country is prepared to undertake, and the extent to which it is prepared to soak its poor, can justify the provision of "Finance" to it, whether from the Fund's own resources, or from the resources we garner for the recipient country concerned from other donors in our role as catalyst for development assistance and balance of payments support. I may be wrong, you know, but I have not come across any rigorous definition of the term by the Fund, or by any outside entity for that matter. It appears that on this issue, the world seem to give the Fund the benefit of the doubt. Or perhaps it has become so skeptical of our attempted rationalization of the madhouse type of conditionality that we brandish indiscriminately everywhere, that it can listen only in mute disbelief and cannot any longer rouse itself to grill us further. A recent Fund study on the "theoretical aspects of the design of Fund- supported adjustment programs" ignored the matter entirely.

You know, Sir, as I write this Letter, a thought keeps recurring; it is this: "How will Mr. Camdessus and the High Priests and others in the Fund choose to respond?". Really, I don't know what may be your tactical approach in the wake of release of this communication, but of one thing I'm certain. Sooner or later some Fund geezer, either with official sanction or not, will come out and say: "Budhoo is absolutely wishy-washy. What he says can never be taken seriously, for really what he's recommending is that the Fund and other donors throw their money down the drain in developing countries, with no conditionality whatsoever and no guarantees that necessary financial and economic adjustment will occur so as to make the country more self- sufficient and less economically vulnerable now, and in the future. What he says can easily be dismissed; it has no merit whatsoever."

Well, that geezer had better start doing some rethinking fast - always a very difficult task for Fund people - because when I speak about Fund conditionality I have in mind something far more comprehensive and analytically rigorous and exact than even the Highest of the High Priests had ever imagined. Yes, Sir. Suddenly, at this late stage, there is another wolf among the sheep.

(i) Leverage Exertion or "Conditionality": A Built-In Feature of the Resource Transfer Relationship

Conditionality or leverage exertion or donor influence on economic policies in developing countries is an inherent aspect of an act of development assistance - whether bilateral of multilateral. To see this it is necessary to look at the aid relationship from the viewpoint of the donor - in this case the Fund. Basically, the latter should be concerned not only with allocative criteria to ensure effective use of aid in a particular developing country, but with allocational criteria to secure an efficient "distribution" of scarce loan funds among all developing countries that qualify for use of its resources. Both set of criteria coincide when the Fund uses, to the full, leverage on economic policies that its financing commands. More specifically, economic efficiency in resource transfer under a stand-by arrangement or Extended Fund Facility, or Structural Adjustment Facility or Enhanced Structural Adjustment Facility is maximized when the Fund provides resources from its own account or from other donors right up to the point where it can have the greatest impact on macro-economic policies of the recipient country. If it lends less than this, its leverage powers become considerably reduced - indeed ineffective - in relation to the amount of financing provided. If it lends more, the leverage impact of "additional" funds decreases sharply and eventually falls to zero; aid is being used inefficiently. A detailed, conceptual framework to show that specific point on the matrix where both financing and leverage exertion (conditionality) are simultaneously optimized in relation to economic efficiency criteria that relate on the one hand to opportunity cost and resource scarcity by the donor, and, on the other, to the social welfare function of the recipient can easily be postulated.

The above prognosis presupposes a conflict of opinion between the Fund and the member country on what is "optimal" or "proper" for national economic development. If such a conflict does not exist either one of two things is implied - i.e., that the Fund is given a free rein in policy-making, or that by a remarkable coincidence, the government's own plans and policies are identical to proposals emanating from the institution. In both these instances, the Fund may provide resources or put together a particular financing package on behalf of donors, without consideration of the "leverage effect" stated or implied, and with no further regard to the social welfare function of the recipient. Really, this defines a situation where the resource transfer relationship is not one that is open to negotiation, involving mutual concessions and "give and take" by both parties over conditionality and other terms and conditions, but crude and explicit "Fund dictation" to the country concerned.

Given such "dictation", our High Priests are quite right in insisting that there is no need to rigorously analyse the concept of "financing versus adjustment". Put another way, it is beside the point to try to determine, in any particular instance, that critical point where the trade off between "financing" and "adjustment" occur so as to maximize economic efficiency in resource provision and resource use. Indeed, no economic efficiency criterion that can possibly relate to the social welfare function of the recipient is built into the calculations of transactors, there is obviously no need to conceptualize resource transfer as a mutually beneficial transaction with rights and responsibilities for both sides. Instead, the relationship becomes one of unbridled power by the donor agency and abject submissiveness by the recipient country. Even under the best of circumstances, this can only define a potentially massive regression in the social welfare function of the recipient.

Let me now summarize my argument. Firstly, unrestrained dictation by the Fund precludes any objective criterion of economic efficiency from emerging in the aid relationship. Secondly, for many Third World countries, it is absolutely impossible to make operational their own set of stabilisation and developmental objectives in Fund- supported programs or to establish anything remotely resembling their own system of priorities. Thirdly, the spectrum of indigenous plans and policies that is a central consideration in all development theory, become totally smothered by omnipotent multilateralism - as said before, our Steamroller (Heaviest) crushes everything in its path. More formally and rigorously - and this is my fifth point - in Fund-developing countries relationships, no set of nationally determined stabilization and developmental objectives can ever be brought to bear on a matrix of choices to show that particular point where the designated transfer, because of its conditionality, ceases to be beneficial, and becomes economically deleterious to the recipient. We have turned all development economics on its head.

By vehemently refusing recourse by Third World countries to any sort of analytical system to determine the economic worthiness of the assistance it is providing, on its own account and on the account of supporting member countries, the Fund has turned all post-war development economics, and all the precepts underlying such economics, on their head. It says: "Accept unconditionally our mickey- mouse monetarist policies that Reagan and Thatcher want you you to accept and which, incidentally, is the only subject in economics that we, as an institution, have any pretensions of knowing anything about. All the fancy ideas that you may have about the content and course of short-term stabilisation and longer term development - just throw it out the window; you have no right to hold any ideas about how you should chart your own economic future or distribute your national cake. These are matters for us, and for our major industrialized countries to decide. To think that you could have the temerity to want to have a say, however small, in what you must do. Just shut up, and fall in line behind us. Or else ..."

In terms of technical analysis and conceptual formulations that may rationalize conditionality that the

Fund imposes and justify it in a formal and rigorous sense to the world, let me point out to you that our meticulous eschewment of this approach constitutes in itself a total admission of our use of naked power to impose economically deleterious programs almost everywhere in the Third World (obviously, we fear to put up these programs to rigorous analysis simply because such analysis will show them to be deleterious). Even more important and damning is our sheer temerity in pushing, at every level, our totally unresearched "financing versus adjustment" theme - the theme of the dictator who is happy in the knowledge that he has banned use of all irritating facts and concepts such as "economic efficiency in resource transfer" and "spectrum of macro-economic objectives of the recipient" and "determination of that critical point where the transfer ceases to be economically beneficial" and "adjustment policies consistent with the social welfare function of the recipient".

Sir, on the next occasion that you stand on a podium and speak glibly of "financing versus adjustment", and Fund conditionality being "flexible" and related to the needs of Southern countries, so as to put presumably the 4.999 billion Fund critics in their place, remember that unless you have a clear and valid conceptual base, and unless your remarks can relate to some specific analytical process and result that can demonstrate a positive welfare outcome in relation to Third World economies, you are speaking, not only as a supra-national Third World Absolute Dictator, but as one who uses power indiscriminately and in a shameful and opportunistic manner to achieve somebody else's aim in other peoples' territory at the cost of everything indigenous and worthwhile there.

That is spoiler action, Sir. That is way, way out spoiler action beyond the scope of economic analysis.

Cases Where Countries May Be Able to Negotiate (with bite) a Fund Program; where their social welfare function become an operational issue in negotiations.

Well, there may be some countries, you know, that may stand up to the Fund and say: "No, we will not accept dictation; we insist on meaningful negotiations of conditionality, with our own social welfare function centerstage" What may be the fate of such countries? What may be the Fund's response?

To answer that question, let us go back to the concept of economic efficiency in aid transfer, and the matrix of choices facing the country concerned, and the existence of criteria for judging its economic performance.

You know, Sir, the choice of perspective for judgement of a country's economic performance can best be understood by a brief review of the impact of international functionalism on national making processes.

The spectacle of UN Specialized Agencies - including the Fund and World Bank - pursuing conflicting and unrelated programs of international assistance in the national economy is one that is well known to developing countries. The difficulties of this process are compounded by the fact that, at the national level, total planning objectives of a country - social goals of integration, fuller employment, greater social security, economic goals of growth, price stability, balance-of payments equilibrium - are meshed together in some sort of explicit or implicit national plan with an order of priority for implementation stated or implied. Criteria for judging country economic performance can be meaningful for the country concerned only when due regard is paid to the latter's own spectrum of objectives - derived through operation of national decision-making processes - and when the uncoordinated activities of all international institutions are taken into account. This implies two things: the standardization of judgment of major international institutions operating in the national economy, and the development of indices of performance relating to national economic and social welfare.

Establishment of development performance criteria along these lines is no doubt difficult - if only because of the existing competitiveness and jealousies among international institutions - but it is not impossible. Indeed, individual researchers have paved the way with meaningful pioneering groundwork over a period of some thirty years. For reasons explained elsewhere in this Letter, the Fund has chosen to forego the opportunity of joining the search for internationally acceptable and verifiable norms and standards for country analysis and evaluation - norms and standards meant to serve predominantly the interests of the international community and of its developing member countries.

In lieu of comprehensive evaluative criteria, the Fund has resorted to an analytical system that takes fiscal and monetary targets as basic determinants of country economic performance. The objective has been to select, in part at the behest of certain major shareholders, a few key economic and financial indicators that presumably should form part of a program approach evaluative system. These having been preselected by our monetarists, all evaluative work are centered around them, without any attempt whatsoever to relate our preselected partial variables to other relevant and longer term elements of evaluative analysis.

As we have seen in this Letter, evaluative criteria by the Fund staff is not a matter of pragmatic experimentation towards an internationally verifiable system geared to the developmental needs of member countries. It represents, rather, that predetermined package that the Fund feels that it can offer an individual developing country at any moment of time, taking into account its own very explicit dogma and analytical and personal (staff-related) subjectivities, its almost complete lack of knowledge of the development process, and the very wide range of "external" constraints including exogenous political pressures from powerful shareholders.

In a matrix system, a developing country that "stood up for its rights" and that managed to keep its head above water and not become overwhelmed by the Fund in the process may expect at best to come to a deal with the Fund at that point where the transfer transaction does not optimize or even increase social welfare, but where it prevents it from falling further. I suspect that the only two developing countries that have managed to get such a "good" deal in recent years have been Yugoslavia and Grenada (before the US invasion of that country served to abort the EFF program that had just been negotiated). In both instances, however, very special "external" circumstances prevailed that were not applicable to other countries of the developing world. As for western industrialized economies that have used Fund resources, one may be quite assured that "conditionality" negotiations and outcome occurred at, or close to the point where the designated transfer increased optimally the social welfare of the recipient. Two good examples are the United Kingdom and South Africa in fairly recent times.

Sir, my remarks here on a proper conceptual framework for specifying Fund leverage in relation to Fund financing, and the postulation and use of appropriate analytical tools for measuring the economic efficiency content of Fund conditionality, are necessarily brief and incomplete. For those of your High Priests and others who may want an extended exposition, may I suggest reference to my book "THE INTEGRATED THEORY OF INTERNATIONAL DEVELOPMENT ASSISTANCE"? It is eminently available in the Joint World Bank/Fund Library.

6. FURTHER THOUGHTS ON THE ISSUE OF DEVELOPMENT INDICES, MEASURING DEVELOPMENT PERFORMANCE AND FUND OPERATIONS' IMPACT ON THIRD WORLD POVERTY

Now that we are so completely in the mainstream of economic development business - every Fund zealot is bragging about the Enhanced Structural Adjustment Facility (I would not be surprised if some of our support staff actually start breaking out in exuberant "official" print) it behooves us to sit back quietly and ask ourselves a few questions, viz: what is the nature of economic development? How has the concept of economic development changed over the last thirty to forty years? Given the tasks that we must now accomplish for Pax Atlantica and Pax Honeypot and for our major shareholders, how can we continue to operate in the Third World without losing all our credibility there? How long can we continue to emasculate the South in our new thrust for Reaganite "privatization" without eliciting concerted official opposition and mass protest? How long can our Chicago School and other such dogmatically designated monetarist economists continue to push their mickey-mouse, absolutely irrelevant concepts of short term financial juggling to score economic and political points for their western bosses down the throat of a screaming Third World? How do they contemplate marrying western monetarist theory to the realities of Third World economic and social change? Or perhaps they do not contemplate to try any such marriage? (It is impossible anyway). Perhaps our institutional expectation is that our relationships with the Third World has already been crystallized into one of Absolute Supra-national Monarch and pliant local slaves? Perhaps we don't have to justify anything that we do there anymore? Just do it, with the nod of approval of our genuflecting well-heeled fellow travellers and nation spoilers, and throw two thirds of the south's population into the garbage heap of lost humanity that I did describe in Part I? Perhaps our long-term plan is mass genocide of half the world's population, with the other half living happily everafter and praising us through all time for our one courageous act of mercy and heroism that changed almost overnight the economic fortunes and perspectives of the world? Perhaps after all, we seek a place in the sun?

Obviously, I cannot take up all these themes here, and even as I start to boil over again with indignation, I will force myself to do the sensible thing and return to the center and speak in sober tones about the nature of development and the Fund's fundamental misunderstanding and misreading of it.

(i) Real World Economic Development Issues of 1988 Versus the Theoretical Corpse that we Dry-Freezed 40 Years Ago, Insisting That It Is Still Alive Today

The preconceptions that we bring to bear on our now highly-touted "developmental role" in the South, and that govern our financial programming, and that determine the structure and content of our PFP under the SAF and ESAF is one that may have held some currency in the late forties and in the fifties, but has long since been overtaken by time and events and real world experience. In everything operational that we do, and in all the statements that pour out from our propaganda machinery, we insist that our aim is to create an environment of financial stability within which GDP growth can occur at some indeterminate stage in the future. Once we bring our brand of adjustment to bear on our Malleable One Quarter of the economy and redistribute resources within that narrow base, and made it to become more "economically efficient", and more "competitive internationally", magic is supposed to take over, with exports growing in profusion, as mangoes on the trees. Unlimited supplies of cheap labor, you know, and foreign entrepreneurship, and international specialization of function and corrupt dictators and their cohorts hiving off both international aid and domestically earned foreign exchange resources to Switzerland and France and England and the United States with us applauding in glee. First World economic equilibrium and optimization of somebody's welfare through the overwhelming (net) transfer of world financial resources from developing to developed countries is really our aim. But we want our myth as Dispensers of Ultimate Economic Wisdom to deepen in the South, proclaimed with fanfare and drum-beating by natives in the jungle clearing in the Comoros, and in Mozambique and in Ghana and Nigeria and Zambia and Tanzania and Trinidad and Tobago.

Hurray! Here at last comes Mr. G.D.P. Growth. He comes haltingly, bashfully, in Half Percentage Points. He comes in the wake of an unexpected upturn in commodity prices, and will disappear again with equal suddenness as these prices fall, but let that rest; let that rest. He comes now, and that's the important point. You see how our policy package is successful? (Never mind the lying and the cheating that we had to indulge in to get Steamroller (Heaviest) off the ground to crush down all in its path). You see how everything becomes justified in the wake of our program? There, we told you so. There's no other way for the Third World to go but through Pax Atlantica and Pax Honeypot. Hail Fund! Hail High Priests! You made it all to happen.

Well, it doesn't work that way. The Malleable One Quarter of the Economy that comprehends Two Thirds of the Population - the Two Thirds that we must round up everyday for economic torture - can never transform the Whole; macro-economic growth can never be attributed to our "Noah and his chosen few in the arc" policies. But let us be generous and give the Fund more credit than it deserves, and assume that its program in Year One did serve to "create" a halting and tenuous economic growth scenario in Year Three. What would we have achieved in eliciting that growth at the terrible human cost that we did impose on the Condemned Two-Thirds?

Development economics tells us that we would have achieved nothing, for GDP Growth can never be an object in itself; it is the means to a more fundamental end of uplifting the poor and transforming society. This is not "compassionate nonsense", you know. Tell your High Priests to start doing some rigorous homework so as to see the world as it is; so as to try to understand how it really works. Tell them to lift up a honey-drenched head from the Honeypot and face Cold, Stark Reality outside a Total Comfort Zone of Blissful Illusion. Tell them that even the development theorists that forty years ago had given grist to the mill with advocacy of "boot strap" economic growth, with unlimited supplies of cheap labor to be manipulated and exploited to an nth degree, have changed substantively their tune, with deepest apologies to the Two-Thirds.

Yes, Sir. Development theory and development practice have moved on from advocating the halting march of Mr. G.D.P. Growth, compliments of the One Quarter Economy and the Two Thirds Population, to recognizing the need for, and making imperative some discernible concept of, and provision for, socio-economic transformation in the South, irrespective of the pace, or the continuous presence of Mr. G.D.P. Growth feeding incessantly from the blood of the Two Thirds, and strengthening further Privileges and Exemptions of the One Twentieth.

Sir, let me quote mainstream modern day thinking in the person of Professor A. Sen, prominent world economist:

> "I believe the real limitations of traditional development economics arose ... from ... insufficient recognition that economic growth was no more than a means to some other objectives. The point is not the same as saying that growth does not matter. It may matter a great deal, but, if it does, this is because of some associated benefits that are realized in the process of economic growth."

Please note the two points being made - ie; the genesis of growth and who pays for it, and the role of growth in the development process once it is realized.

So far we have touched on the first. Let us now move on to the second by bringing up-front the concept of "entitlements".

You know, Sir, over the past decade an international consensus has developed (specifically recognized by most agencies of the United Nations - excepting the Fund - and by the United States and most West European governments) to the effect that provision for, and administration of people's economic "entitlements" is an important purpose of economic management even in the poorest countries of the South, and the ultimate rationale of government. Let me quote again Professor Sen on the definition of "entitlements" and the role of the latter in present day theory and practice:

> "Entitlement refers to the set of alternative commodity bundles that a person can command in a society using the totality of rights and opportunities that he or she faces."

And:

> "On the basis of entitlements, a person can acquire some capabilities, i.e. the ability to do this or that (e.g. be well nourished), and fail to acquire some other capabilities. The process of economic development can be seen as a process of expanding the capabilities of people. Given the functional relation between entitlements of persons over goods and their capabilities, a useful - though derivative - characterization of economic development is in terms of expansion of entitlements."

I want us to have in the back of our mind the "entitlements" concept of development as we try to interpret facts about development as contained in the following table which provides estimates of comparable data for 1980 in relation to 7 countries, viz: Egypt, Sri Lanka, South Korea, Brazil, Tanzania, Nigeria and Zambia. Economic policy and performance in some of these countries have served to bring Fund blood pressure to its highest pitch in recent times. Let us see, in retrospect, where the true battle lines are drawn.

GDP and Entitlements in Selected Developing Countries:

	Egypt	Sri Lanka	South Korea	Brazil	Tanzania	Nigeria	Zambia
1	500	279	1,388	2,002	264	1,035	400
2	...	42	22	38	20	16	20
3	...	85	94	76	70	34	72
4	500	343	608	250	482	1,251	300
5	80	40	34	77	103	135	90
6	61	66	65	63	52	48	50
7	2,100	2,251	2,926	2.513	2,028	2,337	2,150
8	55	22	79	63	39	28	45

Sources: Sivard (1983), as reported in Saadet Deger "Military Expenditure in Third World Countries, 1986 and Social Indicators of Development 1987, World Bank.

Rows: (1) GNP per capital in US$; (2) % of women in total university enrollment; (3) Literacy rate %; (4) Population per hospital bed; (5) Infant mortality rate; (6) Life Expectancy in years; (7) Calories per capita; (8) % of population with safe water.

The above table brings to light the fact that Sri Lanka, Tanzania and Zambia, and to a less extent Egypt, with per capita GDP that is only a small fraction of those of South Korean, Brazil and Nigeria, have taken mammoth strides, comparatively speaking, in effecting socio-economic transformation and in expanding the growth of "entitlements" for their peoples. More specifically, the following are shown:

- The proportion of women enrollment at universities in both Tanzania and Zambia is quite high in relation to the comparable figure for Nigeria, and compares favorably with South Korea, a country with about 5 times their per capita GDP. In Sri Lanka women university enrollment is higher than for all countries on the table, including Brazil, which has a GDP about seven times higher, and South Korea with a GDP five times higher than Sri Lanka.

- The literacy rate in Sri Lanka is comparable to that of South Korea and higher than that of Brazil. For African countries, the literacy rate in both Tanzania and Zambia is double that for Nigeria (with a per capital GDP four times higher than Tanzania, and 2.5 times higher than Zambia).

- Population per hospital bed in the poorest countries - Sri Lanka, Tanzania, Zambia and Egypt, are lower than for all the better-off countries apart from Brazil.

- Infant mortality rate in Sri Lanka compares favorably with South Korea and is almost one-half that of Brazil. In Africa, infant mortality rates in both Tanzania and Zambia are substantially lower than for Nigeria.

- Life expectancy in Sri Lanka is higher than in South Korea and Brazil. In Africa, it is lower in Nigeria than in Tanzania and Zambia.

- In spite of the great disparity in per capita income for countries shown in the table, daily calorie intake per head is very similar in all cases.

- In Africa, the proportion of population with safe drinking water is much higher in Tanzania and Zambia than in Nigeria. In Egypt, it is comparable to Brazil.

Well, Sir, do the above facts have any relevance for Fund policy in the countries concerned?

Certainly they do, and while I do not wish to spell out here our thorough and insidious opposition to countries bold enough to want to transform themselves socio- economically and to increase "entitlements" and alleviate poverty within their borders, and the way that we have tried to victimize and isolate these countries internationally over long time periods, I am duty bound to point out that the issue is by no means one of "progressive" or "radical" countries experimenting with "socialism" and receiving an expected backlash from major shareholding "capitalist" countries who fear that successful "socialist" experiments in the South could develop a momentum and, by some unexplained process, create a security risk for others.

Obviously, the latter type of thinking has always been present in calculations of the Fund and certain of its major Part 1 member countries, but the important point remains that even countries very "friendly" towards the United States, and economically structured along the most diehard "capitalist" lines, have incurred the wrath of the Fund and have felt the sting of its whip at the very first sign of any attempt to give consideration to the "entitlements' sector", or to emphasize economic management concepts that express a concern for economic equity and economic justice among the population. Forget Sir, our thoroughly shameful hounding, at various times over the last two decades or so, of countries such as Tanzania and Zambia and Peru and Chile and Jamaica and Grenada and Ethiopia and the Sudan and Ghana. Think, instead, of Egypt and Nigeria and the Dominican Republic and the Philippines and Brazil and Argentina and Mexico and Venezuela and even Trinidad and Tobago. Set up an independent investigation of why all these countries, and so many more who are so well-disposed to the United States and, by extension, to the "western" brand of "free enterprise" economic philosophy and practice, should have come to such grief, and to such "stop-dead-in your-track-now-on-your-affirmative-stance-on-poverty alleviation-or-else" directive from us. Set up such an independent investigation, Sir, and publish the result, if you dare.

7. THE LITTLE VOICE AND THE MONSTER

There is a tremendous despair within me; its genesis is a Little Voice that says something like this: "The Fund is past all reform; it is in the last throes of shamelessness and ignominy. The only structured approach you'd find anywhere is the imperatives of Pax Honeypot and the dictates of a few strong member countries. There is no principle, no professionalism, no character, no soul."

"The Third World - augh! what is the Third World? It is the place we go to to tow a line and make our name, and gain promotion by being yesmen and head nodders. The irresistible motif of all that we do is our job, and our cherished Honeypot."

That Little Voice keeps murmuring: "What have we achieved through adoration of the Honeypot?" And the Little Voice gets a response from a Monster that appears before me; it is the Fund and I am afraid of its form. But it does not talk unreasonably; it talks in honeyed tones and puts succinctly its own position and its own perspectives; it talks as follows:

"We stop momentarily, you know, to look back at our mistakes in the past, but since we do not want to see mistakes we see images of lost opportunity by the Third World, and perspectives made awry by its peoples - opportunity and perspectives that we in Our Superior Wisdom did give to them in profusion."

"Even as we nibble on the best things of life from the Honeypot, we say in self-congratulation to ourselves: "We and our industrialized western member countries have poured in around $200 billion (gross) into the coffers of Third World governments over the past generation in bilateral and multilateral aid. We have taken over management of Third World economies; we have made every effort to make their poor and destitute even poorer and more destitute and to swell their ranks; we have assiduously kept social security expenditures in the Third World as a minor fraction of arms import expenditures; we have turned back almost totally the concept of developmental "entitlements" and made as Bible truths the ones of "financial stabilisation" and "Reaganite monetarism."

"Frontally and totally, we have aligned ourselves to the ruling classes and the privileged of the Third World, whatever part of the cake they want, we have given it to them. We have set up mechanisms to ensure that the teeming masses cannot touch the entitlements of the fortunate few, the over-privileged One Twentieth".

"Really, we have extended western society to cover the over-privileged of the Third World; in spite of the dreams of Gandhi and Nkrumah and Nyerere and other such like self-proclaimed Third World nationalists, we have split the Third World into two, right down the middle. We have created a Fourth World of the destitute and the diseased and the malnutritioned, and we have made it to be as a monumental garbage heap of earth; outside the pale of everything civilized; outside the reach of any Social Contract; outside the Fold of Humanity."

"Nobody is responsible for that garbage heap and its contents; we will let everything rot there in its own stench."

"Meanwhile, through their own sterling, heroic efforts, the First and the newly-defined Third World are forging a Bodacious Partnership."

"How dare anyone say that the Fund has been a failure? How dare anyone say that we have not furthered the cause of the West in the South? How dare anyone say that the structure of our newly defined Third World society has not been strengthened immensely through our causative role in that World? How dare anyone say that linkages and interdependence between the First and newly defined Third World have not deepened for the mutual benefit of both sides? How dare anyone say that we are not moving towards equilibrium in the First and newly-defined Third World economies? How dare anyone say that there is no international division of labor, no freedom of trade and capital movements, no freedom in the movement of persons?"

Look at our Third World patrons. They come to the western metropolitan centers every day of every year to check their bank accounts and stack more funds in there; and buy real estate in our capital cities; and shop for the most expensive furs to take back to their tropical homes. Look how they finance the United States trade deficit through capital flight! Look how they are good guys politically! Look how they bring peace and security to the West!"

"How dare anyone say that Pax Atlantica was the dream of a few neo-classical economists? How dare anyone say that Pax Honeypot for Our Staff Imbued With Its Unshakably Superior Wisdom was an aberration of all that the Fund, and its creators, stood for?"

"My God, my God, we've made it! In forty years we have achieved all that our Founding Fathers wanted us to achieve, and more; much more. Our task now is to ensure that no one can turn back the tide. Our task now is to deal with the Forth World. Our task now is to wipe it out entirely from the face of the earth, if that is necessary to protect our gains and maintain our peace of mind."

"Little Voice," the Monster continues, "who are you to question our origin, our history, our methods, our results? You are less than a speck of dust, and we - we are like time itself; what we stand for was always there; will always be; we are the very salt of the earth. To want power and to oppress; to covet and to get the substance of others, to build alliances with those who further our cause; to share fruit with those who may rally to us; to destroy those who threaten what we have accomplished - these things define human nature and human life, irrespective of generation, or century, or millennium."

"You say you fight for the destitute and the starving? You fight for an ideal; not for humanity, not for the Two-Thirds who would be just like us if they ever could supplant us (God forbid) centuries from today. Unless there are unlimited natural resources everywhere, like the air that we breathe, an institution like the Fund, to succor the privileged few and desiccate the threatening but unenfranchised majority, will always exist; will always be powerful; will always crush. Who made you the world's policeman to protest so vehemently, at a moment of time, the natural progression of history that can never ever be turned back, that can never ever be changed? Who are you to ..."

"Stop, monster, stop"! says the Little Voice. "Are you trying to make me feel foolish for having a conscience? Are you telling me that there can be nothing good in human nature? And that if, by some improbable miracle, the Fund, and all that it stands for, were to be destroyed, and the Two Thirds were to cast off their chains, the cause of justice and fairplay will not have progressed? That it will just be one power-hungry faction replacing another, and acting with the same inhumanity and callousness that had been there before? And that the cycle of ignominy and worthlessness will thus go on and on?"

"Are you telling me that those who say that they care, and who are striving - futively it may seem, but still striving - to remove mountains, and to restore a fairplay and a justice, are foolish and irrelevant? Are you telling me to go suck my thumb?"

"Yes", said the Monster. "Go suck your thumb. Go dream another dream."

8. REFORM OF THE FUND

The Monster, you know, taught me a lesson that I did not know before. He taught me to try to make everything that I'm saying intelligible within a system that limits my time perspective drastically and that can become operational only in relation to problems about which there is already substantive international consensus. He taught me that if crushing down powerless people is a natural progression, like the flow of water down an incline, I'd be wasting my breath to stand up frontally in the stream and beg it to go uphill. What I could do is to run down the path, and at the bottom where there is no gradient - where the momentum flags; where the flow becomes weak and uncertain now of direction - to ask others to join me in trapping the stream and channeling it elsewhere, away from where it did do so much damage before.

That is not an act of defiance and futility, you know; it is just good common sense.

And so to those who expected fireworks in my proposals for reform, I'm sorry. My task is to try to do what is practical and realizable at any stage; I don't want to contemplate the totality of the Fund's all-enfolding ignominy; it boggles the imagination; it overwhelms me; it makes me feel so helpless. The Monster is right. There can be no cathedrals overnight; let us all, Sir, do our little bit in trying to help build a humble shelter for those who need it now.

Happily, Mr. Camdessus, you will not find me now going out on a limb and isolating myself on the matter of Fund reform. People need people, and I will remain mainstream; in spite of all the evidence that says I shouldn't, I will remain mainstream. I will join forces with all those men and women of reason and goodwill and even permissiveness who would prefer to give our institution a last chance to prove itself. But it must be a last chance; I think the world is ready now to make it a very last chance. The phrase "Reform or Dismantle Now" keeps running through my mind. Will that phrase be in the name of the next international institution that will come to us as the antidote, the anti-hero? Providence knows.

(i) My Perception of the Scope for Fund Reform

One of the most urgent messages that I've been trying to get through in this Letter is that the staff is running amok; it is playing Russian roulette with the developing world; the situation is out of hand; the bureaucracy must be controlled; checks and balances to restore the decision-making authority of the Board of Governors and the Board of Executive Directors must be put into place and must be made operational without delay.

Another underlying theme - and it is closely related to the issue of hegemony of the staff - is the question of the epistemology of the institution as defined in Part IV, and in sections 3 to 6 of Part VI, and our emergence in my words, as the Neanderthaler of the twentieth century. If we are to make any lasting progress in bridging the gap between Third World realities and Pax Atlantica cum Pax Honeypot cum New Nobility we must, as I said before, go back to 1944 and start anew again.

It would be very difficult to make this transition from the Illusion of Dispenser of Ultimate Economic Wisdom to the Reality of Repentant Institution Seeking to Redress Mistakes. Can we do it? Knowing the institution as I do; knowing the self-righteousness and the psychology and motivation of its staff; knowing how sham and posturing have crystallized into operational modes and institutional "truths", I will not bet on it. Certainly, in this Letter I have no choice but to leave that question hanging loosely in the air.

The third matter that cries out for attention of the reformer and adjustment is the one that relates to ultimate power distribution between Part I and Part II member countries of the Fund in terms of voting rights and formal control of the institution. This matter touches very intimately on both aspects of reform identified in the preceding paragraphs of this sub-section. Specifically, if the status of developing countries as owners of the Fund is upgraded to represent anything remotely close to their status as Fund transactors and originators of Fund business, and providers of Fund profit and users of Fund resources, there will be an immediate and automatic reversal of Staff Third World Omnipotence, and of institutional dogma. Perceptions of the intrinsic real world interests that the staff has to "protect" will also be changed.

In such a situation, Pax Atlantica and Pax Honeypot and all operational modules underlying these concepts and principles will just peel off the wall like coats of older paint. Of course this is the most desirable and the most comprehensive solution, but really it requires another Bretton Woods Conference. The question arises: who in the west would want to expose the Bretton Woods institutions, and the Bretton Woods system to public evaluation after forty years of abysmal failure? Who in the west would want to suggest a fairer and more efficient global system, but one that may be perceived as being less advantageous to them? Answer me, who? In this respect, monster's words of "finders keepers, losers weepers" is as wisdom coming straight from the horse's mouth.

So we are left, really, with trying to do some seemingly marginal, yet important things (if that's not a contradiction), that will not change the system fundamentally, but that will be advantageous in modest but well defined ways to developing countries. In this respect all elements of reform action contemplated involve wing clipping of the staff. The chances of implementing these proposals simultaneously as a "package deal" is probably better now than at anytime in the past. Certainly, a very concerted push by the Third World, with support from friends and wellwishers in the west (including certain governments) could never be ignored by the other side.

(ii) Element of a Pragmatic Reform Program for Staff Wing Clipping

A strategy for Fund staff wing clipping must answer two questions, viz: (a) what can be done through direct means that impinge immediately on our over-heavy salaries and allowances and perquisites and "privileges", to reestablish some sort of balance and sanity in our remuneration and terms and conditions of employment? (This Letter screams out that reestablishment of such balance and sanity is an absolute requirement for the restoration of professionalism and perspective and fairplay and humanity in our institution); (b) irrespective of the Honeypot that provides its stream of endless material benefits to Fund people, what checks and balances mechanisms may be created within the organizational structure of the Fund, and in the structure of relationships between the Fund and developing member countries, so as to curb the "absolute" power presently wielded by Fund bureaucracy in the Third World, and ameliorate the growing tendency for wanton abuse of that power?

(a) Fund Staff Salaries, Allowances, Privileges, Immunities

On the first of these questions, I choose at this time to make no substantive comment. In the most recent times internal procedures have been put into place to conduct, as a matter of urgency, a review of aspects of Pax Honeypot, particularly inflated staff salaries and allowances. It is expected that that review will soon be extended to include other elements of the Pot, including the broad structure of absurd privileges, and the wholly unnecessary staff pampering, as described in Part V. While it may be unrealistic to expect the results of these studies to be made public, many people outside the Fund will be waiting for an announcement by Fund management regarding the practical implications of its apparent decision to curtail somewhat the Honeypot, partly in the light of most recent criticisms emanating from a variety of sources, not least of which is the US Congress itself, and other parliamentary and legislative bodies throughout the developed and developing world. Now that the matter of staff salaries, privileges and exemptions and other related subjects discussed in Part V are well in the public domain, it behooves Fund management to come out with a very explicit statement reassuring the world community that urgent and substantial action is being taken to remedy what, by world consensus, is a wholly unsustainable position and a negation of everything that the Fund insists that it stands for. I reserve the right to return to this matter massively at a later date, in the event that a Fund response is deemed inadequate by major elements of its world constituency.

At this stage I am taking an equally reticent attitude with regard to the enormous contradictions and outright absurdities relating to a very wide range of internal administrative and organizational procedures, including the very vexed question of racism at every level of Fund practice and institutionalized processes. Again, on this matter, action seemingly has been initiated in very recent times in response to "outside" pressure, and in the circumstances I fell duty bound to hold fire momentarily. However, as in the case of staff emoluments and privileges, a public announcement will be awaited anxiously by the world community. It is absolutely necessary that the Fund keeps world opinion informed of the specific areas where it sees fit to institute remedial measures, and to advise on the nature, "quality" and timing of such measures. The world community, equally, has the responsibility of instituting some sort of structured mechanism that will allow it to keep abreast of these developments and to exert concerted pressure to elicit further needed change and reform in specifically identified areas.

(b) "Internal" Checks and Balances Mechanisms

In so far as "internal" mechanisms are concerned, the following is suggested, viz: immediate establishment of those safeguards that had been built into the Fund's Articles of Agreement in 1944, but which had never been activated, mainly because of the unforeseen "hijacking" of the Fund by its burgeoning bureaucracy, and the outstanding success achieved by the latter in stifling all other potential power points within the decision making structure of the Fund. In this respect, relatively meaningless "posturing" of the past and present, including creation of the basically toothless and captive Interim Committee and Development Committee and Group of Twenty Four, as discussed extensively in Part V, must give way to a fully independent Fund Council of broad decision making powers and wider geographic representation along lines laid down in our Articles of Agreement. The Council should not be made to operate on "advice" from Fund staff; it must spawn its own small but highly proficient body of technical expertise as a counterweight to the methods and approaches of what initially may prove to be the still all-pervading power of our Retreating Nobility. In any event, it must be expected that in the short term, establishment of an effective regime of "internal" checks and balances that reflects the reality of a previously "captive" institution, will involve, inevitably, some degree of experimentation and perhaps of seeming functional duplication over a "phasing in" period of from, say, three to five years.

(c) "External" Checks and Balances Mechanisms

On "external" checks and balances, a series of closely related, and simultaneously functioning mechanisms are proposed for use by both the Fund and the World Bank. (For a description of problems of the latter with the Third World, and a demonstration of the convergence of its activities with those of the Fund, see Attachment 1).

If the genesis of "internal" checks and balances mechanisms are to be found in the Articles of Agreement of the Fund, the genesis of "external" checks and balances mechanisms are equally to be found in the Articles of Agreement of the World Bank.

Very much aware of the necessity for "checks and balances" in decision-making - and perhaps anticipating the pervasive trend of authority gravitating towards the staff - the Bank's founding fathers had made provision for a series of independent advisory bodies with strategic intermediating roles in decision-making. On of these - an advisory Council - was to be selected by the Board of Governors and was to include "representatives of banking, commercial, industrial, labor and agricultural interest .. with as wide a national representation as possible." Provision was also made for "each loan committee" of the Bank to "include an expert selected by the Governor representing the member in whose territory the project is located." None of these mechanisms are presently operational.

Would restoration of the "checks and balances" mechanism of 1944 contribute importantly to the resolution of present day problems identified above? - problems that are common to both the World Bank and the

Fund? On this matter it can be said immediately that juxtaposition of "independent" decision-making elements with entrenched existing ones can serve as a means for deflating existing or potential conflict between the staff of the institutions and member countries, and for bringing a wider perspective to bear on Fund/Bank policies and operations. Yet merely to restore the instruments of 1944 would be to assume away the problems that have arisen since then. New instruments are needed to neutralize the inordinate and unbalanced growth of power of one stratum of decision-making - ie; the staff - and to keep faith with the intention of the Articles of Agreement of both institutions.

The following are suggested: an Advisory and Review Commission to assume the functions of the now defunct Advisory Council and to act as a final court of appeal on matters relating the administration of the aid relationship, and a series of Regional Coordinating Committees to review on an annual basis economic progress in member countries, and to lay down general guidelines for future Fund/Bank operations in individual countries and regions. A Watch Dog Committee, established by developing countries themselves, is also proposed.

The Advisory and Review Commission

The Advisory and Review Commission, it is anticipated, will act as a final court of appeal on three matters. Firstly, it will arbitrate in disputes between the Fund or Bank or both on the one hand, and member countries on the other, on policy changes deemed necessary to achieve particular economic and social objectives in a situation where the use of Fund/Bank resources are involved. Secondly, it will consider charges by individual member countries of bias or inconsistencies in Fund/Bank attitudes and postures arising from, for example, a change in government, or in national economic and social policies, (eg; institution of an "entitlements vector) or from pressures being brought to bear on the staff by powerful members of the institutions to forego established technical criteria and substitute political considerations that can serve to further the immediate narrow national political goals of such powerful member countries to the detriment of the economic well-being of the developing country concerned. Thirdly, it will examine complaints formally brought to it by the Fund or Bank of non-compliance by member countries with leverage measures or "conditionality" formally agreed to as a condition for the use of the resources under question. The intention in all three instances is to remove disputes from the straitjackets of ultimatums based on imbalance in relative bargaining strengths (staff vis-a-vis developing member country) and place such disputes in the broader and safer perspective of dispassionate, objective analysis from the backdrop of internationally acceptable criteria.

The Advisory and Review Commission will also assume the mantle of the Advisory Council described in the Bank's Articles of Agreement. In addition it should be given responsibility for review of all internal Fund and Bank papers on major policy issues prior to discussion of such papers by the respective Boards of Executive Directors of the institutions. The comments of the Commission should be made available to Directors before initiation of "formalized decision-making processes to define or redefine Fund or Bank policies on operational matters.

As was intended for the Advisory Council, membership of the Commission should be drawn from a wide range of professional disciplines. At least one member should be an internationally renowned jurist. Members of the Commission should be selected directly by the Board of Governors of both institutions and not by the Fund's Managing Director or the Bank's President. To counteract the overwhelming influence of national of developed countries on the staff of the institutions, a majority of members of the Commission should be drawn from developing countries. Provision should also be made for maintenance by the Commission of a small permanent secretariat, including a skeleton staff of technocrats. The Commission should be authorized to seek advice, if and when required, from independent experts outside the institutions.

The Regional Coordinating Committees

The Regional Coordinating Committees will be established to parallel the several Regional Offices or Departments of the Fund and Bank. Operating on lines not dissimilar to CIAP, each Committee will undertake for every country within its jurisdiction a "country economic review" as soon as possible after receipt of the respective institutions' Country Economic Report or similar document. The Committee will examine national economic performance from the perspective of the country's own system of priorities for economic and social development. It will also check the accuracy of each report and call attention to particularly gross oversimplifications or undue use of subjective value judgments that underlie the conclusions and recommendations of reports. The comments and recommendations of the Committee will be submitted to the relevant Regional Department as well as to the government of the country concerned and to the Board of Executive Directors. Failure by the staff to take account of the Committee's findings at successive stages of the decision-making process to formulate a Fund or Bank "lending posture" and "policy package" will provide, a priori, strong justification for recourse, by the country concerned, to the grievance redress procedures of the Advisory and Review Commission.

The majority of members of the Committee will be elected by Fund and Bank Governors for the region concerned; the remaining nominations will be made by Governors from more advanced countries. Only nationals of the region served by the Committee will be eligible for election. Each Committee will operate from headquarters within the region with the help of a small secretariat. To meet the requirements of the Articles of Agreement, the Chairman of each Coordinating Committee will be an ex officio member of the Loan Committee of the Bank and will sit on the latter body whenever necessary. The Regional Coordinating Committees will perform the functions of the regional council as described in Articles 5, Section 10 (b) of the Articles of Agreement of the Bank.

The Watch Dog Committee

In addition to action that must be endorsed formally by appropriate elements of Fund and Bank management, - and all the above fall into this category - it is recommended that developing countries themselves take immediate steps to establish a Watch Dog Committee to oversee their interests in negotiations with the Fund and Bank. It is proposed that the Committee be selected from a panel of eminently qualified persons including political figures, religious leaders, economists, sociologists, jurists and trade unionists from both developed and developing countries. The rationale for the Committee is the existing overwhelming power of the Fund and Bank in the Third World, vis-a-vis individual governments and Ministries of Finance, and therefore the extremely weak position of such governments and such Ministries in processes of multilateral economic negotiations on matters that determine their future, and the well-being or ill-being of their peoples at a particular point of time, and for several years thereafter. The Committee, which may take up the cause of any particular country only at the specific request of the government concerned, will serve to redress a long outstanding imbalance that never ever should have been made to exist. While it will have no authority to adjudicate on Fund horrors and excesses of the past, its work, conceivably, could lead to a less tortured existence for the Third World in the future.

Freezing Relations as an Interim Measure

A general recommendation is as follows: until the above regulatory and control mechanisms, or appropriate varients of them, are established and become operative, developing countries - especially those who at the present time deem themselves to be receiving particularly raw deals from the Fund and World Bank - may consider a strategy of freezing all relations until further notice. This will release their energies to pursue single-mindedly the very urgent, prior task of creating the type of institutional adaptations, as described above, to protect their interest in the face of current gross excesses rampant within the system. In this connection, it is pointed out that while organizational innovation within the formal structure of the institutions (e.g; establishment of an Advisory and Review Commission and of Regional Coordinating Committees) could be unduly delayed by non-Third World elements who may be opposed to the type of change contemplated, there is no reason why developing countries, perhaps through instrumentality of the G-77 or Non-Aligned Movement, or both, could not take immediate action on their own to bring into being the Watch Dog Committee. Indeed, such a critical instrument for protecting the Third World could well be made to function within a six-month period, assuming that there is a reasonable degree of consensus in the South for its establishment.

9. CONCLUSION

Don't fear, Sir. I'm not going to become emotional; I'm not going to will you on to become compassionate; I'm not going to ask you to throw your weight, with eyes closed, behind the world's poor. I have said all I want to say at this stage; I have said it the way I want to say it. It's up now to you to respond the way it suits you best. Your response may conceivably take the form of a non-response, but I think that will be a mistake, I think it will be unsustainable, for this Letter is not a one-shot operation. But more of that later. For now, the ball is in your court.

As I wrote this Letter, you know, pain sometimes gave way to helplessness, and helplessness to a brand of wry humor that perhaps was somewhat unpleasant to ... to our High Priests. So let me make amends with a little nursery rhyme that kept coming to my head today. It goes like this:

"The King was in the counting house
Counting up the money,
(Treasurer's Department checking Third World repayments?)
"The Queen was in the parlor,
eating bread and drinking honey,
(High Priests at headquarters at worship around the Honeypot?)
The maid was in the garden
spreading out the clothes,
(mission staff throwing wool over the eyes of unsuspecting Third World officials?)
There came a little black bird and pecked at her nose.

I don't believe it; I just don't believe it. Really, there's more to it than that; futive pecking just cannot be the answer.

Yours sincerely,

Davison L. Budhoo

87

Attachment 1

DEVELOPING COUNTRIES AND THE WORLD BANK:
THE NEED FOR REAPPRAISAL AND REFORM

I. INTRODUCTION

1. The World Bank Group of institutions - comprising the World Bank proper, the International Development Association (IDA), the International Finance Corporation (IFC), is the most important source of external financing for international development. It contributed in 1987 several billion dollars of multilateral flows to less- developed countries - and these amounts have been rising from year to year. The importance of the Bank, however, does not lie solely in its financing activities - however important these may be. The constitution of the institution imbues it with a managerial role in international development; today it shares with its sister institution the International Monetary Fund (IMF), the distinction of being the linchpin and core of the so-called "international development effort."

2. Its role in this respect is multifarious. It is, with the Fund, the chief advocate of development finance and balance-of-payments support facilities to developing countries, and it assumes constantly as stance of supplication to plead the case for more short-and-long-term financial assistance, whether bilateral of multilateral, from more advanced to less-advanced countries. It coordinates past and future aid pledges of bilateral and multilateral donors to individual developing countries. It establishes international criteria for evaluating "national economic performance", "creditworthiness", "relevance of national adjustment efforts", et al. It makes definitive judgments and assessments to developed countries and to other international agencies on the propriety of development policies of developing country governments - judgments and assessments that become critical in the allocation of bilateral and multilateral aid funds to the Third World. It dispenses, profusely, technical assistance and economic advice to less-developed countries; in some instances it assumes directly, in collusion with the IMF,the reins of national economic management. It influences - in some cases supervises - the operations of national Treasuries, national development banks, major public utilities and other strategic industries. Its joint brief with the IMF extends to cover the volume of public sector expenditures, the level of taxation, movements in real wages, the prices of locally- produced goods and services, the exchange rate of national currencies and, in several instances, employment in the public sector and in the national economy as a whole. It affects directly or indirectly, the lives of hundreds of millions of people in Asia, Africa, Latin America and the Caribbean.

3. Its role as the cornerstone of an international management system for economic development was not meticulously planned in some "grand design" to banish globally the problem of underdevelopment. It evolved haphazardly in response to international economic and political forces and the perception of the staff of the institution on how to channel such forces into specific policies that can best express and further objectives of the institution. As such there is no underlying philosophy - no explicitly stated rationale - for its current, massive involvement in economic decision-making in developing countries. Equally the longer-term implications of such involvement for the organization itself and for its members, have not been carefully worked out. Lack of meaningful theoretical or analytical base for objective judgment on day-to-day activities of the agency is particularly unfortunate in an area of virulent international economic change and of growing dissatisfaction in Third World countries with international development strategies and policies.

4. This submission does not attempt to undertake systematically an examination of the managerial role of the World Bank in international development. Rather, it is designed to provide an interpretation of the structure of decision-making within the Bank Group on critical aspects of the allocation and transfer of Bank resources to developing countries. Some conclusions are drawn on important issues relating to Bank goals, methods and performance in international development. Two questions in particular are raised. Firstly, the extent to which "leverage" or "influence" of the Bank on national economic policies is geared to serve an "internal Bank administrative and management" goal, as against a "country developmental" one. Secondly, the extent to which reform of the Bank on matters relating to (a) transfer and allocation of its resources in develop-

ing countries and (b) implementation of its management role in international development, is now an urgent and necessary task to enhance the Bank's role in international development and to reduce the scope for, and increasing incidence of conflict between the Bank and developing member countries.

II. DECISION-MAKING PROCESSES WITHIN THE BANK ON TRANSFER OF RESOURCES TO DEVELOPING COUNTRIES

5. Decisions within the Bank Group on the allocation and transfer of resources to less-developed member countries involve activation of two decision-making processes: (a) a formal one that requires a confirming vote of the Board of Executive Directors, and (b) a "dynamic" one that skirts the authority of the Board and links directly the technical staff of the Bank to their counterparts in member countries, to national political directorates and to national economic and political decision-making systems there. The two processes identified form a continuum, with the "dynamic" one defining procedures of project and "country" analysis, and evaluation and loan negotiation that are necessarily brought into play prior to a formal submission to the Board for endorsement of resource transfer to a particular country. Remarks here relate to the evaluative "dynamic" process as against the formalized one.

(i) Purpose of Bank's Evaluative and Analytical Work in Developing Member Countries

6. One crucial question to be answered in a discussion of methods and criteria of Bank evaluative work in developing countries is as follows: what exactly is the purpose for which the Bank wishes to have a judgment on a member country? In this respect, it is not enough to say that a judgment is required as part of the process of determining whether or not a loan should be made. This is true but it is not the whole truth. As it operates today, the staff's evaluative work is far more complicated and involved than that required to determine responses to ad hoc application for Bank financing of "specific projects of reconstruction and development."

7. The problem can perhaps best be put in terms of changing loan policies, and the paraphernalia of operational and administrative work in member countries that this involves. Critical in this respect is the policy, initiated over a decade ago, of five-year indicative programming of future Bank allocation to individual countries. Within this planning horizon a major task of operational departments is to provide project "pegs" on which the institution can "hang" pre-allocated disbursements. Responses to individual loan applications are still important, but the resulting Bank inputs of project preparation and appraisal work are conceptualized as an integral aspect of the identification and implementation of an overall multi-year lending program for the country concerned, integrated and assimilated into the country's own medium-term plan, and its financing. The implications of such "project lending under a program approach" are quite far-reaching insofar as the nature, manifestation and effects of Bank leverage on overall economic and social policies of member countries are concerned.

(ii) Instruments and Techniques of Country Evaluation

8. The Bank's program approach work is based on an astonishing range of sustained "country" evaluation studies and reports. The most important of these are the full-fledged country economic reviews that are undertaken on an annual or biennial basis by multi-disciplined Bank staff missions. Complementing such reviews are a series of special reports prepared continuously on economic sectors or on "important" developmental problems. In between country economic reviews is a stream of country updating memoranda to monitor current developments and performance. Crucial instruments of five-year country programming are the annual country program papers and the updating country program notes. These two instruments are prepared after extensive and wide-ranging "dialogue" with individual member governments on "country economic performance," "creditworthiness," country vis-a-vis Bank priorities on the "project list," et al. Leverage conditions for implementing a firmed up lending program for the first three of the five- year "program-

ming" period are sometimes stated, with provision being made for retrenchment or expansion of such lending as circumstances in the judgment of the Bank may justify.

9.   The multiple of reports, committees, departments, et al reflects vividly the authority of the Bank staff in decision-making. Bank staff, in many instances, junior Bank staff, determine the Bank's lending posture, taking into account matters such as savings ratio, GNP growth, governmental efforts at mobilizing domestic resources, priorities in an investment program, export growth, domestic inflation, repayment structure of existing foreign debt. The same staff has authority to negotiate with the country concerned compliance with a policy package of measures that is deemed necessary to make a lending program "effective". In return for a fairly firm commitment to implement the Bank's "package," the developing country is given reasonable assurance of an inflow of resources, to meet at least part of an indicative "foreign exchange gap," on terms that are deemed "bearable" in relation to the repayment burden of existing debt and balance-of-payments prospects.

(iii) New Dimensions of Country Programming Approaches

10. In recent times country programming by the Bank has become more formalized and wide-ranging. The introduction of structural adjustment lending around 1980 defined a major development in this sphere. The emergence in 1981 of Bank/Fund cross-conditionality in resource transfer (in the form of a requirement of the Fund that the Bank must endorse the total investment program of certain developing member countries as a condition for eligibility for use of Fund resources for structural adjustment) and the virtual convergence in 1986 of Structural adjustment lending conditionality with that of the Fund, - has heightened even further the "program" nature of Bank work. Longer-term, pervasive policy trends have also played a part. Three of these may be noted: (a) the Bank's strong thrust into socio-economic lending (in education, population, health, nutrition and rural development); (b) expanded "country" as against "project" technical assistance on its own account and as Executing Agency for other institutions; and (c) an ever-widening involvement in aid coordination for the international community (with a corresponding responsibility, in collaboration with the Fund, to undertake periodic reviews and assessments of overall economic performance in developing countries on behalf of donors and other multilateral agencies).

III. IMPLEMENTATION OF A PROGRAM APPROACH TO RESOURCE TRANSFER FOR DEVELOPING COUNTRIES

11. The widening involvement of Bank staff as described above in economic and political decision-making in developing member countries and the plethora of implications for the countries concerned and for the Bank, have been the subject of very intense concern in recent times. Disquiet about the staff's modern day developmental role, or more specifically, its role in economic decision-making at the national level rationalized in the name of development and development financing, range from the remonstrations of disgruntled groups within individual developing countries, to stifled protests of technocrats and politicians, to open misgivings on independent researchers, and even to explicit attacks by some staff members themselves who have protested publicly the existing state of affairs, and have called for fundamental rethinking of the Bank's role, purpose and methods in national and international development.

(i) Leverage Exertion: A Built-In Feature of the Aid Relationship

12. The present writer holds the view that leverage exertion or donor "influence" on economic policies in developing countries is an inherent aspect of an act of development assistance - whether bilateral or multilateral. To see this it is necessary to look at the aid relationship from the viewpoint of the donor - in this case the World Bank. Basically, the latter is concerned not only with allocative criteria to ensure effective "use" of aid in a particular developing country, but with allocational criteria to secure an efficient distribution of scarce loan funds among all developing countries that qualify for its loans and credits. Both set of criteria

coincide when the Bank uses to the full leverage on economic policies that its financing commands. More specifically, economic efficiency in resource transfer under a country program is maximized when the Bank lends right up to the point where it can have the greatest impact on country policies. If it lends less than this amount its leverage powers become considerably reduced - indeed ineffective - in relation to amounts of financing provided. If it lends more, the leverage impact of "additional" funds decreases sharply and eventually falls to zero; aid is being used inefficiently

13. The above prognosis, it should be noted, presupposes a conflict of opinion between the Bank and the member country on what is "optimal" or "proper" for national economic development. If such a conflict does not exist either one of two things is implied - ie; that the Bank is given a free rein in policy-making, or that by a remarkable coincidence, the Government's own plans and policies are identical to proposals emanating from the institution. In such instances, the Bank, of course, may lend whatever amounts are requested, or deemed fit, without consideration of the "leverage effect" that has been described above.

14. These exceptions apart, leverage exertion is, inescapably, a part of the Bank's operational policies and procedures. At the same time, an admission of the inevitability of leverage exertion does not at all place the Bank above criticism. For while leverage is a fact of life in resource transfer, legitimate doubts can arise as to whether the Bank is using the right sort of leverage, or achieving through leverage the right sort of objective in developing countries.

(ii) Project Approach Leverage Exertion: Limited and Non-Antagonistic

15. A discussion on "problems" of leverage, as distinct from "propriety" of its use, can perhaps best be seen from the perspective of an interpretation of the changing nature of Bank involvement in the internal affairs of member countries.

16. Right up to the formation of IDA, Bank loans were almost entirely project approach loans. The exercise of leverage under the discipline of project approach lending involves a known and unambiguously defined regulatory role over a very limited area of the national economy - for instance, a power plant or an iron steel complex - and it is predominantly technical in nature. Under this approach, fundamental questions - relating for instance to the international political orientation of the government or its role in economic life - are effectively insulated from Bank staff decision-making processes, and the aid relationship becomes predominantly non-antagonistic, with a high degree of consensus as to what is to be done, and how to make Bank loans effective and to further the process of economic transformation.

17. The non-controversial nature of project approach lending by the Bank in the fifties and early sixties need indeed to be emphasized. In every instance of such lending the predominant concern was development and use of evaluative criteria to assess "profitability" (or "productivity") of a specific enterprise, the latter's capacity for financial self-liquidation and its international competitiveness. Such criteria are internationally accepted and technically verifiable; the scope for abuse in use is minimal. By contrast, the problem of measuring "country economic performance" - the concept around which current evaluative work under the program approach has coalesced - raises a hornet's nest of problems for the institution.

(iii) Program Approach Leverage Exertion: Inefficient and Sub-Optimal

18. The choice of perspective for judgment on country economic performance may best be understood by a brief review of the impact of international functionalism on national decision-making processes.

19. The spectacle of UN Specialized Agencies - including the World Bank - pursuing conflicting and unrelated programs of international assistance in the national economy is one that is well known to developing countries. The difficulties of this process are compounded by the fact that, at the national level, total planning objectives of a country - social goals of integration, fuller employment, greater social security, economic goals of growth, price stability, balance-of-payments equilibrium - are meshed together in a national plan with an order of priority for implementation stated or implied. Criteria for judging country economic performance can be meaningful for the country concerned only when due regard is paid to the latter's own spectrum of

objectives - derived through operation of national decision-making processes - and when the uncoordinated activities of all international institutions are taken into account. This implies two things: the standardization of judgment of major international institutions operating in the national economy, and the development of indices of performance relating to national economic and social welfare.

20. Establishment of development performance criteria along these lines is no doubt difficult - if only because of the existing competitiveness and jealousies among international institutions - but it is not impossible. Indeed, individual researchers have paved the way with meaningful pioneering groundwork over a period of some thirty years. For reasons that will later be explained, the Bank, however, has chosen to forego the opportunity of joining the search for internationally acceptable and verifiable norms and standards of country evaluation that serve predominantly the interests of the international community and of its developing member countries. This is in contrast to its attitude of the fifties when project approach criteria were being formulated.

21. In lieu of comprehensive evaluative criteria, the Bank has resorted to an analytical system that takes GNP growth, "country creditworthiness" and "effectiveness" in country mobilization and utilization of resources as basic determinants of country economic performance. The objective has been to select, in kangaroo fashion, a few "key economic indicators" that intuitively must form part of a program approach evaluative system and to orientate all evaluative work around these, without attempting to relate such indicators to one another or to other relevant elements of evaluative analysis. This procedure can conceivably be defended on the ground that it defines for the Bank a gradualist approach to problems of development performance. Under this reasoning criteria may be refined progressively as Bank experience develops in this field.

22. The author, however, thinks otherwise. Evaluative criteria by the Bank staff is not a matter of pragmatic experimentation towards an internationally verifiable system geared to the developmental needs of member countries. It represents, rather, the most liberal "package" that the Bank can offer an individual developing country at any moment of time, taking into account a wide range of internal and external constraints including exogenous political pressures on its operations.

IV. DETAILED ASSESSMENT OF PROGRAM APPROACH EVALUATION WORK OF THE BANK

(i) Superficial and Inadequate Work the Norm

23. As it functions today the Bank is not all geared to the rigorous evaluative work as is demanded by the program approach that the institution has so extensively embraced. It normally does not have a permanent presence in individual developing countries. Its field work for evaluation is generally a cursory affair; with a full-fledged country economic mission remaining in the field for about two to three weeks only and thereafter preparing its report - often running to several hundred pages - in less than six weeks. The fast turnover of staff, the high rate of recruitment and inter-departmental transfers, the perplexing changes in mission personnel - in short, the search for a new equilibrium within the Bank to express its new role in international development - militates seriously against perspicacity and vision in economic analysis of developing member countries, particularly the smaller, and in the Bank's view, the less important member countries. Invariably for the latter, more junior, less competent and inexperienced staff are assigned.

24. These weaknesses and shortcomings, some may say, are an inescapable price to pay during a transitory period. But the question remains: transition to what? As the Bank sees it, the formulation of criteria for program approach lending is a necessary, but undesirable aspect of the resource transfer process. It is the instrument that the Bank must use to allow assimilation by developing countries of its relatively massive loan commitments for 1987, and its even more ambitious targets for the 1988-93 period. Conceptual and methodological problems such as those described above, apparently are not regarded as being inherently important in themselves. Chances are, therefore, that they will be taken into account only insofar as deficiencies in current criteria and policies provoke sufficient questioning and protest in developing member countries, and in the world at large.

25. There is another, more basic factor inhibiting - indeed preventing - the growth of meaningful, evaluative criteria for Bank operations. The author asserts that the entire system of preconceptions underlying the operations of the Bank is intellectually unsustainable and inadequate as a base for allocative/disbursement policies. It is amazing that within the Bank - whose lending is now conducted predominantly under the "program" or "country" approach - there should still be total confusion as to what is "project lending" and what is "program lending."

26. In this respect, the Bank continues to conceptualize program lending in terms of the nature of disbursement (ie. loans not tied to procurement for specific projects) rather than in relation to the purpose of developmental objective of the resource transfer (ie; whether or not it is designed to fill a resource "gap" in a development program approach by the Bank, irrespective of the nature and specific method of disbursement).

27. The difference in concept is far from being a matter of mere classification. By failing to recognize that it is automatically, indiscriminatingly and uncritically making program approach loans through the project instrument in conditions where other instruments of resource transfer under the program approach (ie; sectorial, cross-sectorial, structural adjustment lending, balance-of-payments support facility) may in fact be more appropriate (in the sense of having a higher developmental impact on the economy concerned, taking into account "country" developmental objectives agreed upon by the Bank and the government) the institution is sowing wild oats for the future and compromising importantly and unduly the efficiency of its operations.

28. The effect on the Bank of use of ill-conceived and misguided concepts of resource transfer mechanisms and processes is cumulative. As the existing theory - which in itself is vague and imprecise - proves to be less and less valid for specific transfer situations, the Bank is resorting increasingly to a policy of "playing it by ear" without the benefit of a well-organized and operative epistemology. Over the past few years solutions on an ad hoc, opportunist basis have been arrived at to a number of program approach transfer and allocation issues ranging from pressing policy matters such as "local cost financing", "country creditworthiness", to environmental "structural adjustment lending", problems such as population growth, urbanization and regional economic integration. One difficulty with this procedure is that it widens significantly the scope for arbitrary value judgment in Bank evaluative work.

V. COMPARISON OF FUND RAISING AND FUND TRANSFER AND ALLOCATING DECISIONS

29. We have described above the major mechanisms, processes, problems and issues in resource transfer and allocation, and have demonstrated the overwhelming role of the staff in decision-making and the fragile and unsatisfactory base on which decisions are themselves made. On fund raising - and funds must be raised before they can be allocated - the problems and issues are entirely different in nature. Here it is true to say that although Bank Group staff is entirely free to make proposals that can serve as the basis for determinate action, achievement depends entirely on decisions taken independently by developed countries themselves.

30. Specifically, it is the developed (or "Part I") countries who determine whether the Bank should be allowed to issue bonds in their capital markets at a certain time, in a certain quantum and on certain terms and conditions, and it is the same group of countries that determine the quantum, conditions and phasing of IDA replenishment. All decision-making with regard to such replenishment reflect economic and political considerations of individual member governments in developed countries, irrespective of the recommendations and policy stances of the Bank staff.

31. Ultimately, therefore, what is important in fund raising is not what Bank staff determines, but what developed countries are prepared to do. From this perspective, fund raising decisions can be seen as being made within a relatively self-contained decision-making system of international authority that is exclusive of Bank staff decision-making processes. The views, wishes and priorities of developed countries formulated

in terms of their perceptions of their own national political and economic interests, determine just how effective a role the World Bank Group can play in international development, insofar as effectiveness is measured in terms of the availability of financial resources for transfer, and the terms and conditions on which such transfers are made from more developed to less-developed member countries.

VI. FUND RAISING AND FUND ALLOCATION: A CONTINUUM WITH DEVELOPED COUNTRIES AS CENTERPIECE

32. One question must now be answered. Are fund raising and fund allocating decisions mutually exclusive?

The answer is no. Decision-making within the Bank is in fact a continuum, with the authority of developed countries who provide funds extending to influence the transfer and allocation of such funds in individual developing countries. Can such "outside" influence on decision-making on fund allocation complicate further the problems described above and make more intractable a solution in the interest of developing countries, individually and as a group?

33. The portends are bad. Political pressure extended on the Bank by major shareholders - and in recent times such pressures have become increasingly crude, and more and more explicit - can only deepen, not resolve, the problems identified. Equally, the overwhelming influence, among Bank professional staff, of nationals of a few developed member countries will not serve to establish urgently a greater rapport between the Bank and less-developed member countries. Similarly, the influence on Bank policies of international capital markets, traditionally regarded as a major constraint on effective Bank operations in international development, cannot really be expected to decrease in an era of unprecedented market activity by the Bank and massive concern for existing debt burden of developing countries.

34. Assuming recent policies on fund raising and resource transfer remain unchanged, the most realistic outcome for Third World countries may well be a marginal degree of permissiveness granted by the Bank and by its developed members towards less-developed countries so as to allow the institution to maintain that minimum fund of goodwill and credibility on which its capacity to function is itself dependent.

35. It is the stark reality of their disadvantageous position in the Bank that must propel developing countries to seek change and reform within the institution. In this respect there are certain things that they can do, individually and collectively.

36. All reform proposal, however, must start from a particular set of preconceptions, viz: given its wide-ranging implications for member countries, Bank decision- making on resource transfer should satisfy four basic conditions. Firstly, it should be based on a system of checks and balances designed to prevent arbitrary use of power by any one sector of internal Bank management. Secondly, unambiguously stated and internationally acceptable technical criteria should be used. Procedures should also exist for independent verification of Bank decisions that are formulated through operation of the "program evaluative" process. There should also be a formal mechanism for conflict resolution.

37. Detailed proposals on how the above may be achieved is given in the text of this Part of the Letter, pages 48 to 52.

VII. CONCLUSION

38. We have pointed out, in Section 5, the fragile base for the Bank's continuing operations, with a few advanced countries voluntarily providing the capital funds for transfer to some one hundred less-developed ones, ultimately on terms that donors themselves must approve. In the final analysis, the Bank's existence is justified not on grounds that it raises these funds - they could have been raised by other means - but that it allocates them on criteria that uniquely increase their capacity to contribute to economic development of the recipient entity. In questioning the developmental content of the criteria, as we have done in this submission, we equally have questioned the ultimate usefulness of the World Bank as an intermediary for allocating development assistance.

39. Doubt raising on the meaningfullness of the present day mechanisms for aid disbursement is not new. Almost two decades ago a study by Hirschman and Bird concluded that the problems of administering a "program aid" relationship was insoluble, and advocated an entirely new operational system for aid giving and administration under which the paraphernalia of present day multilateralism would have been allowed to die a merciful death. The present author has rejected this argument, and made an assertion that growth of objective and workable criteria for allocating "program aid" is indeed possible. (See D.L. Budhoo, THE INTEGRATED THEORY OF DEVELOPMENT ASSISTANCE, Institute of Social and Economic Research, UWI, 1973).

40. It is this latter view that has been endorsed in this paper. In doing so, we run the risk of overlooking the importance of entrenched interests who, for reasons unrelated to the needs and circumstances of developing countries, would want to see no change. We take this risk, and appeal now to member countries collectively and to Bank management itself to implement urgently necessary measures to ensure that multilateralism in resource transfers through the Bank be made more effective, and, become designed to serve the interest of both donors and recipients.

This submission is intended as a contribution to this most vital task facing Governors and management of the Bank.

Davison L. Budhoo
May 18, 1988

SUITE 188 □ 4807 BETHESDA AVENUE □ BETHESDA, MARYLAND 20814 □ UNITED STATES OF AMERICA □ TELEPHONE (301) 229-8817

January 10, 1989

Mr. Camdessus
Managing Director
International Monetary Fund
Washington D.C. 20431

Dear Mr. Camdessus,

With reference of my letter of September 20, 1988 that accompanied Part VI of my Letter of Resignation, I am pleased to enclose an extension of Part VI which, with your permission, I will dub as Part VII. The Third World Debt crisis, and the Fund's Debt Strategy since 1983, take pride of place in this new work.

A Postscript to the Letter, dealing with international and Fund reaction to it, will be submitted to you in due course. That Postscript was referred to as a "follow up Letter" in my memorandum of May 18, 1988.

Your sincerely,

Davison L. Budhoo

Attachment

January 10, 1989

Mr. Camdessus
Managing Director
International Monetary Fund
Washington D.C. 20431

Dear Mr. Camdessus,

> Davison L. Budhoo: Part VII of Open Letter of Resignation from the Staff of the International Monetary Fund; the Fund and the Debt Crisis

1. THE FUND AS AGENT OF POWERFUL SHAREHOLDERS TO CHANGE THIRD WORLD POLITICAL AND ECONOMIC SYSTEMS UNDER RIGORS OF THE DEBT CRISIS

It is conceded within the Fund now that the emergence in 1983 of the debt crisis as a live-wire issue and the prospect of debt renouncement or forgiveness that had always occurred in the past in a similar world situation led to a fundamental reassessment of the Fund's role in the Third World. In this reassessment certain major industrialized member countries determined that the multiple uncertainties arising regarding capacity of the Fund to continue to manage Third World affairs from the perception of the narrow self-interests of these few major shareholders demanded urgent strengthening of the institution as the front for achieving their economic and political objectives in the South. The initial intention was not to buttress the Fund and World Bank with new mechanisms and operational modules, and although in the end that became part of the scenario, it was only a concession of convenience to further some more fundamental national objectives.

"Monetarism", as currently defined, was the centerpiece of everything; not only did it tie in with the Fund's past operational practice, but it expressed in a singularly clear way the doctrine of a continuing Fund absolutism in the Third World now fined-tuned, sharply and uncompromisingly, to a political philosophy of the free market economy and a social creed that would buttress, even more than in the past, the well to do, "westernized" strata of Southern Society. Under this system, corrupt dictators with multiple bank accounts in Switzerland and elsewhere, and arms merchants, with the same outlook and concept of the national interest, and foreign investors out to make a very quick buck, and well-heeled nationals who would illegitimately and without the batting of an eye turn around and drain the country concerned of its foreign resources through massive capital flight operations, become even more major actors on the scene than they had been before. Yes, yes, yes, Sir, such dubious fellow travellers and nation spoilers were made to become our natural and constant allies; they were the human resource base on which we were to build the new free-wheeling market economies of Brave New Africa and Latin America and the Caribbean and Asia. For us, they were the salt of the earth.

The corollary is clear enough, and was made very explicit in Fund action from 1983 onwards. Over the past five years and even as "outside" protest against such action was building up to a crescendo, the poor and economically disadvantaged sectors of Third World society were abandoned formally and completely by the Fund.

You know, if one looks closely at the history of our institution, and the evolution of its operational policies, one would see that, over the period 1978-81 - a period of great difficulty for the world economy and of special trauma for most non-oil producing developing countries - the emergence of traces of a flexibility and of a Third World relevance creeping almost imperceptibly into the policies and programs of the Fund. It is not only that it was the time frame within which the three-year Extended Fund Facility saw the light of day (only to feel, soon afterwards, the kiss of death); it was also a time of major experimentation with Fund modules and facilities - Trust Fund, gold distribution, peaked access to the Compensatory Financing Facility, extended quotas, the beginnings of a more human face by our staff and a seeming reduction in conflict and confrontation with Third World governments. Social welfare indices for the South, just becoming available, also show an encouraging, even though gradual upturn over this period. I think that in the broader order of things, historians will see this period as a time when the Fund trembled at the brink momentarily, before plunging down again in darkness.

Well, all that's over; the beast rose with a vengeance in 1983, and he is still rising and crushing down the poor with giant footsteps crunching grains of sand. And what is of relevance to you in all this is not the facts, per se, on the rising of the beast, but the way the Fund specifically altered its policies and stances to play a causative and crucial role, and to manage and supervise the new era of darkness and shame in the poverty-ridden South. You came to us in early 1987 when we were in throes of implementing our mandate to destroy, and quite frankly, almost eighteen months after, that mandate is stronger, and our thirst for blood and ignominy greater than before.

2. OUR MISSION TO PRIVATISE THE THIRD WORLD IN PREPARATION FOR LIMITED DEBT FORGIVENESS IN 1990 THROUGH A PROPOSED INTERNATIONAL DEBT FACILITY MANAGED BY THE FUND

Neither the Fund or World Bank or the three or four major western countries and Japan are as unknowing of, or inflexible in relation to the horrendous implications of Third World Debt as we have led the world to believe. Indeed, there is a consensus in Washington, London, Tokyo, other metropolitan capitals on the one hand, and in the Fund and World Bank on the other on the following matter, viz.; it is impossible under the most realistic assumptions regarding trends in the growth of Third World exports and in the terms of trade, in commodity and energy prices, in protectionism in major western economies, in economic growth in the United States and Western Europe, and in international interest rates, for heavily indebted countries of the developing world to 'grow out of debt' during the remaining years of this century.

In the circumstances, the Fund and its cortege of major shareholders have accepted that debt forgiveness for certain countries of the South is inevitable. The instrument chosen for such forgiveness is an International Debt Facility managed by the Fund, with its capital subscribed by developed countries, and the wherewithal for purchase of Third World debt coming from the proceeds of bonds raised on international capital markets, and guaranteed by the multilateral institutions or by their Part 1 member governments, or by both. The new instrument is projected to become operational in about 1990.

With the question of limited forgiveness seemingly settled, the focus has turned to a different set of issues, viz.; which of the developing countries will be given relief through the Facility? What will be the extent of relief for different Third World countries, and for different groups of Third World countries? Who will determine who gets what? And the answer to all these questions is simple enough: those who have been conditioned sufficiently by the Fund to be free-wheeling capitalist economies will gain; all others will lose.

Amazingly, Sir, as at Mid-May,1988 no one 'outside' has been able to read our lips; no one 'outside' has conceived that there can be acknowledgement in the west of the unsustainability of the Third World debt crisis; no one outside has guessed the establishment of a long-term debt strategy by our organization and by its major shareholders. And that ignorance of our secret plans is good news for us; very good news indeed.

You know, Sir, the battle over Third World debt will not be won or lost when debt forgiveness actually occurs in 1990 (as we have scheduled it to occur).

The battle over Third World debt will be won or lost depending on:

(a) the nature and comprehensiveness of debt Forgiveness;

(b) the conditionality of debt forgiveness in terms of the type of economic structures to be achieved in developing countries before debt forgiveness as a particular level is conceded;

(c) the conditionality for debt forgiveness at the particular level chosen in terms of the reconquest and renewed exploitation of debtor economies by multilateral corporations and other First World economic transactors ("foreign investment" in our parlance);

(d) the conditionality for debt forgiveness at a particular level in terms of the ever accelerating role of multilateral institutions (Fund and World Bank) in designing and supervising implementation of economic and financial 'programs' for Third World 'privatisation' as defined in "Reaganite economics;"

(e) the economic, political and social cost of debt forgiveness, thus presaged, from the point of view of the debtor;

(f) the political gains of debt forgiveness, thus presaged, from the point of view of the creditor.

To date, we have managed to hoodwink the whole world into believing that debt forgiveness, if ever it could come, will be a signal victory for the Third World, achieved in the face of stiff, virulent resistance from major creditor governments and their commercial banks. Quite frankly, we as an institution need to have this particular myth maintained, and indeed strengthened further if that is possible; it is an integral part of our game plan.

And one day, two years from now, we will begin to cash in the chips. One day, two years from now, there will be a lot of debt-crisis related activity by the Fund, with your good self or your successor, High Priests in attendance, jetting from one Third World debt-ridden country to another, and in between making high visibility stops in New York and London, Paris, Bonn and Tokyo. And then ... swish. Suddenly a big announcement will be made. That announcement mentmentmentmentmentwill read something as follows:

"The International Monetary Fund today concluded negotiations between Third World debtors and First World creditors for a restricted form of debt forgiveness. This totally unexpected breakthrough will serve to give new impetus for growth in developing countries, and release resources for their structural adjustment under continuing aegis of the international financial community. The Fund, in collaboration with the World Bank, has managed to achieve this remarkable result for the Third World in the face of ..."

Hurray! In 1990 we will become Third World heroes! From being villain and oppressor with "the blood of millions" staining our hands we will transform ourselves overnight into great benefactors of the poor, deserving finally of Third World trust. All our sins of the past will be forgiven; all our even-greater sins planned for post-1990 will thenceforth be ignored. After all, we delivered the goods when everyone else had given up hope. We delivered the goods the world thought could never be delivered. So now we can be left in peace to go on crushing the poor, as we had always done. We've won the right to crush, haven't we?

You know, Sir, what we would have done in announcing debt forgiveness then, and proclaiming our Third Worldliness in the process of announcing it, is to have chained the Third World into a new era of slavish dependence and naked exploitation and super-power political upmanship, far more comprehensive and intense than anything that had occurred over the past forty years. Under the contemplated scenario, what we would have done in 1990 is to achieve the ultimate logic of Pax Atlantica and Pax Honeypot rolled into one. What we would have done is to justify the fondest dream of Roosevelt and Churchill, and the Bretton Woods Founding Fathers that they had imposed on the Third World. What we would have done is to make 1990 a culmination of the Existing International Order, and to set the stage for an even more burdensome and unjust one for the Third World, with more and more death and destitution and displacement for two-thirds of humankind.

The above is a general statement. But I do not deal in generalities. So I turn now to the specifics of our hush-hush debt strategy, and its consequences, already planned, for the Third World.

3. ELEMENTS OF DEBT STRATEGY, 1983-1990

(a) Scope for Debt relief under the 1983-90 Debt Strategy

In discussing the debt crisis, a prior analytical task is to identify the scope for debt relief, and the specific modules to effect that relief that has been devised by the creditor cartel that we lead and that are being thrust down the throats of screaming Third World governments. In the IMF/World Bank/creditors' strategy for 1983-90, debt relief is defined as case by case marginal interest reduction and/or principal rescheduling exclusive of debt owed to the Fund and Bank, the original terms of which have been declared inviolable and non-negotiable. Now within the context of this basic 'relief' system, a plethora of supporting arrangements find expression - eg; the 'menu' package, the Paris Club approach, the 'swap' arrangement, concerted commercial bank lending, Multi-Year Rescheduling Arrangements. All these in turn rest on issue by the Fund of its seal of approval; invariably this means a Fund program in the country concerned. None of the above seemingly mickey mouse arrangements are benign; all are loaded with a high-powered, irresistible political motif that transcend by far the seemingly innocuous task of providing fleeting economic relief of greatest insignificance.

(i) Protecting all our Flanks by Means Foul or Fair

As we built up, over 1983-88, the interlocking elements of our play that would lead, in 1990, to the grand finale outlined above, certain operative elements become evident, viz:

(a) the need, over the period 1983-1990, to have a watertight system of punishment for those who dared to err from the established procedures for 'interim' debt relief;

(b) the need to fight back any suggestion that debt forgiveness, even in the long term, was a possibility;

(c) the need to make operational a system under which recourse to country 'conditioning' programs with the Fund and World Bank was the only policy path for debt ridden countries to follow;

(d) the need to assert and reassert to the Third World over 1983-90 that the Fund's "Third World debt policy' provides the only hope for 'structural adjustment' and economic growth in the South;

(e) the need to assert and reassert to the Third World that the Fund's 'Third World debt policy' could conceivably impact favorably on what we loosely choose to call 'poverty' and 'the poor'.

Let us review just how we have succeeded in making the above Fund-related imperatives a part of ongoing international ethos.

ii) The Punishment System for Erring Countries

On this matter we have been spectacularly successful. We have drawn the teeth of all countries, or groups of countries, that harboured thoughts of going, or actually attempted to go, against existing orthodoxy, as defined to mean the methods and expectations of the established order, represented by the conclusions of the G7 on Third World debt, and by the creditor's cartel that we have established, and that we so effectively chair. Indeed, our punishment for erring countries have been immediate and withering.

To see this one just has to look at the Peruvian abortive experiment to contain its debt crisis, or the fate of countries like Brazil and Argentina and Nigeria that tried to flirt with 'national' debt solutions, or the outcome of attempts at 'regional solutions'. Concomitantly, the Fund and other members of the creditors' cartel have always managed to repress, immediately and completely, any attempt to organize what can remotely be perceived as a 'debtors' cartel'. We did manage to get this obedience in the South, and to bring protesting debtors to their knees, by unscrupulously declaring miscreants ineligible for use of our resources, irrespective of circumstance - eg; whether external factors beyond their control were responsible for their inability to repay, or whether they deliberately took a decision to defy us thus. By mid-1988 several countries were so declared and others were on the verge of being blacklisted. Our declaration of ineligibility constitutes the kiss of death for all these countries. They immediately became international lepers, with no hope of making operational any other alternative to the Fund's iron fist.

(iii) Ensuring that No Alternatives to Debt Conditioning Programs are Allowed to Exist

Under the 1983-90 debt strategy, the need to make operational an international system under which recourse to 'conditioning' programs of the Fund becomes the only viable path to be followed by countries of the Third World is imperative. And such 'boxing in' of the South by the Fund has indeed been quite successful. To see that, it is important to define more carefully the term 'conditioning' The latter reflects several conceptually different objectives built into our on-going relationship with developing member countries that use our resources. The first refers to the 'program' as a vehicle to achieve the objective of privatising the economy - ie; as the means to convert an economic system, whatever it may have been, or whatever it is, to a preconceived type of free wheeling market system. The initial requirement, of course, is to establish appropriate laws and institutions (for example, foreign investment law, trade and exchange system law, pricing system law, landholding law, company law) through program conditionality. Another definition of 'conditioning' relates not to the objective of conversion in the sense of creating a legal and institutional framework, but to the specific 'program' modules to be used to flesh out the framework, (eg; pre-determined varients of taxation policy, interest rate policy, domestic pricing policy, trade and exchange rate policies).

A related meaning of 'conditioning' is as follows: the final emergence of a system whose social, economic and political costs are absorbed entirely by the "authorities." This requirement, in turn, could lead directly to the government concerned becoming replaced or overthrown because of loss of popular support inherent in the adverse traumatic economic and social impact of the Fund program that it attempts to implement. Such an outcome may well bring into the forefront a military dictatorship aided and abetted by certain major western powers - a dictatorship whose ruthlessness ('efficiency' in our language) in suppressing people's rights in the process of "implementing" our program makes emergence of the type of economic system we want created more plausible than it was before.

For countries with more democratic leanings and resilience, the process of absorbing the economic and political costs of our program may mean substitution of one elected government for another, with the second government finding no more success in implementing the program than the first. Under this scenario, the off-on, on-off, off-on program charade becomes endemic, and continuous political instability becomes a way of life that ensures, among other things, that the program will never be implemented, and the country will never receive international support.

The scenario for such a country is easy to see: an initial IMF declaration that it is ineligible to draw resources pledged under the program because it has violated performance criteria, followed by an announcement that it is ineligible to use any and every form of our resources, because of the build up of arrears in repayment. With this announcement, the country concerned enters into the ranks of international leper countries. In our system, it becomes write off from everything we have to offer, including all forms of on-going debt relief, and designated debt forgiveness scheduled for 1990. The only outcome that may save such a country from our own peculiar jaws of death is another death - i.e.; the emergence of a tyrannical, military dictatorship that would take up the cudgel and implement our program from the ashes of the previous democratic process that we did so deliberately destroy.

Another 'conditioning' factor of our Third World programs is, of course, the timing; everything must be made to occur in concert among countries and across continents at the same time, so that 1990 can become the watershed date when we declare past debt forgiveness in a totally 'conditioned' South, and start anew again on our path of death and destitution.

4. 'CONDITIONING' TO CREATE THE NEW LEGAL AND INSTITUTIONAL FRAMEWORK FOR A FREE WHEELING MARKET ECONOMY

About five years ago President Reagan effectively told us to go out and make the Third World a new bastion of free wheeling capitalism, and how we responded with joy, and with a sense of mission! Of course the entire strategy for propagating Third World economic rebirth into unfettered free enterprise economies was finalized and explicitly stated in the Baker Plan of 1985 and in the eligibility criteria to Enhanced Structural Adjustment Facility to the 62 'poorest' countries of the world. Thus everything we did from 1983 onward was based on our new sense of mission to have the south 'privatised' or die; towards this end we ignominiously created economic bedlam in Latin America and Africa in 1983-88.

It is proper that we take a hard, cold look at the performance of our programs in achieving the country related objectives of economic growth and stabilisation that we said they would achieve. And in doing this 'program review' (if you will consent to call it that) I will subsume our tactic of transforming institutions and establishing new legal frameworks into that of creating new modules and specifying policy instruments to bring our New Jerusalem of "Reaganomics" to a supplicant and traumatized Third World.

(a) The Fund and Free-Wheeling Capitalism in the Third World, 1983-88

There really are two phases of our operations over 1983-88; it is necessary to distinguish these so as to show the disastrous consequences of Fund policies and programs over this period. In Phase I, defined as 1983-85, we reeked havoc in the South. In Phase II, 1986-88, we attempted to use the so-called "Baker Plan framework" to continue our virtual enslavement of the South in an even more comprehensive and systematic way than during Phase 1. The structural Adjustment facility (1986) and Expanded Structural Adjustment Facility (1987) became basic ingredients of our overall debt strategy; they became the major instruments that would lead us to the projected 'glorious' culmination of 1990.

(b) Phase 1

Over Phase 1, our austerity programs, as expressed primarily in 12 to 18 months stand-by arrangements, involved a sharp diminution of the role of the state in economic life, manifested through performance criteria that involved drastic contraction of indigenous public sectors, sharply reduced government expenditures on both current and capital account and far less accommodation than customary in Fund programs on the size of fiscal deficits and external current account shortfalls. In turn, such Fund desiderata dictated unprecedented cutbacks in public sector recourse to central bank and banking system credit, massive devaluation of exchange rates, virtual price decontrol in the domestic economy, rising inflation, precipitous drops in real wage rates, escalating domestic interest rates - all to be achieved within the short, one-year-or-thereabouts period of stand-by arrangements. Of course, the establishment of an 'appropriate' legal and institutional free wheeling market framework was 'built-into' our programs, invariably in the form of 'prior action' and 'program requirements'. Establishment of the new framework involved changes in wage setting and wage arbitration procedures, the rewriting of foreign investment laws and foreign investment incentive schemes, effectuation of new trade and exchange control regimes, new domestic pricing systems, new public utility pricing arrangements, new banking and credit laws, and new processes to diminish drastically the role of the state in economic and social life.

The results of our 1983-85 programs, constructed and implemented under the above imperatives, are now in; our own investigations have brought to light some startling facts. Of the 30 stand-by programs negotiated in 1983 and the 21 negotiated in 1984, fourteen and eleven respectively were aborted in those years. In 1983 only 68 per cent of IMF resources approved under stand-by arrangements were actually drawn (as against 79 percent in 1982); by 1985 this proportion had fallen to 43 percent. On the question of performance in relation to program objectives, the following tell their own story; viz:

- in 63 per cent of all cases in 1983, 59 per cent in 1984, and 58 per cent in 1985, economic growth targets were never realized;

- in 54 per cent of all cases in 1983, 63 per cent in 1984 and 58 per cent in 1985, the inflation rate was higher than programmed.

- On balance of payments aggregates, the current account deficit turned out worse than targeted in 40 percent of all cases in 1983, 44% in 1984 and 53 percent in 1985.

- turning to the debt situation of countries with stand-by programs with the Fund over 1983-85, external debt as a percentage of GDP rose in 70% of all cases during the three year period under consideration;

- the growth in arrears of payment by programmed countries escalated by 61 per cent in 1983, and continued to rise in 1984 and 1985 by 26 per cent and 16 per cent respectively (with Brazil's arrears excluded from the latter year).

- debt servicing obligations as measured by the debt servicing ratio (total debt servicing obligations as a percent of exports of goods and services) rose between 1983- 85 in 75 per cent of all countries with Fund programs. Such obligations more than doubled in a wide range of 'programed' countries, including Ghana, Guatemala, Malawi, Uganda, Uruguay, Zaire, Zambia and Zimbabwe.

These, Sir, are not minor deviations from targeted objectives; they represent a mass failure during Phase 1 of the Debt Strategy of our programs to achieve anything near what we had been promised in terms of financial stabilisation and economic growth. Yet even as these programs were failing so dismally, their mind-boggling costs in terms of the deepening and widening of poverty levels, and the alarming growth in human misery in the South was becoming more and more evident. As you are aware, UNICEF, in its recent study, ADJUSTMENT WITH A HUMAN FACE, has zeroed in on the traumatic and catalytic impact of our programs on poverty and human destitution over the period concerned. This almost unbearable sacrifice by southern people did not lead to any hope for the future. In spite of Fund programs, or more appropriately, because of them, there was more economic bedlam and backsliding in southern economies by the mid-80s than at any time over the past forty years.

Nor should we forget the political cost of these programs in succoring, or leading directly to the emergence of regimes of economic rape and terror in designated countries of Latin America and the Caribbean, Africa and Asia. These costs, inclusive of the drastic diminution of human rights and democracy, are probably as great as the already endless cost of sheer human suffering and degradation.

(c) Phase II

Phase II of the Debt Plot, 1986-88, stemmed from the "Baker Initiative" to maintain the integrity and content of monetarist, market-oriented adjustment programs to change economic structures and philosophies in the south, even in the face of the experience of an almost total debacle of Fund programs in 1983-85.

Our major instigators (shareholders) alarmed by that debacle, came to us and said something like this:-

"The thrust is right, the objectives noble, but hey! Let's do a little fine tuning. To begin with, you must take on a more high visibility role as leader of the creditors' cartel on Third World debt. Go ahead and do that! Stiffen the conditionality so that Free Wheeling Capitalism can roll off the assembly line at a faster pace! Give more economic rewards to our ultra-rightist military dictators and our well-to-do Third World conspirators and fellow travellers. Push the poor more into their little corner, and make sure that they stay there. And to get the ball a-rolling, use

the Baker Plan. Let it be as the base for a new set of instruments for transforming Third World societies."

"And use new jargon; for heaven's sake, use new jargon! Don't say 'Demand Management' anymore. Say 'Structural Adjustment' instead.

That's the magic word. That's the new talisman. And work fast. We don't have much time; all conditioning processes must be completed almost instantaneously in the most heavily indebted countries of the South. Once we have those in the bag, the rest will follow suit. Get on, Fund, with the New and Revised Strategy! Show us the stuff you're made of!"

Well, we tried our best to satisfy our masters, but well ... it just didn't work out as planned. We started to use the structural adjustment jargon, but nothing happened. Over and over we'd ride through in our spanking new Steamroller (Heaviest) shouting "Structural Adjustment Ahoy! Structural Adjustment Ahoy!" But that didn't seem to have the same impact as when Ali Baba said "Open Sesame, Open!" But somehow we could never bring ourselves to believe that there may be no magic, after all, in our words. We really became scared.

Yet we never stopped to think through in our mind what must have happened; we were in a mad rush to complete Privatisation and establish the Free Wheel in the South within our pre-determined time frame. In the circumstances, we could arrive at just one conclusion, viz;- if Bakerite stand-by programs didn't work, something else, already in our control, must do the trick for us.

So again we put our heads together with our First World cohorts and came up with a second New and Revised plan, which was in fact a rerun of the first New and Revised Plan, viz: when the going gets tough and the South cannot perform, stiffen the conditionality; that will serve to put the little devils in their places; that will take good care of them.

Seemingly lacking a capacity to see the South except in terms of our Overwhelming Power there, and its overriding duty to capitulate to our wishes and our myths, we said to ourselves in 1986: "Let us remove all elements of recipient discretion from our programs. Let us state explicitly and unequivocally what the Third World blighters must be made to do, and when and how they must be made to do it. Such a tactic will surely bring Structural Adjustment and Free Wheeling Capitalism into every nook and corner of the world. Let us put Sub-Sahara Africa and Asia under heavy manners. Let us bring, through Expanded Structural Adjustment Facilities, Policy Framework Papers to Ministers of Finance for their signature. Let us state in Policy Framework Papers the particular measures for effecting Privatisation and concomitant construction of the Free Wheel; let us give the countries of the South specific things to do in specific months, and even during specific weeks of specific months. Let us finally put a particular cut-off point for completing our task of effecting Reaganomics and Thatcheromics in the South. Such a timetable will give us just the zip we need to twist the arm of miscreant countries so that all that needs to be broken can become broken well in time for our Grand Finale in 1990."

So did arise the three-year SAF and ESAF, with a deadline of October, 1989 for eligible countries to access the Facility. So, too, did arise our target date of 1990 for making our triumphant announcement that we had become a Santa Clause after over forty years of ...

Hey, Where am I?

I started off resolutely, with every intention of making a no-nonsense technical analysis of our programs, their successes and failures, and their implications for the South over Phase 11 of our on-going debt strategy. But somehow I had to become diverted; somehow I had to reorient and 'personalise' the discussion; somehow I had to get back into my bad old ways of letting my feelings show. Shame on you, Budhoo! When will you ever learn? Do the right thing now before it is too late - tell the good gentleman whom you are addressing that you want to make amends.

No, no I will not take that advice. For really, Sir, I do not want to make amends. I want to keep on the public record what I did say above, for it is the truth. But perhaps I can restate that truth in more formal and precise terms, and make it to be more structured and rigorously analytical. Yes, I'll try my hand at that, so wish me the best of luck as I change the tone again.

5. PHASE 11 RESTATED

The purpose of the Baker Plan that officially ina gurated Phase 11 can be stated simply and, hopefully, non- controversially. It was to create a common policy posture by the Fund, the World Bank, official donors and major creditor banks vis-a-vis heavily indebted countries of the South facing difficulties in debt repayments. The common posture related to the nature and quantum of, and conditionality for, debt relief along lines already detailed. Formally put in terms of a system to ensure that at least some marginal amounts of new funds became available to initiate and help finance "structural adjustment," while 'cooperating countries' continued to service their debt (perhaps on new terms), the Baker Plan soon became the role model for all Fund financial arrangements from 1986 onwards.

In so far as creditor countries and institutions wer e concerned, these arrangements brought to the fore a set of new relationships that challenged the very nature and basis of multilateralism as the latter had evolved since 1946. With regards to developing countries, such arrangements crystallized the system through which free-wheeling capitalism would invade the South, conditioning the latter for some form of debt forgiveness in 1990, while leaving in its wake a legacy of officially-sponsored human destitution unparalleled to anything that had ever happened before.

6. HUMAN DESTITUTION RELATED TO PHASE 11

Let's deal first with human destitution released by Phase 11 in the South. And on this matter the line of enquiry is clear-cut, viz: the way we put "structural adjustment" as traditionally defined and universally understood, to stand on its head so as to pave the way for our grand coup in 1990, and the human and economic cost of fooling the world thus.

In Part VI of the Letter, the very important issue of Fund policies and philosophies, and the fundamental divergence of the latter from mainstream development economics is taken up in the context of the poverty impact of Fund policies through time and our contribution to Third World economic and social woes over the last four decades. Here the analysis, related specifically to our current debt strategy, is far more concentrated, highlighting, as it does, the Fund's role as "hit man" for others in an on-going and well-conceived political plot with well-defined, determinate objectives to be achieved within a specified time-frame. Both types of analysis boil down to the question of the rationale and implications of our own peculiar brand of "structural adjustment".

(a) Redefining Structural Adjustment

You know, Sir, when we use the term "structural adjustment," we wish to convey to those who are being "structually adjusted" the idea of economic and financial policies to get the economy out of an economic hole and place it on a path of sustainable growth and social transformation within a context of indigenously-determined economic and social priorities and trade-offs among desirable objectives, and within a time-frame defined by our 'program.' But there is a big difference what we want others to believe, and what we know to be true. For us the term "structural adjustment" conveys a politically inspired ploy, as against an economic concept that can be measured and evaluated in relation to some criterion of economic efficiency and optimal resource use by the recipient. More specifically, when we talk of "structural adjustment" we have nothing else in mind but an irresistible motivation to implement, in every country of the South, the following political agenda: to call an immediate and complete stop to economic policies that can be interpreted as being in the slightest degree 'socialist' or 'populist' or 'people- oriented', or weighted, however slightly, in favour of the poor and economically underprivileged, or based on the collective, social consensus of the population concerned. All such policies, if they exist, must be summarily scratched, and substituted forthwith with the type of Reaganite free-wheeling capitalism that is so comprehensively built into our 12 to 18 month stand-by arrangements, and our 3 year SAF and ESAF.

Now as we implement, in each country of the South, t his agenda for political transformation, we have no expectation whatsoever that our policies would lead to economic development or enhancement of the social welfare function of our Third World clients; in no instance do we aspire to have our program set the stage for sustained economic and social transformation - a goal that we hoodwink others to believe that we are out to achieve, Yes, yes, Sir. We hide behind the mask of 'structural adjustment' - a concept with great respectability in economics, to do political things in Third World nations that make all known precepts of economics to look like old hat. You know, sooner or later someone will have to start rewriting the economics of developing countries in terms of the basic precept of IMF political imperatives that relate directly to the on-going debt strategy of creditor nations and institutions.

(b) Detailing our Politically Inspired Prerogatives

Well, I suppose at this stage it behooves me to become extremely specific about our politically-inspired prerogatives.

Of course such prerogatives have been stated very explicitly in relation to the Trinidad and Tobago program that was detailed in Parts 11 and 111 of this Letter. That program, I repeat, is the Fund's standard bag of tricks for all countries of the South. Now beyond the Parts 11/111 expose, I have restated our prerogatives in this Section, albeit in a different context. At an even more precise level, I will now proceed to analyse, in as comprehensive and as complete a way as possible, the content and conditionality of the five SAF programs that were made effective in 1986 and early 1987, in furtherance of designated Phase 11 objectives of the Debt Strategy. These programs were designed for, and their implementation attempted in Ghana, Mozambique, Senegal, Tanzania and Zambia.

The Attachment to this Part of the Letter gives details of measures in PFPs that the Fund forced designated countries to agree to as official conditionality for accessing the facility. The inter-country comparison lists macro-economic and sectorial measures along the wide range of economic 'handles' that we use to achieve our own brand of "structural adjustment."

Some very important observations can be made from examining the table. Among them is the amazing volume and multiplicity of policy measures that we demand of countries who aspire to use our SAF resources. In Ghana, for example, 92 specific measures were scheduled for implementation in the PFP, 37 of a general nature and 55 in the sectorial sphere. Comparable figures for Mozambique were, respectively, 48, 15 and 33; for Senegal 60, 19 and 41; for Tanzania 29, 17 and 12; for Zambia 30, 20 and 10. The average number of measures for all the countries considered were 52, of which 22 were macro-economic and 30 sectorial.

With regard to the distribution of measures between the two broad categories some very outstanding facts are evident. On the macro-economic side, the measures laid down for all the countries in the four categories identified - i.e. fiscal policies, monetary policies, exchange and trade system and external debt - were chillingly the same. Virtually all countries were asked to undertake tax reform, reducing the tax burden on the wealthy and increasing it on the poor through more indirect taxation. Calls for expenditure cuts through public sector wage reduction, and cuts in - indeed, in some instances, elimination of - subsidies and transfers to the poor, were widespread. So, too, were curtailment of social services that had previously been targeted to alleviate the plight of the economically disadvantaged. On monetary policies, the core requirement was increases in interest rates to international levels (those prevailing in the United States and Western Europe) irrespective of the developmental needs and and the particular economic and financial circumstances of the country concerned. There were also several directives to 'improve' the banking system through legal action. Also, to make effective the required cuts in government expenditure on the poorest sectors of society, all countries were forced to ration severely banking system credit to the public sector and to increase it to the privileged, well- heeled 'private sector' - invariably to finance the higher consumption levels of the latter group, and to enhance their capacity to import luxury items under a vastly liberalized import system that concomitantly must be instituted as an integral and indispensable part of our 'program'. This latter condition was a basic requirement for all of the countries analysed.

Devaluation, of course, was required everywhere, either directly and immediately, or subsequently, through instrumentality of specific institutional arrangements to maintain 'flexible exchange rates'. (As acknowledged explicitly in Fund publications that were earlier mentioned, devaluation hits hardest the poorest sectors of society through real wage cuts and inflation, and through the welter of Fund-supported measures such as price controls and subsidy reductions that must be brought into force to ensure that the impact of devaluation pervades the whole economy). Another feature underlying all programs was relaxation of exchange controls to allow our favored elite to transfer domestic savings overseas to West European and North American banks.

On external debt, all countries were exhorted to reduce the debt service burden through activation of the "debt relief" package, and through strict limits on new borrowing or other recourse to international finance, thus throwing back the burden of the horrendous 'adjustment' being asked for on the domestic economy, and more specifically, on the poor, and least-able-to-cope economic and social sectors of the domestic economy. Such limitations on new foreign borrowing were being demanded at a time when our favored elite classes of the South were being given more and more of a free hand, through measures deliberately built into Fund programs, including, as already mentioned, the relaxation or elimination of external control regimes, to massively drain the country concerned of its own financial resources (domestically generated savings) through unfettered capital flight. The implications of such capital flight, and our role in energizing that flight, are taken up later in this Section.

The sectorial measures, like the macro-economic ones , comprise a standard, rigid package of Reaganomics applied indiscriminately across the board for all the countries investigated. The core element was privatisation of public sector enterprises; in the five countries concerned, almost 100 enterprises, including public utilities, were earmarked for privatisation. There was also a depressing repetition of agricultural policies being interpreted to mean the removal of state subsidies and price increases to domestic consumers. Turning to the industrial, transport and energy sectors, price increases, privatisation and miniaturisation or removal of state support were common features. Of course, those who suffer most from such "price reorganization" and "market orientation" imperatives of the Fund are the urban poor, trying either to eke out a living as unskilled workers in production or service sectors, or as unemployed shanty town dwellers, already in hopeless destitution.

Now let me turn to another dimension of operations i n the Third World under the "rules of the game" of Phase 11. And in doing so, I will for one moment forget the nature and purpose of Fund programs under the Debt Strategy and their dramatically adverse impact on the poor, and return to the theme of the failure of such programs to achieve anything remotely approaching their smokescreen objective of improving the balance of payments, reducing inflation, eliciting economic growth, et al. And in this respect, let me say immediately that the 1986/87 programs, as analysed by the Fund itself, failed more dismally along the whole spectrum of smokescreen objectives than did the 1983/85 programs that were examined above. It may well be that for the High Priests this issue is of no relevance, since Fund performance in relation to the smokescreen objectives is not really a factor in anyone's calculations. But let us indulge ourselves and examine the question nonetheless. Let us at least make that ex post concession to Third World acute dismay and growing perplexities about what we are doing to them.

That our programs, over the entire period of the Strategy, have failed so dismally to impact positively on the economic and financial conditions of developing countries is related to a simple fact that I think you would readily concede. You know, for the last five years we have been asking countries to transform themselves instantaneously, from whatever they were before, to a homogenized, new packaged brand of free wheeling capitalism, all elements of which are contained in our programs. As we implement thus our "quickie" policy package for changing economic and political systems and ideologies in the Third World, we find the following:- The policy package conflicts fundamentally not only with the financial stabilisation and economic growth objectives that we had promised to deliver through its implementation, but equally importantly, and irrespective of conflict, the airy-fairy idea of changing economic and political systems overnight to suit our purpose just will not work. Yet as we trash around in frustration in the South, intent only on giving more and more unworkable medicine to its peoples, the terrible economic cost of our futile operations - a cost that could be dramatically lightened with a bit more realism on our part - becomes more and more horrendous. And that cost, in our scenario, must be borne entirely by the societies that we are "transforming", and more specifically on its poorest and most economically vulnerable sectors.

Obviously, I cannot go into this matter at any depth in this Letter, so let me just list a few home truths for your High Priests to think about.

As we seek instant, political transformation of countries by forcing them to implement, over the life of our program, the all-enfolding set of measures as outlined in Table 1, we are really asking them overnight to turn straw into gold (or perhaps, more appropriately, the opposite). In the PFP for Ghana, for instance, we asked that country to implement 97 major measures, with more to come for Years Two and Three of the program. Implementation of each of these measures involves very careful preparatory work and the establishment of administrative structures - sometimes very elaborate administrative structures. Neither Ghana or any other Third World country has the type of administrative/organizational/institutional infrastructure to score so heavily for us over so short a time. (Remember that in every program we are asking the administration concerned to cut back on public sector staff). Of course we can continue to fool ourselves that we can go into a country and administer the program ourselves (through a Resident Representative and a continuous stream of other "technical assistance" inputs). Such a ploy, however, is the perfect recipe for the type of abysmal failures that we have been having; it defines the naked recolonialisation of countries still smarting under the economic and psychological wounds of the former master; it will never work. And you must remember that as we are burdening the country concerned with a totally unrealistic load of administrative overwork inherent in our programs, the World Bank, because of us, is doing exactly the same through its reinforcing "Structural Adjustment" lending, whose conditionality is additional to policy measures written into PFPs.

The logic, need one say, is to relax the intensity and comprehensiveness of our politically oriented conditionality. But such a move would be seen as defeating the whole purpose of the exercise, and jeopardizing seriously the integrity of the Debt Strategy Timetable. Doubtlessly it will bring our major instigators on our back, howling with rage.

You know, of course, that this is exactly what happened in 1987. Seemingly concerned about the lack of 'quickie' results in establishing the Free Wheel in the South, one of our mightiest shareholders took matters directly in hand, bypassing your authority and demanding from individual staff members the Free Wheel content of programs negotiated, and the performance of countries in implementing crucial aspects of Reaganomics. I tell you, Sir, this shook us up. It shook us up real good. We didn't know anymore what master we were serving. But let that matter rest; it can only divert attention from the more immediate issues being addressed here. I mention it merely to illustrate the very tenuous base from which we work, and the fact that we are now at zero hour; there is no more time for further experimentation on how best to get the Free Wheel a-moving in the South. There is no time to determine whether our political prerogatives can be attained at less cost to 'program' countries, and with less damage to their social welfare function. From all appearances, the dice is cast, and all we have to do now is let Steamroller (Heaviest) do its stuff, driven by High Priests and Not-So- High-Priests, transformed into Werewolves at Full Moon. But I went through all that in the discussion on Trinidad and Tobago; I don't have to repeat myself here.

7. A NEW SET OF RELATIONSHIPS FOR FIRST WORLD ENTITIES

I turn now to the reorganization of relationships among First World entities and the Fund/World Bank that has occurred over the last five to ensure that the objectives of the Debt Strategy are achieved. In this respect, three different sets of relationships can be distinguished; viz: relationships between the Fund and the World Bank; relationships between the Fund/World Bank and creditor commercial banks; and relationships between the Fund/World Bank and creditor countries.

(a) Fund/World Bank Relationships

The changed nature of the relationship between the Fund and the World Bank since the onslaught of the debt crisis mirrors the complimentary and mutually reinforcing role that the institutions are supposed to play under the Debt Strategy. With "structural adjustment" as the talisman to bring our new act together in the Third World, it was natural that Fund management would see the World Bank - involved traditionally in medium and long-term developmental strategies for the South - as a critical player in its game. It is true that we knew all that was to be done in the type of "structural adjustment" we had in mind, and how to do it. But for appearances' sake, we had to bring in the World Bank and tell the world that we could draw profusely on its expertise in designing and implementing our programs for "structural adjustment." And in addition, of course, we had to use that institution's financial resources and its Third World clout to buttress our watertight, comprehensive, "structurally adjustment" related conditionality.

Before going into the actual relationship of the World Bank and the Fund under Phase 11, a little bit of history is necessary.

You will recall that the origin of the SAF was an initiative of the United States Administration in late 1985 to use Trust Fund repayments to initiate formally our brand of "Structural Adjustment" under the new facility. At that time, it was envisaged that IDA, under Replemishment 7, together with the World Bank African Fund, would come on strongly in providing additional "structural adjustment" lending to countries using SAF resources. No enhancement, then, of SAF resources, funded by donor countries, was envisaged. The expectation was that all official donor concessional financing of a multilateral nature would go to IDA for longer term developmental needs of poor countries.

The Fund's initiative to establish ESAF and to get c oncessional financing for it from major shareholders, was equally an act to dilute IDA's 8th replenishment, and to increase dramatically the conditionality of all IDA-type funds available within the international system - i.e., to put Fund-type conditionality on financial resources - resources that were intended to further longer term transformation of countries via the World Bank's more mainstream perception of that term. Of course, this coup by the Fund was part and parcel of our debt strategy to 'condition' the South.

The World Bank at first reacted with anger and vehemence at our siphoning off of a substantial proportion of what otherwise would have been IDA resources, and also at our attempt to bring into the multilateral system, in the name of structural adjustment, the naked brand of political conditioning of the Third World that we were out to achieve in the Third World.

At this stage, I would not wish to embarrass you or the Bank by going into details of the Bank's "anger and vehemence" at our temerity in 'stealing' its resources. However, it behooves me to mention the Bank's scathing reaction to our design of PFPs. The Bank, of course, prepares PFPs jointly with us, and its management has to approve them before they become operational blueprints for transforming Third World societies.

Towards the end of 1986, some six months after the S AF came into operation, the Bank gave its reaction to the Fund's "blueprint" SAF, including the conditionality elements underlying it. In this reaction, the Bank stated that it would be inappropriate to focus primarily, as the Fund was insisting, "on the fiscal and monetary issues which would affect external and domestic equilibrium, in these growth oriented strategy papers.... Given the adjustments to be undertaken, we believe it essential that governments should be encouraged to address the social aspects of the adjustment process in the PFPs. This is no more a political aspect of the development process than a devaluation. In any event, the Board insists that this issue be covered... (The) growth process has many dimensions."

Well, did we heed the advice of the Bank? No, we didn't. One just has to refer to Attachment 2 to see how it all turned out in the end.

If the Bank, in 1986, was showing a high level of professional propriety, and vehemently protesting our monetarist and "political" approach in the South, how come, subsequent to 1986, that institution became such a pliant and junior partner in our game, towing the line and letting us call all the shots? What was the magic ingredient in this Bank transformation overnight? How come that in Trinidad and Tobago for instance, that institution could change, so drastically and so cowardly, the content of its report, and the objective analysis of its own professional staff, in response to the rantings and ravings of the Fund?

The answer, I suggest, is not simple; there are sev eral elements.

One important reason is that, apparently because of an initial breakdown in communication somewhere along the line, staff and management of the Bank were not sufficiently made aware in 1986 of the perversity and comprehensiveness of the Phase 11 Debt Strategy, and the strength of the imperatives that we were after through "structural adjustment" a la Reaganomics. After its initial outburst and expression of outrage at our conduct in the Third World, the Bank received quick enlightenment as to what the game was all about, and how it should play it. There is ample documentation of the process and methods of this enlightenment; some of that documentation, if revealed, could well put the skids on the some very significant dimensions of the on-going debt strategy. But I'm not prepared yet to raise thus the temperature of the Third World. Let's just leave that matter resting and get on with the analysis in hand.

World Bank enlightenment of the crucial nature of what we were doing for the Cause led, at first, to admiration of us, but admiration soon gave way to slavish imitation of Fund inspired policies and operations in the Bank's own Third World relations. It is not that the Bank succumbed to the Fund under duress, reluctantly recognizing that the latter's narrow focus on "monetary and fiscal issues" must be given equal weight to its broader focus springing from a conviction that "the growth process has many dimensions." Rather, what happened in the metamorphosis is that the Bank embraced the Fund's "focus" as its very own; all its "structural adjustment" operations in the South became defined in relation to the same "monetary and fiscal" elements and perspectives that it was decrying so vehemently as late as October, 1986. Put another way, the crystallization of joint World Bank/Fund conditionality for Third World "structural adjustment" programs after 1986 did not result in the emergence of a series of consistent short and long term economic and financial measures that conceivably could lead to economic development and enhancement of the social welfare function of the Third World country concerned. Instead, the Bank saw its task as follows: - to provide a safety net - a back-up system - that would serve to guarantee that the Fund's politically-inspired "structural adjustment" be given every chance of success.

One instrument through which this major objective is to be accomplished is the Structural Adjustment Loan, reserved for those lower income countries that have satisfied the Fund's "structural adjustment" conditionality for the SAF and ESAF, or for middle income, heavily-indebted countries harnessed to the Fund's pre-packaged, "growth-oriented" stand-by arrangement that is the essential prerequisite for debt relief under the rules of the strategy. Structural Adjustment Loans are predominantly for "Trade Reform" that negates every aspect of the Bank's role as a developmental institution. Elements of "trade reform" to be effected almost overnight under the Bank facility are as follows:- reduction or removal of import tax exemptions to producers for the domestic market, increase in import tax exemptions to foreign investors and others producing for export markets; "rationalization" of taxes and tax rates, with high-bracket income and corporation taxes declining, and indirect taxes, including taxes on essential domestically-produced and imported goods, consumed by the poor, rising spectacularly; institution of VAT or other consumption tax across the board and falling disproportionately on the economically disadvantaged sectors of society.

The significance of World Bank "Structural Adjustment Loans" with this standardized conditionality content, the economic and social impact of which was described extensively in of Part 111, is clear enough. Like the Fund, the Bank is now prepared to denominate its 'program' lending operations not in terms of a determinate impact of its assistance in widening the economic base of recipient economies, or in terms of creating conditions for an improvement in retained domestic savings and domestic investment, or even in terms of an improvement of "absorptive capacity" or a deepening of "developmental institutional infrastructure," but very explicitly and crudely in terms of the achievement of a set of politically-inspired objectives whose economic consequences over the past five years have proved to be nothing but the creation of economic conditions that breed greater unemployment, destitution and social unrest in some of the world's most economically vulnerable and politically unstable regimes. With the World Bank's capitulation, the "scorched earth" Fund system for the South is now totally unbounded.

(b) Fund/Commercial Banks' Relationships

On the changed nature of our relationships with commercial banks, I wish to focus on one matter, viz;- the role of the commercial banks in telling us what to do under the logic and discipline of the Debt Strategy. Everybody's somebody fool, you know, and while the World Bank is our fool, we are the fool of the commercial banks.

However much you may deny it publicly, the only tangible achievement of the Fund since 1983 is to bail out the commercial banks from the logical consequences of their self-serving Third World lending during the 70's. This signal Fund achievement can be seen by looking at three inter-related factors - the evidence of commercial bank lending over the period of the Debt Strategy; our own mad stampede in the last three years to compel governments to go into "Structural Adjustment" programs without adequate financing; and our forcing of the self-same governments into accepting speculative financing packages that are outrageously overpriced, inefficient and short-term, with no certainty regarding quantum of funds or time schedule for disbursement. In return for honoring the Third World with net funds amounting to -US$16 billion in 1986/87, the commercial banks embarked, through us, on a heady and independent program to establish their own macro-economic conditionality, the logical consequence of which was the destruction of more Third World children, on top of the millions already destroyed, or earmarked for destruction, through our own Sentence, and that of the World Bank that we ourselves had written.

It seems to me that we are putting all "logic of the marketplace" to stand on its head - a "logic" that we refer to ad nauseam in our dealings with the Third World, and that guides, according to us, everything that we do there - when we make, as we do everyday, a statement like the following to the commercial banks: -

"In the 70's you were very imprudent in your accelerated lendings to certain Third World entities. As you were fully aware then, your lendings did not go into the financing of economic development. They were used for the purchase of military hardware from our major shareholders, for the financing of wasteful construction projects ordered by corrupt dictators and their cohorts, and for capital flight. Sometimes the loans that you made - and you know this and have concurred in it - never even got to the shores of the country that you were lending to; they ended up instead in private bank accounts in New York and Geneva and London. Bribery, kickbacks and commissions were the order of the day. You got your full share, and you made sure that your principals and co-conspirators in the Third World got theirs too."

"The line between legality and illegality was thin, very thin; but you and yours straddled every atom of it. You knew the risks you were taking, and the risk premium that you were demanding was high, very high. You knew fully well the chances of what is happening now actually occurring, and you discounted for that possibility in your price."

"The laws of the market that we swear on and live by tell us that you must now cut your losses and weasel out of this yourself. The laws of the market tell us that as an international manager we should only be involved in the task of helping to provide orderly conditions within which the market process of resolving the debt crisis could run its full course. You as an independent transactor should get together with the other independent transactor involved (the Third World country concerned) and try to find mutual accommodation within the logic of the marketplace - a logic that to date has guided every inch of your operations, and determined every cent of your profit."

But, you know, commercial banks, we are not talking about a rational line of reasoning here; we are not talking about evenhandedness and justice in the international system; we are not applying the same maxims of the market to you that we are applying to the Third World. You and us; we are one. We are kith and kin; we are of the First World; we obey the same master; we were born to kick around the poor of the South, and to murder little children there. We were born to connive with each other to achieve a common end."

"Discipline of the marketplace for us? What utter nonsense!

Our calling goes far beyond that. We do not even need to put up a smokescreen; we do not even need to pretend that we are trying to practice what we preach. Lucky, lucky us, and lucky, lucky you!"

"Well now, commercial banks, back to business in the wake of our studied forgetfulness about market forces and market motivation and entrepreneurship risk and the reality of total bankruptcy in all these southern countries. Between now and 1990 we will keep the pot boiling over for you so that you can get on with your shady deals, and get and give more kickbacks and commissions, and continue in all the sleaziness and shoddiness of the last twenty years - sleaziness and shoddiness that have been brought out so vividly in recent research by independent investigators. We will not only open up the South for you to make more shady deals than you had ever made in the past, but will share with you our own boundless power there. Yes, yes, we'll give you authority to make or break governments, and we'll put out the little children for you to kill too. We are brothers, you know. What are brothers for if not to help each other realize a full potential? "

You say I'm exaggerating? Well, consider the following facts, and explain them to the survivors of our continuing holocaust.

- over 1983-88, the Fund's Executive Board repeatedly approved stand-by arrangements with Third World countries that were contingent on the commercial banks, ex post, agreeing to provide specified levels of concerted lending; only in 1 case out of 27 between 1983-86 did the banks come good by the time of Board approval. In multiple 'brinksmanship' exercises after Board approval, the commercial banks were given the authority to determine whether or not the Fund arrangement should go forward on the conditionality negotiated by the Fund with the country concerned, and with the performance criteria specified. If the commercial banks said no, the whole arrangement would go astray, and the country would be left in the lurch.

- This procedure has been used by the commercial banks to demand their own regime of macro-economic conditionality for countries seeking use of Fund resources, and already submitting themselves to the harshest conditionality of the Fund and World Bank. Effectively, what this entails is a commercial banks' capability to veto arrangements between the Fund and developing member countries, if such arrangements are not perceived by the banks to adequately protect their own interests the way they want them protected. The implications are clear enough: private multinational corporations whose recent record has shown them to be interested only in making and taking out maximum profit from the Third World in the shortest possible time, have the power now not only to veto Fund arrangements, but to demand in such arrangements government action to feather their own nests, and allow them to operate unfettered, undeterred by social or economic or political consequence in the country concerned.

- given their central role in dictating the broad thrust and specific details of conditionality for Fund programs in Third World countries, the commercial banks have wasted no time in spawning their own institutions to make that role effective. Thus has arisen the Institute of International Finance (IIF) in Washington DC, and related organizations elsewhere (e.g., the Japan Centre for International Finance). Consultation with commercial banks on Fund conditionality for individual countries, and more broadly, on our relations with such countries under the Articles of Agreement of the Fund, occur constantly, and at a fast accelerating pace, particularly in relation to Multi-Year Rescheduling Arrangements (MYRAs). We even undertake mission work in the South on behalf of commercial banks under Enhanced Surveillance Arrangements. In this respect, it is not inconceivable that in the near future, the commercial banks will be directly represented on Fund negotiating and consultation missions to designated Third World countries, thus formalizing the reality of such banks being full partners with us in our task of crushing down everything with Steamroller (Heaviest) at Full Moon.

the commercial banks have managed thus to call the shots in relation to Fund conditionality and country performance criteria demanded by the Fund from developing countries in conditions where the net contribution of such banks to external financing for Third World heavily indebted countries have been massively negative (by over -US$16 billion during 1986/87). Lending under concerted schemes - a major instrument used to achieve the results discussed above - fell from about US$30 billion in 1983/84 to just US$3 billion in 1986 and US$7 billion in 1987.

Sir, the emergence of a cortege of commercial banks as a crucial entity that importantly structures and determines, through the Fund, economic policies and perspectives for Third World countries, bring into focus a series of issues other than the critical one of the fate of the South now, given the peculiar convergence of disparate Third World forces and institutions and policies and perspectives as described above. Among these issues are a series of 'internal' ones that you would rather forget. Quite frankly, the emergence of the commercial banks as our constant bedfellow and our co-conspirator is pregnant with implications for the staff, and its personal integrity, and the accelerated decadence of the Fund as a multilateral institution - a decadence that has been so clearly highlighted in Parts 11 to V, and certain Sections of Part V1 of this Letter. But leaving all this aside for the moment, I want you to consider the following broad questions:- did the debt crisis change substantively the nature of our institution and the way we must perform our day to day tasks because of the strident demands of our masters and the successful 'upmanship' of the banks? Did we go further into Hell because of shameful scheming and prior action of others? Or did the final caving in occur because of an internal rot, and irrespective of the strength and persistence of outside forces?

(c) The Fund/World Bank and Developed Countries

As matters stand, the G7 proposes and the Fund/World Bank disposes; technically and intrinsically there can be no conflict of interest between our major shareholders and ourselves: we stand ready at every stage to do what the master tells us to do.

Of course, the G7 itself never sticks to the 'rules of the game' for properly functioning multilateralism; it is riddled with conflicting interests and perspectives. However, on one thing there is well-nigh consensus; it is this: the major cause of fundamental imbalance within the system is the U.S. fiscal deficit, and the inevitable need, because of that deficit and given domestic policies in certain G7 surplus countries, for a reverse net flow of funds from the Third World over a continuing time period and on a fairly massive scale.

Let me be a bit more specific. Capital flight, without doubt, has become institutionalized as the critical variable that makes possible some degree of minimal balance within the international system. Without such flight, the system would be incapable of functioning; it would become inherently unstable; the world would go back to the unmitigated financial disorders and rampant 'beggar my neighbor' policies of the inter-war period. In the Fund, we have come to accept as a fact of life that the United States has the right and privilege to live beyond its means through the accumulation of foreign debt. Equally, we have come to accept as a fact of life that others in the G7 have the right and privilege to refuse to make themselves less competitive internationally, thus precluding the United States, with no further effort on its part, from exporting more to reduce its balance of payments deficit (closely linked to its fiscal deficit). In this conjuncture, Third World domestic savings, siphoned off as capital flight, has become the most crucial element to maintain Quality of Life in the west. Blood money of the poor and poverty stricken of the South, legally and illegally exported to the west by our well-heeled fellow travellers resident in the South, is now the most essential prerequisite that allows the existing system to limp along. The death and stench of the shanty town allow the west to enjoy Life in Super-Abundance, with all the paraphernalia of Cadillacs and Porches and and nuclear weapons and SDIs and B2 bombers.

While the Fund and World Bank force developing countries, through "Structural Adjustment" programs to open up their exchange systems so that all necessary capital flight can occur without impairment, G7 and related countries - including Switzerland, the United States and the United Kingdom - meet their responsibilities under the so- called "management system for development and development financing" by opening up themselves to become major havens for Third world capital flight. These countries, and several other western ones, provide a wide range of government incentives, including tax exemptions and other highly favorable legal provisions, for attracting Third World capital flight. The purpose, of course, is to dynamise such flight, ensuring thus that the floodtide of Third World domestic savings going to finance consumption levels in developed countries becomes an established, legitimate feature of the the Phase 11 Debt Strategy.

What quantum of blood money from the poverty- stricken of the South is required to keep the existing system afloat? Well, there is no exact measurement of the stock of Third World capital flight in the West, but most informed recent research puts the figure in the region of from US$500 billion to US$800 billion, probably more than equal to the market value of the entire stock of outstanding Third World debt (nominal value of around US$1.3 trillion). The implications of this is clear:- if Third World savings in the West in the form of capital flight by a handful of well-heeled transnational residents, undertaken mostly illegally sometimes with the connivance of banks and always under Fund official or unofficial auspices, were allowed to remain in the South, where they were generated and where they belong, there would be no Third World Debt crisis at all, and no Third World Debt Strategy of the Fund and its First World cohorts! In other words, the debt crisis really is staged, to provide the occasion and the instrument for the Fund to force its politically inspired "Structural Adjustment" down the throat of the South. Without the capital flight that we so deliberately generate in our programs, the rug would be pulled from off the feet of our master, and modern-day multilateralism would become as a fish out of water, devoid of its irresistible purpose to emasculate the South and destroy its peoples for glorification of the Fund/World Bank and a few misguided countries of the West.

Yours sincerely,

Davison L. Budhoo

MACROECONOMIC POLICIES
(number of measures in parenthesis)

Policy	Ghana	Mozambique	Senegal	Tanzania	Zambia
1. Exchange and trade system	Flexible exchange rate (auction and liberalize trading system (8)	Exchange rate action and liberalize trading system (7)		Exchange rate action and liberalize trading system (6)	Flexible exchange rate (auction) and export promotion (4)
2. External debt	Reduce debt service burden, limit new borrowing, eliminate arrears (2)	Reduce debt burden, rescheduling, limit new borrowing (2)	Limit debt burden and normalize relations with creditors (3)	Limit external debt burden, limits on new borrowing (1)	Normalize relations with creditors, limit new borrowing (4)
3. Fiscal policies					
a. revenues	Improve domestic resource mobilization, tax reforms (8)	Increase revenue, tax reform (2)	Increase revenue, tax reform, new customs code (8)	Reduce deficit and more efficient expenditures, new taxes, limit wage increases (5)	Increase government revenue, tax reform (3)
b. expenditures	Strength expenditure control (11)	Contain expenditures on wages, subsidies, and transfers (2)	Reduce expenditures especially wages and subsidies (3)		Reduce expenditures, limits on subsidies and wages, public expenditure reform (7)
4. Monetary policies	Mobilize savings, control credit, and strengthen banking system, auction market for Treasury bills (8)	Control credit and increase savings through increased interest rates (2)	Control credit and improve banking system, flexible interest rates (5)	Reduce inflation and improve banking system, interest rate adjustments (5)	Control credit and mobilize savings, flexible interest rates, Treasury bill market (2)

114

SECTORAL POLICIES
(number of measures in parenthesis)

Policy	Ghana	Mozambique	Senegal	Tanzania	Zambia
1. Agricultural policy	Rationalize producer incentives, raise producer prices, phase out subsidies, institutional reforms (22)	Increase producer incentives, price adjustments, liberalize marketing system (9)	Expand and diversify production, price and subsidy adjustments (12)	Improve incentives, increased prices for export crops, liberalize marketing (2)	Rationalize price and marketing system, price adjustments, subsidy reductions (3)
2. Public enterprises	Rationalize public enterprises (17)	Reform of 25 industrial and 15 agricultural enterprises (1)	Promote efficiency, liquidate or privatize certain enterprises (9)	Improve productivity, rehabilitation or restructuring of certain enterprises (1)	Promote efficiency, tariff reform, restructuring or liquidation of certain enterprises (4)
3. Public sector management	Strengthen management (12)	Improve control and effectiveness (6)	Strengthen investment programming (8)		
4. Price and marketing liberalization	(Part of agricultural policy above) (4)	Liberalize price and marketing system (6)		Eliminate most price controls (3)	Decontrol of most prices (1)
5. Industrial policy		Price adjustments, institutional reform (4)	Tariff reform, price adjustments (11)	Prepare action program for restructuring (3)	
6. Transport		Increase tariffs, rehabilitation of port and rail facilities (7)		Improve capacity and efficiency (3)	
7. Energy			Develop local sources (1)		Raise domestic petroleum prices
8. Mining sector					Revitalize sector through 5-year investment plan with IBRD